Entirely Up to You, Darling

ENTIRELY UP TO YOU, DARLING

Richard Attenborough
and
Diana Hawkins

HUTCHINSON
London

Published by Hutchinson 2008

2 4 6 8 10 9 7 5 3 1

Copyright © 2008 Richard Attenborough and Diana Hawkins

Richard Attenborough and Diana Hawkins have asserted their right under the Copyright,
Designs and Patents Act 1988 to be identified as the authors of this work

First published in Great Britain in 2008 by
Hutchinson
Random House, 20 Vauxhall Bridge Road,
London SW1V 2SA

www.rbooks.co.uk

Addresses for companies within The Random House Group Limited can be found at:
www.randomhouse.co.uk/offices.htm

The Random House Group Limited Reg. No. 954009

A CIP catalogue record for this book
is available from the British Library

ISBN 9780091797089 (Hardback)
ISBN 9780091920999 (Trade paperback)

The Random House Group Limited supports The Forest Stewardship
Council (FSC), the leading international forest certification organisation. All our
titles that are printed on Greenpeace approved FSC certified paper carry the FSC logo. Our
paper procurement policy can be found at www.rbooks.co.uk/environment

Mixed Sources
Product group from well-managed
forests and other controlled sources
www.fsc.org Cert no. TT-COC-2139
© 1996 Forest Stewardship Council
FSC

Typeset by
Palimpsest Book Production Limited,
Grangemouth, Stirlingshire

Printed and bound in Great Britain by
Clays Ltd, St Ives plc

CONTENTS

List of Illustrations

ACKNOWLEDGEMENTS

The authors would like to record their gratitude to the following:

Sir David Attenborough, Clive Barnes, Sue Barton, Martin Baum, B. J. Bjorkman, Neil Bradford, Tess Callaway, Don Card, Gabriel Clare-Hunt, Terry Clegg, Jake Eberts, Lord Evans of Temple Guiting, Michael Grade, Trevor Griffiths, Tommy Hanley, Kay Hawkins, Roy Margrave, Professor Alan McGregor, Caroline Michel, Frank and Katherine Price, Paul Sidey, Judy Wasdell, Wendy and the late Donald Woods . . .

. . . and, of course, Sheila Attenborough, for contributing our foreword.

FOREWORD

ON BEING ASKED to write the Foreword . . .

When Richard and Diana asked me if I would like to write the fore-word for their book I remember I felt a warm glow and a slow smile overtake me – secretly, you understand, not to be seen. They were kind enough to remember that the book was my idea. So, they were saying 'get on with it – write the foreword'.

What fun, I thought. But, could I do it? I'm not one of those spec-tacular people who punch the air with their fist and jump onto someone's back at sudden happenings. I tend to go the other way and remain silent and rooted to the spot.

Even when Dick won the Oscars for *Gandhi* the same thing happened, resulting in my finding myself alone in that vast auditorium except for darling stalwart Diana when everyone else had left. I needed time to absorb it all and I wasn't sure how to react.

Having been an actress myself for quite a considerable period many years ago, I was then of course 'part of the business'. Now I am not but I am alongside it, as it were, partly involved and partly witness, buffeted or elated according to what's occurring. I try very hard to keep up but I am married to a grasshopper and just when I think I've caught up – he's jumped somewhere else. So I will read the book with a certain interest.

Now I've rambled on and taken up most of my allotted space and I haven't said anything. Well, of course, if you, dear reader, are sweet enough to go on and read the book then I needn't bother, need I?

Perhaps as I have now reached a certain age I might be allowed a little sentimental bit. Looking back, I have felt extremely fortunate to have been able to see so much of the world, and I value beyond anything the love of my husband and that of my family and loyal and trusted friends, who have stayed with us – Dick and me – supporting us in tragedy and failure and cheering us in happy and successful times.

We have travelled so far and have come back home.

Sheila Attenborough, 2008

I

AND THE WINNER IS . . .

DH— A COUPLE OF hours ago, Dick, Sheila and I were on our way to the Oscars, Hollywood's glitziest event of the year. We hardly spoke in the limousine but Dick kept yawning as he stared out of the smoked-glass windows; a sure sign of tension.

For him, this evening marks the end of a very long journey. Over the past two decades, Sir Richard Attenborough's pig-headed determination to make a film about Mahatma Gandhi has brought him close to bankruptcy, made him a laughing stock and obliged him to accept a whole series of acting assignments he really should have declined.

A former viceroy and two prime ministers have helped to bring him here. Four billionaire brothers, a maharaja and a maverick movie mogul have cruelly let him down. And, over and over again, Hollywood refused to invest a single cent in his epic project. One studio head summed up the attitude of the whole community when he spat: 'Who the fuck wants to see a movie about a little brown guy dressed in a sheet carrying a beanpole?'

Tonight, amazingly, the film that Tinseltown derided is up for eleven Oscars. Dick has two of these nominations; one for Best Director and the other as producer of Best Film.

With the ceremony under way, he and Sheila are seated close to the stage, with Ben Kingsley and his wife, Alison, a couple of rows behind. As the film's director of marketing, I'm further back, as is flame-haired

Marti Baum, Dick's Hollywood representative, known as Agent Orange. Close by is Jake Eberts, the tall Canadian who stuck his neck out to save *Gandhi* from extinction, and our supportive distributor, the enigmatic and quietly spoken Frank Price, head of Columbia Pictures. Dotted around the stalls are fourteen of the film's technicians, all but one British.

The cavernous Dorothy Chandler Pavilion is packed with stars and moguls, movers and shakers, players and hangers-on. With television cameras trained constantly on the auditorium, no seat must ever be left vacant, so if anyone takes a comfort break, their place is immediately filled by one of the extras in evening dress hovering in the aisles.

Our main competitors are *E.T.* and *Tootsie*, both apple-pie American to the core. Dick and I are convinced that *E.T.* will sweep the board.

We've known this since we saw Spielberg's wonderful movie at a matinee in Manhattan several months ago. The theatre was full of kids with their parents and, unlike any British audience, they'd all stood up and cheered as the end credits rolled. When the lights came up, we looked at each other, knowing we didn't stand a chance.

As usual, the Oscar ceremony is overrunning. Everyone, it seems, is breaking the two-minute rule by making rambling acceptance speeches. I'm incredibly nervous and sneaked out a little while ago for a cigarette, my seat being taken immediately by a stunning girl in a satin gown. This was after John Williams's original score for *E.T.* had beaten our east–west collaboration of Ravi Shankar and George Fenton. As I returned, our brilliant make-up artist was also losing out to the French film, *Quest for Fire*. Now, with Best Visual Effects and Best Sound Effects both going to *E.T.*, it's beginning to feel ominously like a landslide.

Next up is Best Film Editing and I'm clapping like mad because, although Spielberg's film was expected to take the prize, the worthy winner is our own John Bloom. So at least *Gandhi* has one Oscar. But depression descends again when *E.T.* walks off with Best Sound.

Our rival is not in contention for Best Costume which traditionally goes to a movie displaying a great deal of extravagant and innovative design. Although *Gandhi* required more than a thousand authentic period costumes, it's inconceivable we can beat the science fantasy, *Tron*, or Zeffirelli's lavish screen adaptation of *La Traviata*. So it comes as a total surprise when John Mollo and his Indian colleague, Bhanu Attaiya, receive an Oscar apiece.

Back at the hotel this morning, Bhanu was optimistically rehearsing her acceptance speech. Certain she wouldn't win but not wanting to deny her the pleasure of anticipation, we said nothing. And now onstage, Oscar in hand, this shy woman in a sari who's travelled all the way from Delhi is totally speechless.

Suddenly, unbelievably, *Gandhi* is on a roll. Our art department, headed by Stuart Craig, wins Best Art Direction and Set Decoration. Billy Williams and Ronnie Taylor win Best Cinematography, and Jack Briley collects the statuette for Best Original Screenplay. We've won five and lost out on three. But the big ones, the ones that really matter, are still to come.

First of these is Best Director. Dick's competing with Wolfgang Petersen for *Das Boot*, Sydney Pollack for *Tootsie*, Sidney Lumet for *The Verdict* and, of course, Steven Spielberg, director and producer of *E.T.*

The revered Billy Wilder is to present this award. Since his arrival in America during the 1930s, this extraordinarily creative producer, director and screenwriter has been nominated twenty-one times, receiving three Oscars for *Lost Weekend*, one for *Sunset Boulevard* and two for *The Apartment*.

In a voice that still bears traces of his Austro-Hungarian origins, Wilder announces, 'The winner of the Best Director award is . . . Richard Attenborough for *Gandhi*.' Dick joins him onstage, accepts the statuette, places it on the podium and stands there for a long moment, gazing out at the audience.

'Ladies and gentlemen,' he eventually says, 'and fellow members of the Academy. Without Jake Eberts and the National Film Development Corporation of India, *Gandhi* would never have been made. Without my agent, Marti Baum, I would not have been able to maintain my courage. I am also enormously indebted to Frank Price and Columbia Pictures for the risk they took in agreeing to distribute this film. Finally, I should like to say to my fellow nominees, I am profoundly honoured to be in your company.'

Now it's Best Actor. Essentially a theatre actor, this is the first time Ben Kingsley's appeared in any major film, let alone carried a whole production in a pivotal role that spans sixty years of his character's life. And this total newcomer is up against Jack Lemmon, Peter O'Toole, Dustin Hoffman and Paul Newman. Is O'Toole perhaps empathising just a little with Ben in the nail-biting moments before the vital enve-lope is opened? Exactly twenty years ago, he was nominated for his own stunning debut in *Lawrence of Arabia* and, in the event, lost out to Gregory Peck.

But Ben does not lose out. Deservedly, but incredibly, this young Anglo-Indian – real name Krishna Bhanji – has won the 1982 Academy Award for Best Actor in a Leading Role. It's an amazing moment and one that will determine the entire course of his future life and career.

With the ceremony drawing to a close, we've finally arrived at the last, most prestigious and influential prize of all. This is the Oscar which goes to the producers of the movie which, uniquely, has been voted Best Film by the entire membership of the American Academy of Motion Picture Arts and Sciences. The contenders are *E.T*, *Missing*, *Tootsie*, *The Verdict* and *Gandhi*. All the other pictures have two producers; we have only one.

Television star Carol Burnett is about to open the envelope containing the winning title, so far known only to the scrutineers at PricewaterhouseCoopers. Nine television lenses zoom in on nine tense nominees.

'And the winner is . . . *Gandhi*!'

A split second of silence as the losers rearrange their facial expres-sions, followed by a burst of applause. Then, in a tuxedoed and bejew-elled Mexican wave, the whole huge audience gets to its feet; stalls and balcony, front to back, row by row, until everyone is standing.

They remain on their feet, clapping, cheering and whistling, as Dick kisses Sheila, moves into the aisle, climbs onto the stage, makes his way to the podium, kisses Burnett and accepts the gleaming trophy. *Gandhi* has won eight Oscars; more than any other British film in the entire fifty-five-year history of the Academy.

Struggling to collect himself, the winner embarks on his second accept-ance speech. He doesn't know it yet, but the catch in his voice and the tears on his face are creating an image which will remain embedded in the public consciousness for many years to come. Dick says:

'I deeply regret that my late partner, Moti Kothari, to whom *Gandhi* is dedicated, is not here to share this award. To his widow, Dorothy, and his two children, I send my love and my gratitude because it was Moti who, in the very beginning, inspired this film.

'Members of the Academy, you have tonight honoured a number of the people who helped to make *Gandhi*. And without them, I would not be standing here. But I'm sure they will agree that the person you really honour, as Ben said in his terrific speech, is the Mahatma himself.

'He was an inspiration to millions and millions of people and to this day he remains an inspiration. Your great folk hero, Martin Luther King Junior, was inspired by Mahatma Gandhi. When Lech Wałęsa, that noble Polish patriot, recently came out of prison, he said he now realised that violence and confrontation would never bring about true freedom in his country. The only way to preserve human dignity was to seek peaceful change through the philosophies and teachings of the Mahatma.

'Gandhi simply asked that we should re-examine the manner in which we attempt to solve the world's problems. He said that in the twentieth century the answer is no longer to be found in blowing the other man's head off. He spoke to and for all of us; the whole world.'

RA— Diana claims I cried. Typical exaggeration; I was of course overcome but I don't recall shedding any tears. What I remember most is that I couldn't get the words out. The point being, that I am, and always have been, an actor and actors' emotions, being close to the surface, sometimes appear without conscious volition. It was the standing ovation that choked me up. I don't think it had happened with any other award that evening.

I first experienced a standing ovation in my teens at the first night of *Brighton Rock* in the theatre. That was as exciting as anything I can ever remember. It also happened at the premiere of *Oh! What a Lovely War*, my first film as a director. But when everyone got to their feet at the Oscars, it absolutely jammed me in the solar plexus. I do remember thinking how proud my ma and pa would have been.

What really got to me, though, was that all those people, the same people who'd told me for so many years that I was mad to pursue this project, were now on their feet, saluting, as I saw it, not me but the 'little man in a sheet carrying a beanpole'. There, gathered under one roof, was this extraordinary assembly of talent, the people who made movies and the executives who controlled Hollywood, finally acknowledging that this was a subject worthy of recognition.

I don't think they voted for *Gandhi* believing it was the best film of that year because, as I've always said, technically and emotionally *E.T.* was by far the better movie. But in subject terms, *Gandhi* was unique. And yes, there was a sense of vindication . . . and of triumph. I would hate not to use the word triumph but at the same time I'm ashamed of using it. I felt vindicated because it really shouldn't have taken twenty years to raise the finance.

I don't regard my two Oscars as trophies; they're memorabilia. I like having them, as I like having BAFTAs and Golden Globes. There are people who use them as doorstops. I find that self-conscious. Ostensibly, they want to show they don't care. Bollocks. Of course they care. Mine are on a mantelpiece in the office. I don't pretend they don't exist, but I don't display them in my house.

The Oscars are very, very special and hundreds of millions of people all over the world watch the ceremony on television. And like them, that night it was as if I was witnessing it all from a distance. It was Mahatma Gandhi who won Best Film, not me. And it seemed unreal because I genuinely never believed we'd win.

I was also astonished at the way the press latched onto the tears Di continues to assure me I shed. Why else, she asks, would my puppet in *Spitting Image* have jets of water spurting out of its eyes? And what about the endless weepy cartoons? I do have to confess, being the ham that I am, I took the mockery on board. Afterwards, whenever I had to make a speech that needed to start on a laugh, I only had to produce a box of Kleenex . . .

Today, people have mostly forgotten. Those Oscars were a long time ago and I'm now in my mid-eighties, so bloody old. The ribbing did go on, though, for years and years and years. I suppose it was because men used to be admired for keeping a stiff upper lip. Things are very different and so much better today. For instance, when I was young, husbands were always excluded when their children were born. It's a wonderful experience I missed because, at the time, it just wasn't done.

I think it is good that we are now able, even encouraged, to show our emotions and be really involved, as is my son, Michael, in caring for our children. I would have been a far better father if I had spent more time with Michael, Jane and Charlotte when they were small. It's something I wish I could go back and change – particularly since the

Asian tsunami at the end of 2004. I bitterly regret that I didn't see my kids as much as I should have done, that I didn't make more of an effort. I was so sure they'd always be there and, whatever I missed, could be made up later on. Stupidly, I always thought there'd be plenty of time . . .

DH— After Dick had finished his acceptance speech and been escorted into the wings, Sheila and I waited and waited for him to return. The ceremony came to a close and the huge theatre emptied as most of the audience sped off to the famous, unofficial Oscar parties.

Most coveted was an invitation from the legendary agent, Swifty Lazar, who held court at Spago on Sunset Boulevard. He represented a host of the biggest stars and was reputed to be so powerful he could clinch deals for actors who weren't even his clients, cheekily collecting a percentage from their actual agents after the event.

When the two of us were almost alone in the darkened auditorium, Sheila and I finally persuaded 'security' to allow us backstage. It was mayhem. All the press who'd been lining the red carpet when we arrived were now surrounding the winners, clamouring for pictures and interviews. And Dick, of course, was in the thick of it. As we knew all too well, he's always the last to leave. It's to do with manners. He will not walk away from anyone who has waited to talk to him or get his autograph.

True to form, he wouldn't leave the Pavilion that night until every picture was taken and every interviewer satisfied. Then, having linked up with Ben and Alison Kingsley, we set off in our chauffeured stretch for the staid official party, known as the Governor's Ball. Dinner was finishing by the time we arrived. At such events in Hollywood nobody stays for dessert. They pick at their rubber chicken, grab the table decorations and head for the hills.

We were escorted into the ballroom by Jonathan, a young publicist from Columbia Pictures. Dick and Ben plonked their three Oscars on the reserved table and looked around for someone who might bring us a much needed drink. Behind them, our minder was in quiet conversation with an unhappy older man who was muttering that something had to be done to stop 'these people grabbing our awards'. It turned out, when he was introduced, that this was Jonathan's father, Sid Sheinberg, the much feared head of Universal Pictures.

The sour grapes were understandable. Only a year earlier, when David Puttnam's *Chariots of Fire* had won four Oscars for Twentieth Century Fox, screenwriter Colin Welland had brandished his statuette, shouting provocatively; 'The British are coming!' And tonight we'd fulfilled his boastful prophecy, with *Gandhi* winning handsomely for rival studios, Columbia, while Universal's anticipated shoe-in, *E.T.*, had come away with just four technical awards.

Dawn was breaking when we finally made it back to the Beverly Hills Hotel. The night staff in the lobby lined up to applaud Dick and Ben as they entered. We asked if the loot could be put in their safe and learned it was nearly full as the rest of the *Gandhi* crew had made the same request. Because some awards had gone to a team, we'd actually walked out of the ceremony with twelve of the unexpectedly heavy statuettes.

In a haze of euphoria, I took Dick and Ben's Oscars into the back office. The safe was opened. How satisfying, how profoundly satisfying to see this squad of shiny brittannium sentinels, hands clasped on the pommels of their swords. And how strange that these trophies of so little intrinsic value but huge professional worth should be the end result of Dick's twenty-year quest.

RA— Without any exaggeration, it was a twenty-year quest and it began in 1962. I'm not a great one for superstition but the two events which started it all, one immediately after the other, do imply some kind of kismet.

The first happened at a charity auction in London. Everyone present had either donated an item or undertaken to buy one. I was a buyer. The catalogue simply said, 'A bust by Epstein', and, regardless of the subject, I decided to try for it. I'd always hankered after an Epstein; not one of his monumental sculptures, but something small that could, maybe, live in our hall.

If memory serves me right, my winning bid was £250. The bust, cast in bronze, happened to be the head of Pandit Jawaharlal Nehru who was, at that time, Prime Minister of India. I carried him home in my arms and, at half past one in the morning, placed him close to our front door where he remains to this day.

Soon after dawn while I was still asleep, the phone rang on my bedside table. The person on the other end of the line was a complete stranger. He told me his name was Motilal Kothari and that he'd obtained my private number from a mutual friend because he had an idea and it was vital he put it to me in person. Mr Kothari was very insistent and, despite some misgivings, I was persuaded to meet him for lunch a couple of days later.

At the Waldorf Hotel, a grave, middle-aged Indian greeted me with the polite Hindu *pranam*, placing his joined hands in front of his face. Little did I know that this gesture, which seemed so unusual and so, well, exotic in 1960s London, would become as natural as a handshake.

Mr Kothari proved to be a dedicated follower of Gandhi who had left India in disgust following the Mahatma's assassination by a fellow Hindu at the end of 1948. Having emigrated to London, my host had taken up a post at the Indian High Commission in the Aldwych.

After many years of reflection, Mr Kothari had come to believe that, in deserting his homeland, he'd also deserted Gandhi. And he was now determined to put this right. His mission was to disseminate the story of the Mahatma's life as widely as possible, making his philosophies and achievements known to the whole world. And what better way, he said with disarming simplicity, than through the film which I was to make.

His confident assertion took me by surprise. I'd acted in films since 1942 and been fortunate enough to achieve star billing and all the trappings of celebrity before becoming typecast in stories which lacked, it seemed to me, any real artistry or substance. In an effort to achieve something worthwhile, together with my then partner, Bryan Forbes, I'd recently become an independent producer, but I could only lay claim to two low-budget films with a third still in production when Moti Kothari put forward his extraordinary proposition.

Now, call it kismet, love or simply a need to validate myself, but there was a reason which prevented me from rejecting his proposal out of hand. My father had always wanted me to follow in his footsteps and become an academic. Long before Tony Blair came on the scene, his mantra was education, education, education. My brothers, Dave, Johnny and I, called him the Governor. Why we did so is lost in the mists of time but the nickname was almost certainly devised by Dave and me, the family pranksters.

Frederick Levi Attenborough, who was born in 1887, was a working-class baker's son from Stapleford in Nottinghamshire, not far from the eponymous village of Attenborough. It was education, newly compulsory for children up to the age of twelve, which took my father in 1911 to a teacher training centre in Long Eaton, just over the county border in Derbyshire where one of his instructors was the remarkable English educationalist, Samuel Clegg.

This was my maternal grandfather, described as 'a high-voltage cable, electrifying the local community', who had just set up one of the first secondary schools to offer free places to children over the age of twelve. In 1913, the live-wire headmaster offered my newly qualified father a teaching post at the ground-breaking Long Eaton Higher Elementary School and, since the salary was meagre, took him into the family home as a lodger. The Cleggs had three beautiful and intelligent daughters and, within a couple of years, the Governor had wooed and won the eldest. Her name was Mary.

Education then took my newly married parents to North Wales, where he underwent further teacher training at Bangor Normal College and then on to Liverpool where he taught. From there, amazingly, the village baker's son won a foundation scholarship to Emmanuel College, Cambridge, where I was born and he eventually became a don. Dave and Johnny arrived during our father's tenure as principal of Borough Road College in Isleworth, now part of Brunel University.

Then, at the age of forty-five, the Governor found his true vocation in Leicester. He became principal of the city's College of Higher Education and devoted the rest of his working life to steering it towards full university status.

At the family home on campus, my adolescent school reports made it abundantly clear that the principal's eldest son did not apply himself and was unlikely to enter higher education. It was equally clear that animal-mad Dave, two years younger, was the clever and assiduous student most likely to scale the academic heights.

Instead of concentrating on my exams, I spent every spare moment at the Little Theatre, a vibrant and remarkably professional hotbed of amateur dramatics, of which my very supportive mama was president.

If the Governor was the studious visionary, beavering away behind the closed door of his study, my mother was the doer. As teenagers, we called her Mary which, I suppose, was very avant-garde at the time. It was Mary who'd been a crusading suffragette, Mary who took part in marches protesting against Franco's Fascist regime in Spain and Mary who eventually worked herself to death as one of the founders of the Marriage Guidance Council.

I'm sure she wanted all her sons to grow up happy and fulfilled, no matter what career they chose. But I'm equally sure that the Governor, who'd pulled himself up by his own bootstraps, yearned for us all to follow in his footsteps. For him, a university degree was the be-all and end-all. I would have been seventeen when he called me into his study for a showdown.

'Dick, you say you want to become an actor. Well, you have to prove to me that you can do it. We can't afford to send you to drama school, so you'll need to win a scholarship and I'm afraid there's only one which also carries a grant for living expenses. It's called the Leverhulme and it's offered competitively by the Royal Academy of Dramatic Art in London. If you win it, I give you my word I will do everything in my power to help you. Otherwise, you must promise to give up acting and buckle down to get your matriculation.'

I did win the Leverhulme and the Governor said he was very proud. But, nevertheless, I knew in my heart of hearts that he was disappointed. So Mr Kothari's proposal that I should make a film with something important to say which could use cinema to reach, entertain and, yes, teach vast numbers of people, had enormous appeal.

Even in 1962, at the age of thirty-nine, I still desperately wanted to prove myself. I wanted the Governor, who'd lived partly with Sheila and me since Mary's untimely death the previous year, to take real pride in what I was doing. And, in addition, I knew that Mahatma Gandhi was someone he held in very high esteem.

Back in 1931, when I was eight years old, the Mahatma had come to England to take part in round-table discussions about the future independence of India. And we'd seen him together, the Governor and I, at the local cinema in some grainy black-and-white newsreel footage.

I remembered the sneer in the commentator's strangled upper-class vowels as he described the high hopes this small, nut-brown man had for his people. I remembered that Winston Churchill had famously shrugged him off as 'that naked fakir'. I remembered Gandhi had sat on the floor at the House of Commons, chanting the Bhagavadgita, and taken tea with the King at Buckingham Palace, clad only in his loincloth and sandals. When reporters asked if he wasn't somewhat underdressed for the occasion, the Mahatma had retorted gravely but with his characteristic twinkle, 'I believe His Majesty was wearing enough for both of us.'

All this came back to me in bits and pieces while I sat facing Moti Kothari across the lunch table. But what I remembered most, and with great clarity, was what the Governor had said as we sat together in that cinema all those years ago. People around us had sniggered as the news-reel showed the defeated Indian leader emerging from 10 Downing Street. And the Governor had told me; 'They don't understand, Dick. Mr Gandhi is extraordinary. He is truly a remarkable man.'

That was good enough for me. And so I acceded to Moti Kothari's initial request; that I should read what he believed to be 'a jolly good biography' of the Mahatma by the American author, Louis Fischer.

DH— At the time of his first meeting with Moti Kothari, Dick was co-producing *The L-Shaped Room*, starring Leslie Caron, and I was the film's impressionable 24-year-old publicist.

Before she started filming, Miss Caron had warned Dick she would never be able to work on the first day of her period. This did not go down well. Professional actresses in his view soldiered on, no matter what. Nevertheless, he asked her to provide a list of dates so that shooting could be scheduled around them. This she did, but phoned him one evening to tell him her date was wrong and she would not be at the studios the following morning.

Richard, she told me in a worried call immediately afterwards, had responded in a way she didn't understand. He'd refused to cancel Leslie's car and told her it would be outside her Montpelier Square home at the appointed time in the morning. Then to her bewilderment, he'd added, 'But whether you choose to come is, of course, entirely up to you, darling.'

It was far too complicated to explain that she'd just been subjected to the favourite arm-twist in our producer's impressive canon of reverse psychology. So I translated. 'He means you'd better come in, or else.'

So in she came, very French, very grumpy, and it only took one look at her puffy face and the dark circles under her eyes to know that any close-up was out of the question. Leslie was sent home and throughout the remainder of production she and Dick hardly spoke; I became their go-between.

Part of the incredible tenacity that made Dick persevere with *Gandhi*, even when all seemed lost, is his own ability to soldier on, no matter what. Setbacks, exhaustion, illness . . . none are a good enough reason to give in or give up. He seems to believe if you ignore any impediment it will eventually evaporate.

For years and years, he had tinnitus; the result of gunfire during the Second World War. He'd sometimes get crotchety for no discernible reason and, when put on the spot, reluctantly admit that the 'bloody noise' in his head was driving him mad.

Then came deafness. I remember a time in post-production when we kept adding the chirping of crickets to a film's soundtrack until they threatened to drown out everything else. And still Dick kept saying, 'I can't hear the bleeding crickets.' He'd completely lost the upper register of his hearing. Only many months later did he agree to have an ear test and, eventually, to wear the hated hearing aids.

These had a downside and an upside, both to do with the fact that hearing aids whistle when they're covered. The downside is that Dick, who lives on the phone whenever there's nothing else to do, either has to have a specially adapted receiver or hold an ordinary one so far away he can't hear the voice at the other end. The upside is that his grandchildren learned to play musical hearing aids by covering and uncovering each of his ears in turn.

Gout was another affliction which he ignored for a long time. Once, when we were filming in Montreal, he could hardly bear to put his foot to the ground as he climbed down from his camper van. But, as soon as he saw the waiting actors, crew and camera, the pain seemed magically to disappear. He was immediately on his toes, both physically and metaphorically.

Harder to bear, I believe, is the more recent onset of diabetes. All his life, Dick has been the ultimate chocoholic. He told me one of the only times his mother smacked him as a child was when he stole chocolates and then lied about it. And in my own experience, every location caterer knew the way to the guvnor's heart was to produce a monster bar of Toblerone.

However, not one crumb of chocolate has passed his lips since his diagnosis. It was the same when he gave up smoking, going from sixty Woodbines a day to none at all in a matter of weeks, through sheer willpower. Once Dick sets his mind to something, nothing but nothing will blow him off course. And so it was with *Gandhi*.

RA— As I'd promised Moti Kothari, I took the biography with me to Switzerland at the beginning of 1963 when Sheila and I went on a post-Christmas holiday with Bryan and Nanette Forbes. And less than a tenth of the way through the book, I read something that knocked me for six.

The young Gandhi, then a newly qualified lawyer practising in South Africa, was walking along a street with a friend. They were on the pavement. Two white South Africans were approaching from the opposite direction, also on the pavement. Before they drew level, Gandhi's friend pulled him into the gutter to let the lordly white men pass unimpeded, as was customary at the time.

After they'd gone Gandhi thought for a while and then said calmly to his companion: 'You know, it has always been a mystery to me that men should feel themselves honoured by the humiliation of their fellow human beings.'

I was thunderstruck. He was then in his early twenties and, for me, this mild observation demonstrated a perception far beyond his years and one that was indeed, as the Governor had said, truly remarkable.

I carried on reading and finished the book in one sitting. Immediately after, I was shouting on a crackly payphone in the hotel lobby to Mr Kothari in London. Having told him how impressed I was with the biography, I asked if the project had any backers. He had no idea what I meant. 'Money,' I yelled. 'Have you got any money to make the film?'

'Money?' he said. Despite the atrocious line, I could hear the total bewilderment in his voice. 'Ah . . . no, Mr Attenborough, I don't have any money.' I took a deep breath and told him in that case I would assemble the necessary funding because I was determined that this film must be made. What was more, I would direct it myself.

This, of course, was totally insane. Why would anyone in their right mind entrust the direction of a major production, set in a faraway land and no doubt costing a fortune, to an actor totally devoid of any relevant experience?

The only person who supported me in this patently absurd ambition was, naturally, Sheila. She said if this was something I really cared about, a story I desperately wanted to tell, then I shouldn't let anything or anyone put me off. What neither of us realised was that *Gandhi* would impact on every aspect of our own lives, and those of our three young children, for years and years to come.

By the time I met Moti, we owned our Queen Anne house on Richmond Green outright. We'd bought it for a song just after the war, with not a little financial help from parents and friends.

Having lived for a long while with newspaper instead of carpet on the floor, Old Friars was by now pretty much as we wanted it. I had a Rolls with a personalised number plate and Sheila had her Jag. The art I'd started to collect simply because I liked it was beginning to appreciate significantly in value. We had help in the house and in the attached suite of offices, together with a nanny and a chauffeur. Bills came in and they were paid. School fees fell due and they were met. All this, with that one phone call, I was placing in jeopardy.

In the years which followed, bills often weren't paid on time and I was absent more and more, either trying to raise money for *Gandhi* or acting in faraway places, just to keep the project afloat. At one point, I sold three paintings by Stanley Spencer, the pride and joy of my collection, for a pittance to tide us over until I got another job. I can't bear to think what they would fetch today.

Then later still, just as we were about to start shooting in India, I took the biggest gamble of all, by volunteering to forgo my entire salary until *Gandhi* went into profit. To make matters worse, I knew full well by then that film distributors' balance sheets, even for hugely successful worldwide blockbusters, rarely show any profit at all.

This is creative accounting as an extreme art form. It is also why the really big stars now insist on having a gross percentage, right off the top, straight from the box-office take. Somehow in Hollywood the receipts never exceed the cost. You suspect the private jets, the executives' holiday trips with one short 'meeting' in some far-flung outpost, the shortfall on this, the overhead on that all get charged to your film. And probably to half a dozen other films as well. So labyrinthine is this system that only twice, to the best of my knowledge, has anyone challenged it in the American courts and won.

As it happened, because of what seemed like a series of disasters at the time, *Gandhi* was saved from this fate. But that was way in the future. What preoccupied me when I committed to Moti Kothari was finding sufficient cash to fund an initial script and, of course, overcoming the not inconsiderable problem of learning to be a director.

First and foremost, though, I believed I had to take soundings in India. Would they allow an Englishman to make a film about their Mahatma? The country had been free of British rule for just sixteen years and it was possible, I reasoned, that memories of colonialism were still too raw for our project to be even accepted, let alone welcomed.

And, as Moti had drummed into me, Gandhi had been so much more than a political leader. The very word, mahatma, means 'great soul'.

On a more prosaic level, I knew the sheer logistics of the epic story I intended to tell would require the cooperation of the Indian government, the armed forces, police, railways and, above all, the huge and lumbering bureaucracy that we, the British, had left behind.

How was I to make contact with someone powerful enough to set all this in motion? The answer came at a lunch in Mayfair organised by the Variety Club. One of the other guests was Admiral Sir Ronald Brockman who worked with Earl Mountbatten of Burma, the last of Britain's long line of British viceroys in India and the man who, after independence, was invited to stay on as first Governor General of the new republic.

I was already acquainted with Lord Louis, as I called him, because my first film, *In Which We Serve*, was based on one of his own wartime naval exploits and we'd met a number of times since. So, at the end of the Variety Club lunch, I collared Ronnie Brockman and asked how best to approach his boss.

In another of those kismet moments, he invited me to accompany him back to their offices, saying he knew the great man had a spare twenty minutes before his first scheduled meeting that same afternoon.

We walked over to the Ministry of Defence where Lord Louis kindly agreed to see me straight away. I told him about the film and asked if he might be willing to put my case to the Indian Prime Minister. He responded by asking me to write a summary of everything I'd told him and to end this aide-memoire with the all-important question: was my proposal one which might in principle gain official approval?

I promised to let him have such a document within a couple of days. That was too late, he said. Too late? Yes, he was leaving for Delhi the following morning and, since he'd be spending a week as Pandit Nehru's house guest, would put my request to him in person.

Three days later, the meticulous Lord Louis sent me a telex – no fax or email in those days – saying the Prime Minister had given the approval in principle I'd sought. That was the first time I experienced the decisiveness that emanates from real power.

Years later, when I most needed it, Pandit Nehru's daughter, then herself India's Prime Minister, would demonstrate the same ability to cut through red tape and make everything possible.

By the end of May 1963, I was in Delhi with an appointment to meet Pandit Nehru in his office early one Sunday morning. Moti had been taken ill at the last moment with a recurring heart problem and it was his brother, Vala, who greeted me with a *pranam* as I emerged from the airport. He suggested I might like to visit the Gandhi Samadhi at Rajghat on my way to the hotel. Despite the long plane journey and the intense heat, I could think of no more fitting way to begin my first passage to India.

If, like me, you have never been further east than the Mediterranean, India immediately impacts on every one of your senses. You taste dust and hear klaxons, music, street cries, laughter, bells, song, traffic. You smell tuberose and excrement, spices and petrol fumes. You touch hot metal and wipe ineffectually at the sweat that seems to spring from every pore. And, above all, you see an intensity and a combination of colour you never dreamed existed.

I sat forward in the taxi, trying to fix all this in my mind as we made our way to the River Yamuna and the spot where Mahatma Gandhi had been cremated on the last day of January 1948. His samadhi is, in essence, an open-air funerary platform, made of brick, which has been overlaid with polished black marble. After his body was incinerated on a pyre, some of the ashes were interred close by and the remainder scattered in all the seas and principal rivers of India.

On this, my first visit, the place was crowded with people. Vala and I removed our shoes, as is the custom, and placed a garland of marigolds in tribute. If I had been religious, I would have said a prayer. Instead, I thought of the man and what I had undertaken, hoping I could do him justice. On later visits to India and when we were making the film, I often visited the samadhi at dawn when it was deserted. It became a place to reach inside myself and, when the going was tough, to find new strength.

Next day early, another taxi took me up Rajpath towards the imposing government complex of Rashtrapati Bhavan, the series of imposing ochre buildings designed by Lutyens, originally the seat of the viceroys.

Mr Nehru's office was in South Block. Although it was not yet eight thirty, a number of people were already waiting to see him. As I was first, I was told it would be greatly appreciated if I did not exceed my allotted thirty minutes since his diary was tightly scheduled.

At precisely the appointed time, I was shown in. Mr Nehru got to his feet and greeted me with the now increasingly familiar *pranam* and, without hesitation, I responded in kind. In manner and appearance he was exactly as I had expected; calm, courteous and extremely focused. He encouraged me to tell him what I knew of the Mahatma and my plans for the film.

It was all going extremely well and we seemed to have been talking for no time at all when I glanced at my watch. To my horror, my half-hour had already elapsed. I started to make a move. 'I don't believe we have finished,' he said. 'Do please sit down.'

He then produced an album of snapshots and professional photographs; his own priceless collection of intimate and formal images recording India's long march to independence. Some of the pictures were loose and, so that we could pore over them together, he laid them out on the floor.

We got down on our hands and knees. Throughout, he referred to Gandhi as Bapu, which, he told me, was the respectful Hindi word for father. Here was a snap of Bapu spinning cotton at his ashram. There was another with the young Nehru himself, laughing together like naughty schoolboys. The Prime Minister, now sitting back on his heels, was telling me stories; touching and funny anecdotes mixed up with his personal interpretation of historical events. This was gold dust. Wishing I'd had the foresight to bring a tape recorder, I tried desperately to commit what he said to memory.

A civil servant came into the office. Seeing the Prime Minister on the floor, he stooped, somewhat embarrassed, and handed him a note. Still on his knees, Mr Nehru glanced at it. 'Yes, yes, yes,' he said dismissively. With a reproachful look at me, the man left.

Eventually, Mr Nehru returned to his desk. He said he wanted me to remember that, when asked if he had a message for mankind, Bapu had responded: 'My life is my message.'

He also said he would arrange for me to see a number of people who would be helpful and that I must meet his daughter. He dialled a number and, when the call was answered, said, 'I am sending the English film actor and producer, Richard Attenborough, to see you. He is going to make a film about Bapu.'

I was elated. He hadn't said I hoped or even that I wanted to make a film about Bapu but that I was *going* to make it. With this endorsement ringing in my ears, I left for his official residence, Teen Murti, and my first encounter with Indira Gandhi. She was not in any way related to the Mahatma, as many in the West suppose. Her husband, Feroze Gandhi, a Member of the Indian Parliament had died in 1960, leaving her with two sons, Rajiv and Sanjay. The widow and her boys moved in with the Prime Minister, who was also alone, and she became his official hostess.

It is hard, now, to reconcile the shy, softly spoken woman who greeted me at Teen Murti with her later public persona. When she entered the room, the sari which covered her head was also drawn modestly across the lower part of her face, revealing only her eyes and part of her hairline, untouched as yet by the famous white streak.

There was nothing hawkish or imperious in her manner, nothing to indicate that in eight years' time, as Prime Minister herself, she would lead her country into a war. Neither was there any sign that, prior to Independence, this polite woman with an Oxford degree had been jailed for eight months by my fellow countrymen.

She was obviously knowledgeable about cinema, both Indian and Western. I asked if she believed an Indian film-maker would be better suited to my project.

There was, she said, only one who could make a film which would reach out to every nationality. That, of course, was the great Satyajit Ray, but he was not a devotee of the Mahatma. With her expressions of interest and, indeed, enthusiasm ringing in my ears, I took my leave, saying I would return with a script before the end of the year.

Back in London, I set to work producing and acting in *Séance on a Wet Afternoon*. My partner, Bryan Forbes, had written the script and was directing. Because my make-up was extremely complicated, requiring a prosthetic nose, I had to arrive at Pinewood by six thirty in the morning in order to be ready on set at eight. We'd shoot for the next ten hours, with a break for rushes and lunch. Then, by seven in the evening, I'd be back in my Richmond office and work until gone midnight with the newly engaged *Gandhi* screenwriter, a scholarly and mercurial Irishman called Gerry Hanley.

DH— *Séance* was a difficult film for me. Playing opposite Dick was the middle-aged Kim Stanley, a highly regarded method actress in her native America, but virtually unknown in the UK. Being averse to air travel, Miss Stanley had insisted on crossing the Atlantic by liner. Dick and Bryan drove down to Southampton to meet her and, having been asked to ensure that the press turned out to record the occasion, I went with them.

During the journey, the two men decided they ought to greet their leading lady with a bouquet. The problem was that none of us was carrying a chequebook and our pooled cash amounted to very little. So it was a pitifully small and slightly wilted bunch of flowers that Dick presented to his underwhelmed co-star in her stateroom. Worse was to follow. On learning that two men from the *Southern Daily Echo* were waiting – after a great deal of undisclosed arm-twisting on my part – to interview and photograph her on deck, Miss Stanley haughtily informed us she did not 'do' publicity.

The film, essentially a two-hander, was shot in moody black and white. The story ended with a twist which could not, on pain of death, be revealed. The female lead, having taken against me on sight, was not posing for pictures or giving any interviews. No matter how hard I tried, I couldn't get any publicity. Feeling very bad about this, I remember offering to take a cut in salary which Dick, as producer, turned down.

Towards the end of shooting, he passed a kidney stone, reputed to be the nearest a man can come to childbirth. The pain must have been bad because our leading man was absent from the set for a whole day while his pal, the director, doubled for him in long shot.

I should add, despite my own shortcomings, that *Séance* did very well at the box office. Many believe this was Dick's finest performance and it won him the BAFTA Best Actor award in 1964. For me, though, his most outstanding characterisation was in *Guns at Batasi*, our next film together, which won him a second BAFTA in 1966.

RA— I'd raised the money to pay Gerry Hanley for a first-draft screenplay from a very unlikely source.

John Davis, who ran the Rank Organisation, was probably as ruthless a man as I have ever come across. He was disliked intensely by almost everyone on the creative side of the British film industry because he was a bully who brought an accountant's rationale to bear on every artistic decision. The subject of a film was irrelevant. All that mattered to JD was the balance sheet. Under his aegis, Rank began to pander to the lucrative US market by putting American characters played by failing American stars into British stories. As a result, the pictures lost their identity and, like the Europuddings of later years, became bland mid-Atlantic tosh that ended up pleasing no one.

And yet, when I went to see him about *Gandhi*, JD was remarkably kind and very straightforward. Despite his fearsome reputation, he didn't humiliate me. He just said, 'I don't think anything of the subject and I don't believe it will work. But I do accept your commitment and I think you should be given a chance.' He immediately wrote a cheque for £5,000 without any conditions attached.

Impressed by this, Moti Kothari now disclosed that he too had been seeking funding and believed he was on the verge of success. Since a major portion of the film's budget would be spent in India, which had very strict currency regulations, we needed to find either a cash-rich Indian company or an extremely wealthy individual willing to invest a great many rupees.

Fateh Singh Rao Gaekwar, known to his chums as Jackie, was every inch the Asian potentate. When he became the Maharaja of Baroda in 1951, he had inherited a fabulous fortune, then estimated to be worth £15 million and today, I would imagine, close to a billion. This expansive and jolly man adored cricket and, as a Member of the Indian Parliament, went on to become the Gujurat Minister for Health, Fisheries and Jails.

Moti introduced us just as shooting on *Séance* was coming to an end. To my delight, Jackie proved very keen to supply some rupee funding for pre-production and ultimately some or all of the total *Gandhi* Indian expenditure. This was the start of a relationship which, over the next seventeen years, would all but drive me crackers.

DH— In the autumn of 1963, I was asked to publicise a Rank film about beauty queens which started out as 36:18:36 and later became *The Beauty Jungle*. The star was Janette Scott, daughter of Thora Hird and the girlfriend of a vicar's son called David Frost who did rather bad stand-up in nightclubs but was just beginning to make a name for himself with a highly irreverent TV programme, *That Was The Week That Was*.

After we'd filmed location scenes with Tommy Trinder in Weston-super-Mare, *The Beauty Jungle* moved to the French Riviera. I'd brought onto the production a stills cameraman who worked for *Weekend* magazine and it was this friend, Tommy Hanley, later the Beatles' photographer, who introduced me to my second husband.

Peter Hawkins was a former Fleet Street news editor who'd inherited a small fortune from his father and gone to live in Valbonne where he acted as a freelance stringer, mainly for the Sunday tabloids. As Tommy pointed out, I needed editorial space, he needed stories, and the film had plenty of bathing beauties. How could we not get on?

I hated Peter on sight. He was tall and blond and appeared to be perpetually looking down his Roman nose. But he was fascinated by the film business and we persevered, trying to be polite to each other, until, a week later, I realised I was totally in love. When the film crew flew back to London, Peter came too. He was still there with me, in my one-room Chelsea flat, when I started work at Pinewood on *Guns at Batasi*.

Dick was playing the lead, this time without the added responsibility of being the film's producer. That position was taken by his RAF friend, George Brown, father of a ten-year-old daughter called Tina who would eventually take New York society by storm when she became editor of *Vanity Fair*.

In *Guns at Batasi*, Dick played an old-style regimental sergeant major serving out his time in an unstable African colony on the verge of independence. For this he had to assume a ramrod posture, a closed mind and a stentorian parade-ground voice. But what made the characterisation so special was his subtle depiction of the gradual breakdown of certainty in a career soldier facing a huge moral dilemma not covered, or even envisaged, in Queen's Regulations.

With this film, I had no trouble at all in gaining huge amounts of publicity, though not for the leading man.

At the outset, the juvenile lead was to be played by an unknown Swedish model in the Bardot mould called Britt Ekland. She was young, shapely and a natural blonde. We put her up at the Dorchester and arranged a press conference to announce her casting.

Meanwhile, however, Miss Ekland bumped into one of the hotel's other guests, Peter Sellers, who had taken up residence in the Oliver Messel suite. Within hours, it seemed, Britain's best-loved comedian had proposed and Britt had accepted. Our press conference was a riot.

They were married almost immediately on a snowy day in February 1964 at Guilford Register Office. Their haste was due to an imminent parting. Britt was about to start work on *Guns at Batasi* at Pinewood, and Sellers was contracted to *Kiss Me, Stupid* in Hollywood.

I was roped in to help cope with the hordes of reporters and photographers who besieged the wedding reception at Sellers' Surrey home. My new love, the other Peter, was thrilled to accompany me to this huge showbiz event. I remember him sauntering, glass of champagne in hand, down to the gate to greet his shivering Fleet Street mates. He came back with a proposition. The photographers were close to their deadline. If Mr Sellers would agree to be photographed carrying his bride across the threshold, they would all go away. This was duly done, with my Peter, poacher turned gamekeeper, enjoying every minute.

A week or so later at Pinewood, I became aware that the new Mrs Sellers was not a happy camper. Having arrived late on set, a cardinal sin, she confessed that her groom had kept her awake most of the night with a long-distance phone call. Missing her desperately, he'd convinced himself she was having an affair with her pop idol co-star, the young John Leyton. Peter was going crazy, Britt said. She was afraid he'd do something silly.

This went on for several more days. Then, one morning, Britt failed to turn up at all. We learned, at lunchtime, that she'd flown to Los Angeles to be with Sellers. Shortly after their passionate reunion, he suffered his first heart attack.

Back at Pinewood, producer George Brown and the prickly director, John Guillermin, needed a new juvenile lead and they needed her quickly. Britt's replacement, who flew in from Hollywood, was a shy, softly spoken girl of nineteen with brown hair long enough to sit on. Her name was Mia Farrow and she was the convent-educated daughter of Maureen O'Sullivan, the original Jane to Johnny Weissmuller's Tarzan.

As if fulfilling Peter Sellers' fears at second remove, Mia and John Leyton got on extremely well; so well I expected them to marry. But nothing happened and, when shooting finished, Miss Farrow returned to the States, where she amazed everyone by promptly becoming the third wife of 49-year-old Frank Sinatra.

RA— The news reached me on 27 May 1964 while I was shooting an emotional scene with Mia and Dame Flora Robson. In the early hours of that morning, Pandit Nehru had died. I was devastated; India had lost a wise and charismatic leader, the world had lost one of its few truly great statesmen and, just as *Gandhi* seemed to be making a break-through, I had lost my most valued advocate.

Just two months later, with shooting on *Guns at Batasi* completed, I joined forces with someone as far removed from Pundit Nehru as anyone could possibly imagine.

Joseph E. Levine was one of America's greatest showmen and a one-man band in the land of giant corporations. He was born in a Boston slum in 1905, the youngest of a Russian immigrant tailor's six children. Joe became a hustler almost as soon as he could walk, working as a newsboy, shoeshine; anything and everything to help his widowed mother. He told me his introduction to the movie business came when he was hired to run cans of film from one nickelodeon to another, enabling a group of exhibitors to maximise box-office receipts by showing each reel to as many audiences as possible in the space of a single evening.

The brainwave that propelled Joe into the big time came in 1959 when he went to Rome and purchased distribution rights to an existing film for peanuts. *Hercules* was a dire Italian action adventure which boasted, in his own words, 'musclemen, broads, a shipwreck and a dragon for the kids'.

He risked a lot of money dubbing on a new track, cleaning up the negative, making hundreds of prints and literally flooding the media with advertising. When the picture opened simultaneously at over six hundred movie houses across America, Joe made an absolute fortune before bad word of mouth could kill it stone dead.

With this one huge gamble, he had created a method of transforming a turkey into blockbuster that endures to this day. And, once he hit the big time, Joe began to splash out. He bought a vast estate in Greenwich, Connecticut, and a hundred-foot yacht which he named after his beloved wife, Rosalie. He travelled with an immense retinue, staying always in the largest suite at the world's most luxurious hotels. His Manhattan office on East 52nd was above his favourite 'fast-food joint' – the swanky Four Seasons.

Having been recognised by Hollywood as a player, albeit through distributing some truly awful pictures, Joseph E. Levine reinvented himself as a man of taste. At the start of the sixties, he bought the De Sica film *Two Women*, and lobbied expensively to get an Oscar nomination for its unknown lead player, Sophia Loren. She became the first star of a foreign-language film to win Best Actress. Many other Oscars followed for the films Joe backed, including one for Katharine Hepburn in *The Lion in Winter*, perhaps his favourite of them all.

I met him through a friend of my London agent, John Redway, in the summer of 1964. Mr Levine was ensconced in a huge suite at Claridge's where lawyers and number crunchers were wheeling and dealing in every room, including both bathrooms. While cruising between the different groups, the bulky dreadnought at the centre of all this frenetic activity came across me. He said, almost without stopping, 'Why the hell d'ya want to make a film about Gandhi?'

The fact that he scarcely paused gave me time to compose my answer. What I told him when he cruised back again seemed to go down well and, incredibly, by the end of the morning, Joe had agreed to finance a major research trip to India and to assume all the financial obligations which Moti and I had already undertaken, allowing me to repay John Davis.

Mr Levine flew back to Los Angeles with Gerry Hanley's completed script and all the legal and financial information he required. Within a matter of days, we heard that Paramount had agreed to distribute the film under their existing agreement with Joe's own production company, Embassy. As soon as Jackie Baroda committed, *Gandhi* would be up and running.

DH— *Guns at Batasi* was the last time I would see or work with Dick for over a decade. As a unit publicist, unless I was working on one of his films, I never felt part of the tightly knit creative crew, but merely a crass, uber-annoying female appendage, forever jeopardising the sacred shooting schedule or producing unwelcome journalists. This was never more evident than during the making of *The High Bright Sun*, a film about Cypriot independence.

As was usual, there were just three other women on the unit: the costume designer, the continuity 'girl' (a chauvinist job title if ever there was one) and clever, glamorous Betty Box, Britain's first and, at that time, only female producer. The stars were Dirk Bogarde and Susan Strasberg.

Calabria, way down in the boot of Italy, was doubling for Cyprus, and everyone was struggling in the intense summer heat to meet the end of shooting deadline. My main concern was that I was lacking a posed two-shot of the lead players which was crucial to the poster design. Susan and Dirk, who didn't get on, had continually made all kinds of lame excuses not to pose together. And so, on the very last day of the location, I was obliged to ask the first assistant director to give me just five minutes with both of them in costume so that the stills cameraman could get this vital picture.

He snarled in his Old Etonian drawl: 'In case you hadn't noticed, we're trying to make a film here.'

I snarled back: 'And I'm trying to make sure somebody bloody well pays to see it.'

I got my shot but the episode epitomised everything I disliked about being a publicist. On returning to London, I gave up the lease on my Chelsea flat, loaded all my possessions into my MG Midget and drove to the French Riviera.

There, Peter and I rented a painter's eyrie in the old quarter of Antibes overlooking the ramparts, the Baie des Anges and the snow-capped Alpes Maritimes beyond. Having erected a narrow shelf all around the huge studio and filled it with bottles of wine, we threw a party for everyone Peter knew, emptying them in a single evening. Not surprisingly, we soon ran out of money.

My lover decided to try his hand at writing a novel. With nothing to do except rattle around, making it impossible for him to concentrate, I started to write too.

RA— Now that *Gandhi* was, to all intents and purposes, up and running, Moti felt able to resign from the Indian High Commission to concentrate on the film. With the same intention, I turned down an extremely lucrative offer to appear in MGM's *Operation Crossbow*.

We hired the Savoy Hotel's River Room to announce that our project, then called *Mahatma Gandhi*, would go into production on 2 October 1965, the ninety-sixth anniversary of his birth. *Daily Cinema* described the event as 'one of the largest and most enthusiastic press receptions seen in London for many a year'.

With hindsight, I realise everything that followed was inherent in the occasion. Jackie Baroda had sent last-minute apologies and Joe, who'd once described himself in a press handout as 'a colossus, towering above the lesser moguls of filmdom', was conspicuous only by his absence.

2

ENTIRELY UP TO YOU

RA— I REMEMBER OUR MA and Pa sitting with their backs to the autumn sunlight flooding through the big bay window, their faces wreathed in hopeful smiles.

It is September 1939 and, unusually, Dave, Johnny and I have all been called into the Governor's study. Normally, we'd be summoned individually to receive one of his dreaded more-in-sorrow-than-in-anger lectures. But now we sit here in a row, facing him and Mary; three ordinary boys aged sixteen, fourteen and ten, squinting as we try to take in the enormity of what we are being asked to decide.

Since Kristallnacht, when the Nazis staged violent attacks on the entire Jewish population of Germany, the Governor has chaired the Leicester branch of the British Jewish Refugee Committee. In response to this organisation's urgent representations, Parliament has allowed an unspecified number of Jewish children to enter Britain temporarily, provided each is backed by a £50 bond 'to assure their ultimate resettlement'. Chillingly, this emergency measure also stipulates they must make the long journey across Europe unaccompanied and in sealed trains.

In less than a year, ten thousand children have been brought out of Germany, Austria and Eastern Europe in a massive rescue operation, known as *Kindertransport*. Most have gone on to find safe haven with relatives in the USA and Canada.

Then, a few days ago, we'd all gathered round the wireless in the drawing room to hear Prime Minister Neville Chamberlain admit his policy of appeasement had failed; Britain was at war with Germany. Hours later, a German U-boat had sunk the British liner, SS *Athenia*, carrying over a thousand passengers to America.

This means, the Governor now tells us, that civilians are no longer able to cross the Atlantic, even if they manage to obtain visas. So the two fearful little girls occupying our guest bedroom cannot go, as arranged, to their uncle in New York.

Irene and Helga Bejach, neither speaking a word of English, arrived in London alone. Mary met them at St Pancras and brought them back to Leicester with their pathetic little suitcases; two pale waifs whose Jewish mother had been dragged from her bed in the early hours of the morning and dispatched to a concentration camp. Now, their Gentile father, the Medical Officer of Health for Berlin, was also facing internment, for refusing to issue an anti-Semitic statement, publicly disowning his wife and children.

Irene is eleven and has a nervous tic that constantly wrenches her face. Helga, aged nine, came covered in sores. More traumatised than we can possibly imagine, both wet their beds. And now Mary and the Governor are asking Dave, Johnny and me if we will agree to accept these two little strangers as our sisters.

No one's pretending this will be easy, the Governor says. He carefully details the significant difference it will make to all our lives. Irene and Helga are very shocked and frightened. He and our mother propose to treat them in all respects as their daughters while helping them to follow their own religion. To maintain the hope that they will eventually be reunited with their parents, the girls would call our ma and pa 'aunt' and 'uncle'.

Two extra children will mean the family income, now supporting five, stretching to seven. Household economies will need to be made, clothes made to last longer, treats and holidays curtailed. Mary goes on to warn us that, much as she loves us – and she does, dearly – Irene and Helga need her to show them love even more than we do. Because these changes will affect us all, the Governor concludes, he and our mother feel the decision should not be theirs alone.

As I sit there with Dave and Johnny, trying to take in the consequences of this bombshell proposal, I'm aware that both our parents are silently willing us not to let them down. But it is Mary who adds the words which make it utterly impossible to refuse. She says gently: 'It's entirely up to you, darlings.'

Irene and Helga became our sisters and remained so for the rest of their lives. When the war was over, we learned that both their parents had perished in the Holocaust. As teenagers, the girls went to live with their uncle in the United States where they married and became American citizens. Dave, Johnny and I remained in close touch and they joined us in mourning Mary and the Governor when they died. Irene and Helga have gone too now and I miss them very much indeed.

They brought into our ordered, middle-class household an awareness of a wider and more dangerous world. It was their presence which allowed the Governor and Mary to show us in an immediate and practical fashion that actions do indeed speak louder than words. And their enduring faith gave us all some understanding of what it means to be Jewish.

Many years later, I believe it was this, together with the presence of my two adopted sisters in America, which was largely responsible for the undeniable bond I had with Joe Levine. Indeed, during the time we worked harmoniously on two films, Joe bestowed on me the highest accolade in his colourful vocabulary. I was, he said, a real *mensch*. It was this evident affection which was to make our final severance so unexpected and so very painful.

DH— In the South of France, the Swinging Sixties had completely passed me by. By the early seventies, barely eking a living as novelists, Peter and I had gradually moved to the less fashionable end of the Riviera and then across the border to Italy, where the living was cheaper still. We wound up renting a small apartment in an idyllic but isolated medieval hill village, perched fifteen hundred feet above the Mediterranean.

The three hundred inhabitants of the ancient principality of Seborga had recently taken the quixotic decision to secede from Italy, by proclaiming independence and creating their own frontier, painting a wobbly blue line across the only access road. After some initial suspicion, they took us to their hearts. When funds were particularly low, I'd find little gifts on our doorstep first thing in the morning; a clutch of eggs, zucchini with yellow flowers attached or just a single huge and fragrant tomato.

By now Peter had been commissioned to write an authorised biography of Prince Rainier of Monaco and, having sold three adult novels, I'd been asked by my agent, George Greenfield, to ghost a new book for the ageing Enid Blyton, then in the grip of Alzheimer's. This I felt unable to do but found myself wanting to write for children, mainly, I think, because I so longed for a child of my own.

My story was called *Zozu the Robot.* I dashed it off very quickly, and then, convinced it was a load of pretentious tosh, chucked it into the dustbin. Unbeknown to me, Peter rescued the typescript and sent it off to London where hardback rights were bought by the prestigious Sidgwick & Jackson. Years later, a steady stream of royalties from the eventual Puffin paperback would be all that stood between me and the British bailiffs.

Blissfully happy in zany Seborga and on the strength of the two book sales, we decided to get married. A British consulate was the easiest place to solemnise our expat union and the nearest was across the border in Nice.

My parents were coming down for the occasion. Before they arrived, we visited our friends, mostly yacht crews, along the Côte d'Azur, inviting them to the ceremony and on to a party afterwards at a sailors' bar on Monte Carlo harbour.

One of the intended guests was a rich American widow who had a large house on Cap Ferrat. When we went there to issue an invitation, however, our friend was absent. She'd rented the house to a somewhat eccentric English couple who were still unpacking. He was Jonathan Routh, who'd fronted the first reality television programme, *Candid Camera*, and she was Bobbie, bubbly ex-wife of the multimillionaire publisher and philanthropist, Paul Hamlyn.

When we explained our mission, these two complete strangers insisted on acting as our best man and bridesmaid. Jonathan said he'd provide the bouquet, which proved to be a bunch of greenery bearing chilli peppers and, because someone had to do it, Bobbie promised to cry.

She had her handkerchief at the ready as the marriage ceremony got under way. Halfway through his preamble, the consul stopped and looked around the room, counting under his breath. 'Oh dear,' he said prissily, 'I see there are thirteen present.' He bustled out and returned with a sullen French cleaner who shut the door and took a seat at the back.

Having appeased superstition, the consul stood behind his desk which, being covered by Union Flag, looked remarkably like a coffin and started again from the beginning, frowning because of the giggles. He'd reached the bit about anyone knowing of any lawful impediment when he stopped for a second time.

'Is that door shut?' We assured him it was. 'It won't do,' he snapped. 'Someone, please open it. We'll have to begin again.'

It transpired that our marriage wouldn't be legal unless any last-minute protestor was able to storm into the room unimpeded. By the time the consul finally pronounced us man and wife, he could hardly be heard above the guffaws. Our bridesmaid was laughing so hard that tears were coursing down her face.

Maybe thirteen was indeed an ill omen. Bubbly Bobbie committed suicide a few years later. It's the only time I've ever heard of a woman slitting her own throat. And among the wedding guests at the sailors' bar in Monte Carlo was an unknown redhead. Some years later, she would help to break my heart.

RA— It's clear to me now that, despite his avowals, Joe Levine never really shared my passion for *Gandhi*. The very qualities I so admired in the Mahatma – self-deprecation, renunciation of worldly goods, passive resistance – all ran counter to what made my maverick mogul tick. Above all, Joe was motivated by the desire for prestige as a film-maker and, strangely, because there was no outward sign of this, by his racial heritage.

He was not overtly Jewish; I never saw him wear the yarmulke or knew him to attend synagogue and, when I spent long weekends with his family, they did not keep the Sabbath. Nevertheless, after India formally recognised the Palestine Liberation Organisation in 1975, Joe was angry. And when the PLO was granted full diplomatic status, again under Indira Gandhi's leadership, he was incandescent.

1980 had begun so propitiously. I'd managed to secure a deal with the BBC whereby, at some future date, they would pay £1 million for a British television premiere and subsequent screenings of *Gandhi*. This would enable us to raise a matching amount of production funding against their guarantee.

Even more importantly, a prickly, superstitious and utterly brilliant American by the name of Jack Briley had delivered a new version of the screenplay which was by far the most moving and insightful I'd ever commissioned. Even Joe greeted it with praise. He said it was 'bankable'.

Although I'm convinced international politics lay at the heart of it, the event which precipitated our rupture was, of all things, a birthday party. Jackie Baroda had resurfaced again in February, promising to invest the rupee equivalent of $10 million in the film and Joe immediately flew over to meet him at the Dorchester, bringing his lawyer. In their presence, Jackie finally signed a contract which, Joe was certain, together with the BBC deal and Briley's script, would enable him to raise the full dollar component without any difficulty. Jackie, Joe and I shook hands on the deal and, in an atmosphere of euphoria, promised ourselves that, together, we would make one of the great movies of all time.

Joe returned to New York and Jackie departed for Delhi. The very next day, however, the maharaja's London advisers informed me the document he'd signed could cause him huge legal problems in India and must be withdrawn immediately. For twenty-four hours, I tried frantically to reach Jackie on the phone, only to discover he was incommunicado in Lahore with the Indian cricket team.

At the end of March, he suddenly reappeared in London and, after further negotiations with his lawyers, I was again given an assurance that the necessary rupees would be forthcoming. A few days later it was Jackie's fiftieth birthday.

Sheila and I hosted a party for him at Old Friars and, as Joe was in Connecticut, invited his London representative, Eddy Bryson. Jackie arrived in full brocaded maharaja regalia and formally announced to the assembled show-business guests that he was the principal backer of the *Gandhi* film. At that, I proposed a toast and we all drank to the munificent birthday boy and the success of the project.

A couple of days later, on Easter Sunday, Joe rang me. In one of the most unpleasant phone calls I can ever remember, he chose to interpret the whole birthday celebration as a huge, calculated insult to himself. 'That shit Baroda' was not be trusted. Moreover, he'd been told that I'd never so much as mentioned his name in any of the toasts. Going on to call the Indian Prime Minister 'a two-timing bitch' among a tirade of Yiddish expletives, Joe suddenly announced, 'That's it!' He had no intention of proceeding with *Gandhi* and, without him, I'd never be able to raise a single dollar. When I disputed this, he snarled, 'OK, you have it, Dickie,' meaning copyright in the script, 'I'll let you have it.'

The copyright in question was vested in three versions of the screen-play by different writers, together with the core material on which they were based, Louis Fischer's biography of the Mahatma and another of his books, *The Essential Gandhi*. Because Fischer believed so fervently in our project, he'd sold film rights to Moti and me, as a partnership, for just £1 and I'd become sole owner after Moti's untimely death from a heart attack in September 1969. Some time later, convinced that Joe's enthusiasm and commitment matched my own, I'd signed all the rights over to him; free, gratis and for nothing. Tautology apart, that was to prove one of the biggest and costliest mistakes of my life.

Immediately after his ranting phone call, I wrote to Joe, saying I'd invested nearly twenty years in this film and was not about to abandon it. I was determined to stick with the project until it went ahead or went under.

My letter crossed with a telex, obviously written at Joe's behest, from Bill Goldberg, his in-house accountant. This stated in terse legal jargon that I was not at liberty to make any representations or commitments whatsoever in regard to *Gandhi*, since all rights were the sole property of Joseph E. Levine Presents Inc.

I rang Joe and explained a letter was on its way to him. He didn't budge an inch, saying harshly, 'I want a severance.'

My belly churning, I replied, 'All right, Joe. I accept.'

Worse was to follow. Less than two weeks after the birthday party, I learned that Jackie Baroda's much trumpeted investment was nothing of the sort. What he was actually offering was a rupee loan, equivalent to just under $1 million with interest computed daily at 2 per cent over base rate. Furthermore, the whole amount had to be repaid within three months. Bearing in mind the legal constraints imposed by Joe and with no other funding on the horizon, there was no way I could take up such a loan, even if the terms had been remotely acceptable.

In April of that year, carrying Jack Briley's revised script, I flew to India in a last-ditch attempt to save the production.

DH— Life had happened while I was making other plans.

In Seborga, I was approaching forty. Working on an outline for a new novel, I suddenly found myself unaccountably exhausted. I'd see our bedroom from my desk and think, I'll just lie down for a while. Three, four, five hours later, Peter would be shaking me awake.

Because I was more fluent in French, I went to consult a doctor in Menton, just across the Italian border. After taking my medical history, this jovial man invited me to undress and considerately stubbed out his Gauloise before conducting an examination. Then he smiled, rather smugly I thought, as he pressed some kind of instrument to my stomach and reached across to turn a dial on a box beside the couch. To my total amazement, the room was filled with a rhythmic squelching. Spreading his hands in one of those infuriatingly self-satisfied Gallic gestures, the guru announced, 'Your baby's heart, madame.'

I'd heard of dozy women who claimed to have no idea they were with child until they actually gave birth. And here I was, sixteen weeks pregnant according to this Frenchman, without a clue.

He proceeded to give me a lecture. It was not good for a first-time mother of a certain age to be living up a mountain, *surtout* an Italian mountain, many kilometres from the nearest medical facility. Such a late pregnancy must be closely monitored at every stage. I paid for the consultation and went out into the blazing August sunshine.

Peter and our red-headed best friend, Jeannie, were waiting for me in Italy. I knew that he, twelve years older and already a father of three from his first marriage, would not exactly welcome my unexpected news. But alone in Menton with hordes of holidaymakers milling around, I was filled with such joy. With my last couple of francs, I ordered a beer at a pavement cafe and silently toasted my longed for child.

In the event, Peter was remarkably sanguine. Our problem was that we had no money, no entitlement to free treatment and no medical insurance. The answer, we decided, was for me to go to England and throw myself on the mercy of the NHS just long enough to be sure that all was well. Peter, still working on his Rainier biography, would stay in Seborga with our two dogs and Jeannie would come up and cook for him whenever she could.

With hindsight, it was a recipe for disaster.

I went to stay with my parents in Berkshire and made an appointment at the local hospital. There, as an 'elderly primate', I was warned that the odds of my having a Down's syndrome baby were extremely high and agreed to undergo a test. The result was promised within a few weeks and, if it was positive, I'd be urged to have an abortion. I stayed on in England, the weeks went by, my belly swelled, the baby kicked and still no test result. It finally came just two months before my due date: I was expecting a healthy girl.

By then, I was being scanned, assessed, weighed and monitored at ever decreasing intervals. I'd also enrolled in antenatal classes with a group of much younger women who were all intent on having a fashionable, drug-free, 'natural' birth. To help us attain this nirvana, we learned something called the distraction exercise.

Peter came over for the event. He was loving and supportive, although the very idea of my refusing any form of pain relief made him snort with derision. Believing it would help him bond with the baby, I begged him to stay with me during the actual delivery and, somewhat reluctantly, he agreed.

My due date came and went; there were complications and the birth had to be induced. The process was started at nine in the morning and I was in full labour by lunchtime. Whenever the midwife offered an epidural or gas and air, I refused, concentrating like mad on the famous distraction exercise which involved saying 'one hundred' very loudly when a contraction began and counting down until it abated. What had seemed ridiculously easy at antenatal classes now took every ounce of concentration but it worked.

By three in the afternoon, with the baby imminent, Peter couldn't be found. He'd bonded so well with the other expectant fathers that they'd all taken themselves off to the nearest pub. He sidled in eventually; a sheepish bloke of fifty, wearing a mask and gown. Placing himself at the head of the bed and averting his eyes from the business end, he reached for my hand. I was pushing now. And grunting with effort. Peter's nails dug into my palm. 'Easy as shelling peas,' he said bravely, and out the baby came.

We agreed I would stay in England until after the six-week checkup. Peter, meanwhile, went back to rescue the dogs from our Italian neighbours, taking with him all the cash I could muster to pay back rent and settle the grocer's bill. He was waiting at Nice airport when eventually I flew in with baby Kay Iona. Jeannie was not very well, he said; could we stop off and see her on the way home? Not long afterwards, she came to stay in Seborga.

Within a matter of weeks, I discovered Jeannie and Peter were lovers. Life stopped. A decade of love, laughter, trust; all gone.

I rented a car and somehow held it together as I drove non-stop back to my parents' house in England with my five-month-old daughter, the clothes I stood up in and not a penny to my name. On arrival, I had a complete nervous breakdown, rendering me unable to take up my recent commission to write a novel for Doubleday, and joined the feckless army of single parents dependent on government handouts.

RA— Dawn was breaking as I removed my shoes. Somewhere in the sprawling city of Delhi I could hear the morning call to prayer and a screeching flock of parakeets flying towards the nearby river.

Barefoot, I approached the Gandhi Samadhi and stood there for a long while, reflecting on the make-or-break nature of this pilgrimage. Then, as the cremation site filled with light, my thoughts turned to my final encounter with the Mahatma's most trusted ally.

Sixteen long years ago, on my second trip to India, Pandit Nehru had invited me to his official residence, Teen Murti. I'd found him markedly aged in the months that had elapsed since we'd knelt on his office floor to look at photographs. However, despite failing health, he'd remained intensely interested in the film and, during our brief time together, had made two observations I would never forget. The first concerned the huge problem of finding an actor to play Gandhi.

I needed a trained professional, not just a good lookalike; someone with both the skill and the physical attributes to conjure up the passionate young firebrand just as convincingly as the revered octogenarian. The Prime Minister's own somewhat surprising choice had been Alec Guinness. This had taken me aback; not because Alec lacked ability – in my eyes he was remarkable – but because he was English.

'The nationality is unimportant,' Nehru had declared. 'All that matters is that he should be very good.' Then, having reflected for a moment, he'd added with an impish grin, 'And besides, the idea of being portrayed by an Englishman would have made Bapu laugh a great deal.'

When the time had come for me to take my leave, he'd courteously accompanied me to the door of Teen Murti, where we exchanged a farewell *pranam* before I made my way towards the waiting car. Then, as I'd turned to wave, he'd followed me down the steps and taken hold of my hands to underline the importance of the only injunction he ever issued: 'Richard, do not turn him into a deity; he was too great a *man* to be deified.'

Pandit Jawaharlal Nehru had died a few weeks later and his samadhi, Shantivan, was now close to where I stood. As the sun burned away the last vestiges of morning mist over Rajghat, I put on my shoes and made my way back to my hotel. There, I found a message from the present Prime Minister inviting me to dinner.

Indira Gandhi had been appointed Minister of Information and Broadcasting by her father's successor, Lal Bahadur Shastri. For me, this had been enormously helpful, since for two years it placed her in charge of the government department which dealt with film. During that time, I came to understand that, in trying to help me, she was honouring her late father's wishes. Then, following Shastri's sudden death in 1966, Indira herself had become Prime Minister and, in so doing, created a dynasty that would bring her family enormous power and untold personal tragedy.

Over the years since our first meeting, her shyness had completely evaporated and it is true to say that we'd become friends. We'd meet whenever I went to India in an effort to move the film forward, and also in England, where her sons were at school, remaining in touch while she was out of power, following the 1975 State of Emergency. Now, after a landslide victory at the polls just four months earlier, she'd been reinstated. And, following Joe Levine's volte face, I needed her help and advice as never before.

Teen Murti having been turned into a museum, a bungalow complex at 1 Safdarjang Road, within New Delhi's diplomatic enclave, was now the Prime Minister's official residence. Mrs Gandhi lived there with her extended family; the two now adult sons, their wives and children. Sanjay, the younger of the boys, was her undoubted favourite, a hot-headed political heir apparent who was to die only two months later at the controls of a stunt plane. Rajiv, whom I greatly preferred, was then a mild-mannered airline pilot who, having unwillingly assumed his mother's mantle and become Prime Minister himself, was to be killed by a suicide bomber in 1991.

Dinner that night was informal. We all sat laughing and chatting round the table until it was time for the children to go to bed. I'd brought with me a copy of Jack Briley's new script, which Indiraji, as I now called her – the 'ji' being a sign of affectionate respect – promised to read as soon as possible.

Then, with only the adults present, conversation turned inevitably to the film. My hostess wanted to know what exactly was the cause of the long delay. I explained that hard-currency funding could almost certainly be raised, provided I could secure the rupee element. But, unfortunately, all my efforts in this regard had proved fruitless. Jackie Baroda had finally pulled out and I would welcome any advice that might lead me to a new Indian backer.

It was then that Indiraji came up with a proposal. She would arrange a meeting with the present Minister of Information and Broadcasting to see if there was any way in which the government, possibly through an organisation called the National Film Development Corporation, could help find the required rupees.

I was overwhelmed. I couldn't count the number of times I'd flown out to India, totally broke, or the endless humiliating hours I'd waited in the stifling corridors of ministerial buildings, seeking permission to film in various places, only to get bogged down in layer upon layer of bureaucracy.

As her sons and daughters-in-law continued to chat over the dinner table, Indiraji invited me into her study. I occupied one of the armchairs and she slumped behind her desk, looking all of a sudden infinitely weary. I remember thinking how much office had aged her. And then I saw that her body was heaving with huge sobs. Concern overcoming respect, I went and put my arm around her shoulders. And it all came pouring out.

The country was so vast and every area had its own irreconcilable problems. So many different languages, sects and castes. So much hunger and abject poverty. So much potential for religious rioting and bloodshed. No sooner had she attended to one flashpoint than another exploded and then another. It was never-ending. 'Richard,' she said in despair, 'sometimes I just don't know what to do.' It seemed to me, as I searched in vain for some words of comfort, that this must be the loneliest woman in the entire world.

The following day, I discovered Indiraji had been as good as her word. I was given an appointment with Suresh Mathur, the new Joint Secretary to the Minister of Information and Broadcasting, and also met the female managing director of the National Film Development Corporation, Malati Tambey Vaidya.

No more waiting in corridors; suddenly I was making enormous progress. The final breakthrough came at the end of the week when an official letter was hand-delivered to my hotel. This confirmed that I could call on the unpaid collaboration of all three armed services, the police and the entire railway network.

Almost unbelievably, the letter went on to state that, via the NFDC, the government would also supply all the required direct rupee expenditure. In short, India was prepared to invest the equivalent of $8 million, a third of the total funding needed to make the film.

I saw Indiraji once more in Safdarjang Road before I left for London and, of course, thanked her profusely. She, meanwhile, had made time to read the script in the early hours of two successive mornings and said she considered it remarkably successful. Her only suggestion – and she stressed it was only a suggestion – concerned omissions. She believed, for Indian audiences in particular, it would be helpful if the film could acknowledge what we'd been obliged to leave out in order to tell the story of a whole historical epoch in just over three hours of screen time. This was an excellent idea and the finished film began with the following legend written by Jack Briley:

> No man's life can be encompassed in one telling. There is no way to give each year its allotted weight, to include each event, each person who helped to shape a lifetime. What can be done is to be faithful in spirit to the record and try to find one's way to the heart of the man . . .

The Prime Minister then went on to address my greatest concern. Since receiving the official letter, I'd worried that accepting government funding would entail a whole host of quibbling scholars and civil servants, all completely unversed in the medium of film, wanting to meddle with the script. That would be a nightmare scenario and one which, despite my situation, I knew I could never accept.

But Indiraji had already foreseen the problem. Government, she said, should not have right of script approval because the film must be the creation of its makers. Those at the ministry should merely be satisfied, as she was, that the manner in which the subject was envisaged was a proper one.

As I was driven away from her residence, the turbaned Sikh body-guards on either side of the gate snapped to attention. Indiraji was to say: 'When I have men like this around me, I don't believe I have anything to fear.'

How wrong she was. In 1984, as the loneliest woman in the world went to greet Peter Ustinov in the garden behind her house, two of those same bodyguards shot her dead. Both were religious extremists, protesting a government order to storm the holiest shrine of Sikhism, the Golden Temple at Amritsar.

Another friend and mentor had also been assassinated five years earlier in County Sligo, Ireland. Lord Louis Mountbatten and his family were out fishing on their annual seaside holiday when the Provisional IRA detonated a bomb, smashing their little boat to smithereens. Lord Louis, one of his teenage twin grandsons and his son-in-law's mother were killed. His daughter, Patricia, and her husband, my much loved colleague, John Brabourne, were both seriously injured. Neither ever fully recovered.

I loathe any form of physical violence. I can't, for instance, bring myself to watch a boxing match. Through the centuries, different faiths have sanctioned, incited, rewarded and even blessed all kinds of appalling acts. I hate organised religion so much I can't embrace it in any form, although I do believe in a supreme being. I found it utterly depraved that an amazing woman like Indiraji and a man of courage like Lord Louis should be cold-bloodedly murdered in the name of a doctrine.

Unaware of this future tragedy, at the end of April 1980 I boarded an Air India 747 for the long journey home, alternating between jubilation and dread. Jubilation because at long last *Gandhi* was becoming a reality. Dread because of the showdown with Joe which lay ahead.

DH— Holed up in my parents' back bedroom, sleep eluded me and, despite ever increasing doses of prescribed antidepressants, I kept having panic attacks. Worst of all were the voices in my head, conducting this never-ending slanging match, trying to make sense of how my marriage had ended, over and over and over again. Yet, astonishingly, my baby seemed contented; bald as a coot, funny and adorable, my only reason to keep going.

The first pinpoint of light in this dark void came when she outgrew the drawer which served as her bed. I applied to social security for a grant to buy a cot and an official was sent to vet my circumstances. My parents had a pleasant house in a sought-after Berkshire village and, after a good nose round, this woman arbitrarily decided they must be supporting me – they weren't – and turned my application down. It was the best thing that could have happened; I knew I had to get a job.

The phone call I received from Dick shortly afterwards, engineered by our mutual friend, Ann Skinner, was the first time we'd spoken in many years. After we'd exchanged news, he told me he had a problem. Another mutual friend, his devoted personal assistant Maureen Goldner was leaving to get married. Might I be interested in taking over her job? Having kitted myself out courtesy of Oxfam, I went to see him.

Dick and Sheila have lived in the same house since 1949. The face Old Friars presents to the world is a substantial, double-fronted Queen Anne family home. Linked to it is a walled garden, a conservatory filled with orchids, a private cinema and a former eighteenth-century gambling club which Dick converted into his office annexe, Beaver Lodge.

Here, he led the way up the stairs, past his framed collection of good, bad and downright ugly cartoons of himself, and into his corner sanctum with *oeil-de-boeuf* windows overlooking the garden. Then as now, his desk was piled high with scripts, minutes and masses of correspondence. What particularly caught my eye was the bookshelf, crammed with works on Mahatma Gandhi and topped by portraits of the three Attenborough children. Cheek by jowl with their smiling faces was their father's chosen reminder of how the other half lived; the world-famous photograph of a screaming, napalmed little Vietnamese girl, running naked along a road.

I sat nervously in the visitor's chair as Dick outlined what he wanted me to do. As a publicist, I'd been vaguely aware that he didn't only make films, but only now did I begin to grasp the mind-boggling range and time-consuming nature of these other commitments.

Although he would virtually double this workload over the years to come, by his early fifties Dick was already the very active chairman of the Actors' Charitable Trust, the Combined Theatrical Charities Appeals Council, the Royal Academy of Dramatic Art and the UK's first independent music station, Capital Radio. A football fanatic and director of Chelsea FC, he was also the pro-chancellor of Sussex University. He'd helped to establish and was vice president of BAFTA and, as a board member, actively participated in the day-to-day running of the Young Vic Theatre Company.

In 1970, at the invitation of the feisty Labour Arts Minister, Jennie Lee, Dick had become a founding governor of the National Film School. Now, in a further fusion of his socialism with his film-making, he'd been approached by the only prime minister ever to take an ardent and active interest in cinema and was currently a leading member of Harold Wilson's Film Working Party.

Finally and most time-consuming of all, this unrepentant workaholic was the ardent 'face' and president of the Muscular Dystrophy Group, which entailed making continual personal appearances up and down the country in an effort to raise £1 million a year for research.

As his PA, he told me, my responsibilities would include being the day-to-day link with all these organisations, dealing with the press, answering the phone, organising his insanely crammed diary and making sure he had all the information needed to chair a whole gamut of monthly meetings. Oh, and there was just one other thing, he said airily. A magazine had asked him for some biographical background material. Would I mind writing a suitable press handout before I went home?

Needing the job so badly, I'd omitted to mention that I couldn't so much as string a sentence together. Or that my short-term memory was completely shot. Or that I was taking enough Valium to fell a carthorse.

Dick's faithful secretary, Gladys Barnes, was a crack typist and I sat for two hours at her daunting electric typewriter. Darkness fell, no words came. In the room behind me, the Attenboroughs were watching the evening news on television. I started to panic. When Dick came to see how I was getting on, I asked if I could bring the work back to him later in the week.

Within two days, I'd found a childminder I trusted enough to look after Kay and, after a whole day at my Olivetti portable, had cobbled together a very short biography. It was clumsy and pedestrian, but Dick seemed happy. I had the job.

Almost imperceptibly, life began again.

RA— Two days after my return from Delhi, I flew Concorde to New York and went straight from JFK to Joe's palatial office on East 52nd Street. He greeted me coldly, remaining seated behind his massive desk. When I told him the wonderful news about the rupee funding, it provoked nothing but contempt.

He'd heard, he sneered, about my activities in India; peddling his subject to every third-class distributor. I told him this was totally untrue. The only discussions I'd had were with government officials and the NFDC, both at the request of the Prime Minister.

Joe snorted derisively and went on to say I had no right to bandy his name about. The subject belonged to him, as I'd been clearly instructed in Bill Goldberg's telex. I told him I hadn't so much as mentioned his name. And, furthermore, he should bear in mind that a great deal of the subject was mine, since I was responsible for the original concept and had paid many expenses, including travel and a large proportion of the screenwriting fees, out of my own pocket. Joe was unmoved. He ordered me to go down the fucking corridor and see Bill Goldberg.

Bill's office was anything but palatial and, despite the accountant's bluntness, I detected a smidgeon of sympathy as he set out Joe's demands. The first was that I had to purchase a sixty-day option if I wanted to set up the film on my own. This would cost me $250,000. I needn't put up cash because Joe was already holding $150,000 of my profit share from the two films we'd made together, A Bridge Too Far and Magic, and intended to pocket the remainder from the same source.

However, in order to exercise the option, I had to pay Joe $750,000 on the first day of shooting and an additional $1 million on the last. He was also demanding a hefty percentage of box-office receipts. Stunned, I asked what would happen if, having exercised the option, I failed to set up the film. The answer was that I would lose any money owed to me and all rights would revert to Mr Levine.

I was aware that Joe prided himself on striking a hard bargain but this was way beyond the pale. I felt sick and angry and utterly betrayed.

On my return to his office, Joe looked at me without any discernible emotion. 'Do you accept?' When I replied his terms were extortionate, he responded, 'Do you, or don't you?'

Taking a deep breath, I said that a sixty-day option was totally impractical. I needed longer. Eventually, Joe grudgingly agreed to nine months.

It was now May 1980; this meant I had until the following February to raise all the hard currency needed to make the film, plus an extra $1,750,000 for Joe. Failure would mean I'd lose the subject forever. I left, saying he would have my answer within twenty-four hours.

Having checked into my hotel, I immediately rang Martin Baum in Los Angeles. Marti was and remains my mentor, my dear friend and my sheet anchor in times of professional trouble. Now in his eighties, he has become the totemic father figure at CAA, one of the most powerful agencies in Hollywood. It was his astute representation which enhanced my earning power as an actor, keeping me afloat financially throughout the *Gandhi* years in a succession of big budget international movies: *The Great Escape*, *The Flight of the Phoenix*, *The Sand Pebbles* and *Dr Dolittle*.

When I told Marti what had transpired that morning, his immediate response was that Joe personally had never invested so much as a nickel in *Gandhi* and under no circumstances must I accept such swingeing terms. If I did, he would never speak to me again.

I said, 'Marti, I know Joe. He's not going to back down and I can't pull out now. Not after all these years. I'm sorry you disapprove but I'm going to sign the severance.'

'And supposing you do set up the movie, where are you going to find the cash to pay off Levine?'

'I'll give up my fee.'

'You plan on working for nothing? Dickie, you are totally insane!' So saying, and for the first and only time in our relationship, Marti hung up on me.

DH— It would be many years before I learned the details of Dick's rupture with Joe Levine. He returned from New York, telling me only that he no longer needed reminding to wear his Bulgari watch whenever he went to the States. This hugely expensive gift from Joe had two dials, one set to GMT, the other to Levine time. Whenever they were to meet, Dick had swapped the treasured gold watch his parents had given him on his twenty-first birthday for the Bulgari, henceforth consigned to the back of a drawer.

Although it was never discussed, both of us had the same problem. Money, or rather the lack of it, was on my mind, morning, noon and night. I'd divorced Peter, who was now living in England with Jeannie, but the few pounds he was supposed to pay in maintenance soon stopped and half my wages went on childcare. Only the royalty cheques from *Zozu the Robot*, now stocked by many primary schools, kept the bailiffs from my door.

My biggest fear was that Kay might fall ill and I'd need to stay at home to look after her. To store up goodwill for this eventuality, I never called in sick and, because Beaver Lodge was so busy, always took money in lieu of holidays.

Wages were the responsibility of Dick's in-house accountant. Len sat in a tiny yellowed room, chain-smoking and tut-tutting at the Attenboroughs' perceived extravagance as he struggled to balance the books. One particular purchase irked him more than any other. This was a small but valuable painting by Rouault, a head of the crucified Christ, to which Dick and Sheila had accorded pride of place over their drawing-room mantelpiece. Whenever the figures failed to add up – which was often – Len would announce with sombre glee: 'That's it. Laughing boy's got to go.'

'Laughing boy' remained in situ but what I didn't know, as Dick became more and more frenetic during the summer and autumn of 1980, was that every painting he owned was in hock to the bank. Neither was I aware that his anticipated income stream from *A Bridge Too Far* and *Magic* had been cut off by Joe Levine.

He didn't confide in me a great deal in those days; we lived in different, upstairs–downstairs worlds. I could only guess at the pressures which made him go so red in the face he looked ready to drop dead from a heart attack. I called these terrifying episodes the purple poppy-eyed screamers.

Gradually, however, I learned to avert them. What irritated him was waffle. When he asked for information it needed to be presented in a single, succinct sentence which could be amplified if necessary. He was also very stubborn and, having made up his mind, the only one way to change it was to present him with irrefutable logic. A climbdown, if it came, was almost imperceptible; he'd merely pause fractionally and say, 'Anyway,' before changing the subject completely.

With India five hours ahead of Greenwich Mean Time and Los Angeles eight hours behind, Dick's working day usually started before dawn and ended around midnight. Nevertheless, he continued to chair the monthly meetings of all his business and charitable commitments and was continually travelling in aid of the Muscular Dystrophy Group.

As if this was not enough, he also became involved with a break-away group of Labour MPs, known as the Gang of Four, who were in the process of forming a new political party, the SDP. Then, almost defiantly, towards the end of 1980, as the pressures surrounding *Gandhi* continued to mount, he entered the world of television, becoming deputy chairman of the fledgling Channel 4.

RA— Having signed the severance with Joe, I assumed total responsibility for *Gandhi* and, despite the magnitude of the challenge, found myself hugely energised, if somewhat lacking in patience.

It sounds cocky, but I have known ever since I became a Scout leader that I am good at being in charge. Maybe it's something to do with being the eldest son, but I am not afraid of responsibility. I'm happiest when I'm heading an enterprise; be it as chairman or as producer-director in sole charge of a film.

On my return from New York, I'd learned of a Canadian who, through a new venture capital consortium called Goldcrest, might be persuaded to invest some seed money in *Gandhi*. I immediately arranged to meet him.

In complete contrast to Joe Levine, Jake Eberts worked in a poky attic, totally devoid of ostentation. He was then in his late thirties; thin as a rake, bespectacled, inordinately tall and slightly stooped, as if to avoid cracking his head on the low ceiling. He also had an incapacitating stutter, frequently getting stuck at the start of a word and continuing to struggle while you fought the urge to say it for him. And, like me, Jake was a gambler.

His background was unusual. He was a qualified chemical engineer, born in Quebec, who'd graduated from the Harvard Business School and worked on Wall Street before coming to England where he'd become managing director of the renowned brokerage and investment giant, Oppenheimer. Then, suddenly, he'd changed direction, embarking on the highly speculative business of film finance by putting together the money for Martin Rosen's animation classic, *Watership Down*.

It's my belief that Jake fell in love with the movies as a result of the box office and critical success of that one film. What I didn't know when we met – and neither, it eventually emerged, did his gorgeous wife, Fiona – was that he'd recently made the cardinal mistake of staking his own money on a flop called *Zulu Dawn* and, as a result, had plunged heavily into debt. Some years later, the knock-on effect of this disastrous invest-ment would have a major impact on the whole of the British film industry.

So when I first went to see him, Jake had every reason to be cautious. Nevertheless, having heard me out, he agreed to read the *Gandhi* script that same evening. Early the following morning, he phoned and told me he'd read it twice. He said, 'I think it's the m-most m-magical subject I've ever come across and, like you, I would give a-anything on earth to get it m-made.' Again not unlike me, he then started to cry. I remember it so clearly.

Marti Baum has a description for anyone brave or foolhardy enough to commit unsecured finance to an embryo movie. 'They are,' he says with a twinkle, 'just a little bit pregnant.'

Within a month of our first meeting, due solely to Jake's enthusiasm, his two fledgling investment companies, Goldcrest in London and International Film Investors in New York, run by his business partner, Jo Child, were jointly in the *Gandhi* club to the tune of $750,000. It was enough to keep the project moving forward.

By then, with just one exception, every major Hollywood studio had declined to finance the film; many pouring scorn on the whole idea. My last hope of major traditional funding resided with Twentieth Century Fox, whose managing director in London, Ascania Branca, had kindly recommended Briley's new script to his bosses in Los Angeles. Soon after Jake came on board, I flew out to see them.

As always, I stayed at the Beverly Hills Hotel. As always, now he'd decided to speak to me again, Marti came for a council of war after his weekly Saturday-morning manicure. Like all top agents, he kept himself exceptionally well informed on the politics and inner workings of every Hollywood studio. The word was good, he told me. A number of people at Fox were crazy about the script.

On the Monday morning, we set off optimistically for a crunch meeting on the Fox lot. Although Marti had briefed me beforehand, in male-dominated Hollywood it was still a surprise to see a very attract-ive young woman heading up the five executive 'suits' in the conference room. This was Sherry Lansing, a former teacher and actress, whose appointment as the company's newest, youngest and first female president had been big news only a short while before.

The meeting lasted three hours and went, I thought, extremely well. The late Herbert Morrison, a politician whose arm I'd twisted when he headed the British Board of Film Censors, had told me I could sell ice cream to Eskimos and I certainly pulled out all the stops at Fox that day. Before we parted, the most senior of the male executives was strongly urging Sherry to commit and she was giving every sign of it being a done deal. They promised to get back to us before the day was out.

Marti and I returned to the hotel in high spirits and repaired to the Polo Lounge where I tucked into a chef's salad while he, who dines but never lunches, had a celebratory glass of mineral water. The big letdown came with my coffee. Our waiter appeared with a phone which he plugged into the booth and handed to Marti. I knew at once that the news was not good. Sherry, perhaps wanting to demonstrate her newly acquired clout, had had second thoughts and decided *Gandhi* was not commercial. The answer was no.

There's always a tipping point when I'm trying to set up a movie, a moment when I have to choose between a leap of faith or playing it safe. Despite Sherry's adverse decision, the relatively small but vital amount of hard currency Jake had so swiftly amassed proved to be my tipping point with *Gandhi*. With his support, I elected for the leap of faith.

Although the bulk of funding had yet to be raised – not to mention the little matter of finding a suitable leading actor – if I was ever to make this film, pre-production work in India had to get underway immediately.

It was now June. The script called for twenty-six weeks of principal photography and I had to start shooting by the end of November if I was to have any hope of finishing before the onset of the next monsoon, five months later. Failure to start on time would entail all the rights reverting to Joe.

I flew out to Delhi to make final decisions about location sites. With me went Terry Clegg, our stalwart line producer, and a core group of British technicians who began to recruit a local crew, build sets, amass costumes, rent premises, hire transport and embark on the thousand and one negotiations which would set the whole production in motion.

At this point, with Jake taking the lead, we had just five months to raise $15 million.

Since I'd already been turned down by every conventional source of film funding, Jake began to approach unconventional sources on both sides of the Atlantic. Over the summer of 1980, he was constantly on the move between Switzerland, France, Britain and the States; personally pitching the film to over a hundred merchant banks, insurance companies, pension funds and venture capitalists. Not one displayed the least interest.

Meanwhile, with the Indian government pouring rupees into pre-production and their own speculative $750,000 already spent, Goldcrest and IFI somewhat nervously increased their stake to $1 million. At the end of September, when Jake finally located a couple of promising leads, these two companies bravely agreed to plunge even deeper, committing an additional $2 million.

The first of Jake's new leads was Barclays Bank. Jo Child specialised in applying tax breaks to film finance. In America, this had allowed the two of them to form a limited partnership which had taken advantage of Small Business Administration incentives to build up a significant film investment fund.

Turning their attention to British tax law, Jake and Jo came up with a novel scheme under which a particular arm of Barclays would buy Gandhi and lease it back to us. This would result in the film accruing an interest-free cash injection of $8 million. As Jake said triumphantly, it looked like a bonanza.

With the hard currency shortfall now down to $4 million, a secretive and fabulously wealthy family of Indian industrialists came onto the scene. They were the Hinduja brothers – Gopichand, Srichand, Prakash and Ashok – collectively estimated to be worth $8 billion.

Some years later, three of the brothers would be accused of corruptly persuading Indiraji's son Rajiv to buy a large quantity of field guns from the Swedish company, Bofors. The case dragged on for well over a decade before being dismissed by the Indian High Court.

Meanwhile, Gopichand and Srichand, the two Hindujas based in Britain were seeking citizenship; networking among the great and good, contributing to both Labour and Conservative coffers and making substantial charitable donations through their family foundation.

1924: With my mother

1924: With my father

Circa 1933: With my brothers, Johnnie (*left*) and Dave (*centre*)

Lydies Wot Come to Oblige, 1935:
In drag with Dave (*right*)

Sussex University, 1979:
Dave receives his honorary degree.

(*Main Image*) *In Which We Serve*, 1942:
Making my screen debut
(*Above*) *In Which We Serve*, 1942
'Dysentery in every ripple'. Noel Coward
(*left*) confers with co-director, David Lean

(*Right*) 1944: Sheila and I celebrate
our engagement at the family home
in Leicester.
(*Left to right back*) Dave, Sheila, Johnnie, me
(*Front*) Pa, Ma and my dog, Seamus.

(*Top*) Called up, 1943: AC2 1808294 Attenborough R
(*Above*) *Journey Together*, 1946: With Edward G Robinson (signed).

January 1945:
With Sheila on
our wedding day

Brighton Rock,
1947: As Pinkie

Chelsea FC, 1948:
An early photo
opportunity with
star players,
Albert Tennant
(*left*) and Tommy
Lawton (*right*)

Signing autographs
with Sheila

Passing the
driving test

1950: With our firstborn, Michael John Attenborough

Record Rendezvous, 1952: The new DJ chooses records with Michael

1959: Our three children, Michael, baby Charlotte and Jane

The Baby and the Battleship, 1956:
With Johnnie Mills

The Angry Silence, 1960:
Crossing a picket line

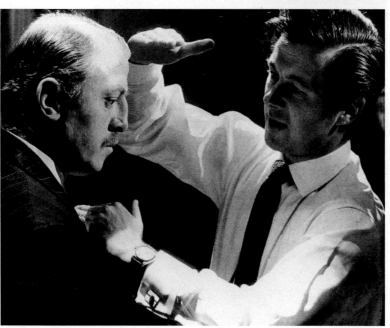

*Séance on a
Wet Afternoon*,
1964: Directed
by my partner,
Bryan Forbes

One such donation would become headline news many years later when the foundation contributed £1 million to cost overruns on London's ill-fated Millennium Dome. Peter Mandelson, then in charge of the project, would subsequently resign over allegations he had helped Srichand secure his British passport.

Back in 1980, after numerous meetings in Bombay, Geneva, Paris and London, Jake had struck a deal with Gopichand Hinduja who agreed to put up the final $4 million for *Gandhi*. Although the terms were tough, Jake believed they were acceptable. This vital injection of cash would be made available some months hence, when I was due to be filming in Pune. The relief was enormous. At long last, the film was fully financed.

It was by now July and still I had no leading actor. Alec Guinness had long ago rejected the idea of playing Gandhi on the grounds that he was 'too grey-eyed, too heavy and just plain too old'. Since then a number of other stars had been approached or suggested. One American studio had intimated they might be prepared to back me if I cast Richard Burton because he was sexy; an idea so idiotic it was not even worth a further thought.

My own first choice had been the brilliant and charismatic Anthony Hopkins, whom I both admired and knew very well, having already cast him in *Young Winston*, *A Bridge Too Far* and *Magic*. Tony was really keen to play Gandhi and even checked into a health farm, losing a couple of stone before concluding it would be physically impossible. And, over the years, Dirk Bogarde, Peter Finch, Albert Finney and Tom Courtenay had all excluded themselves for the same reason.

Finally, I approached John Hurt, who had just received rave reviews for *The Elephant Man*. John was interested but again doubted he could look convincing as Gandhi. So we agreed on a full make-up and wardrobe test.

I was already in the process of setting this up, when my theatre director son came up with another suggestion. Mike had remembered an actor who'd been a magical Hamlet some years ago at Stratford. In his opinion, this young man was now one of the best classical actors in the country, and as he was currently playing Squeers in Trevor Nunn's acclaimed production of *Nicholas Nickleby* at the Aldwych, surely I had nothing to lose by going to see him?

The actor's name was Ben Kingsley. I saw the play, thought him absolutely wonderful and immediately went backstage to ask if he would test on the same day as John Hurt. Ben, thirty-six at the time, believed my sudden appearance had some kind of mystical synergy because, only days earlier, his wife had bought him a biography of Gandhi which he'd just started to read. When he heard about the test, Trevor Nunn told him presciently: 'This is the part you were born to play.'

What I didn't know until I met him was that Ben's original name was Krishna Pandit Bhanji or that the paternal side of his family came originally from the north-western Indian state of Gujurat – Mahatma Gandhi's birthplace.

Ben was born in Yorkshire, the son of an English mother and an Asian GP, Rahimtulla Bhanji. When he became an actor, it was his father who'd advised him to adopt a British-sounding name in the belief it would help to get him better and bigger parts.

As Ben Kingsley, he'd worked his way up the ladder of the Royal Shakespeare Company from spear carrier to leading man. However, his screen experience was limited to a few brief television appearances in *Coronation Street* and one film in which he'd had a small part as a gangster.

I very rarely screen-test any actor or actress and never ask them to give a reading. I watch some of their previous work and then arrange a meeting in relaxed surroundings where I can ask a few questions, observe very closely and listen.

Since John and Ben were both superb actors, testing them for *Gandhi* was merely a matter of appearance. We filmed them, sitting, standing and walking, on the smallest stage at Twickenham Studios, ten minutes from my home. Both had full body and facial make-up and were clad only in the dhoti, a loincloth of white homespun cotton draped from waist to knee.

After I'd seen the rushes, I thought it best to invite John to a private screening. We viewed his test first. 'Oh, Christ,' he said after a moment or two, 'I look like a bloody front-row forward.'

Then we saw Ben. Suddenly, here was a lithe Indian man, totally at home in his skin, who seemed to have worn a dhoti all his life. And, miraculously, he radiated a charisma which, you instantly believed, could bind millions to his cause. The lights came up in the screening room;

John shook my hand. 'Dickie, my dear, you've found your Mahatma. Best of luck to you both.'

DH— By October 1980, the sedate Regency offices in Richmond were buzzing with activity; budget, script, set and schedule meetings, a stream of hopeful actors and actresses turning up on the doorstep, constantly ringing telephones and the newly installed telex machine – our most reliable contact with Terry Clegg's office in Delhi – chattering away incessantly.

Chalky White, Dick's newly appointed sketch artist, was preparing storyboards for all the film's major scenes, while Michael Stanley-Evans, his producing partner, was continually poring over a series of complicated charts.

Also beavering away at Beaver Lodge as the start of shooting grew ever closer was Lorna Mueller. When Dick was awarded a knighthood at the beginning of 1976, he'd employed her as a temp to help answer over a thousand congratulatory letters and Lorna had stayed on, carving a niche for herself as the dogged *Gandhi* researcher. And now, this married mother of two was confiding that Dick had agreed she could join the unit in India.

Suddenly it hit me; within weeks, all this activity would cease. Everyone else would fly off to Delhi, leaving me behind. It wasn't sensible but suddenly I found myself yearning to be part of this huge enterprise.

I was forty-two with sole responsibility for a small child. But I'd escaped the benefit trap, found a job and put a roof over our heads. And, distrusting psychotherapy, I'd silenced the voices in my head by allowing them to rant unchecked until I was so bored with their endless repetition, they'd simply faded away. I'd even managed to kick the Valium habit.

In nine months, Kay would start school. It was now or never. Knowing he hadn't yet engaged a publicist, I sounded Dick out. The response, typically, was both generous and immediate. If I wanted the job, it was mine. And of course I could take Kay; it shouldn't be too difficult to find her an Indian nanny.

I thought it over for all of twenty-four hours, weighing the security of a nine-to-six job against this daunting leap into the well-paid but precarious freelance world I'd left behind so long ago.

Then I thanked Dick for believing in me and started packing.

3

BLOODY TINKERBELL

DH— NOVEMBER 1980. WE are installed in the vast pink and terracotta Ashok Hotel, New Delhi. Outside in the grounds, my five-year-old daughter, Kay, is riding in the howdah of a weary old elephant with painted trunk and tattered ears under the watchful eye of her new ayah, Felicia. This will remain her most vivid memory of India.

At the rear of the hotel, shaded by its massive bulk, is a small swimming pool, very deep and icy cold, where the wives of the British film crew socialise during the day. Set apart from this group, a near naked man with oiled body and shaven head is meditating in the full glare of the sun. This is the light-skinned Ben Kingsley, preparing physically and mentally for his defining role of a lifetime. Soon he will retreat to his suite for another lesson in spinning cotton on a wheel called the charkha; a technique he must practise until he can spin and talk at the same time.

Below Ben's suite, on the ground floor, a whole corridor has been turned over to film production offices. The core unit is fully assembled now; some seventy technicians from the UK, their fifty Indian counterparts and an army of local workmen building sets. Hundreds more people, both skilled and unskilled, and many thousands of extras will be hired over the next six months as the film team criss-crosses the subcontinent; from Delhi to Bombay and then on to Pune, Patna and, finally, Udaipur.

A succession of stars playing cameo roles – John Mills, Edward Fox, Martin Sheen, Candice Bergen, Ian Charleson, Nigel Hawthorne – will join the caravan en route, film their scenes and fly home again. The final shooting script also contains over a hundred smaller speaking parts, many consisting of only a single word. Dick will cast each of them personally, choosing from the hordes of hopefuls who hunker each evening outside his hotel office, waiting.

Rohini Hattangady, the highly regarded Indian actress who will play Gandhi's wife, Kasturba, and the actors portraying the Mahatma's group of followers, including Pandit Nehru, are already engaged. Some are theatre players, with little or no film experience. Others appear regularly in the lengthy Bollywood melodramas, leavened with song-and-dance routines, which are the mainstay of their thriving indigenous industry.

It's not just the style of Indian movies which is so different; production is spread over a far longer period with the actors contracted for as much as a whole year. This is proving a nightmare for our line producer, Terry Clegg, and his thirty behind-the-scenes staff, busy compiling the charts, schedules and lists which dovetail, down to the very last detail, the different personnel, equipment and transport which must all be assembled at the start of every working day.

The object of all this meticulous planning is cost-efficiency. Every conceivable item of expenditure is listed in the film's budget. The grand total, always expressed in US dollars, stands at just under $24 million which, at the prevailing sterling exchange rate, amounts to £10 million.

Certain fixed and known costs, including the stars, director, producers and writers are known as 'above the line'. All expenditure which can vary due to unforeseen circumstances appears 'below the line'. To this is added the contingency, a fixed percentage for overruns. As the producer and director responsible for this vast enterprise, Dick prides himself in not exceeding the contingency. Ever.

This means the production team, and particularly the film's financial controller, must be able to quantify the 'what ifs' at the drop of a hat. If a thunderstorm appears on the horizon, is it cheaper and more efficient to sit it out, or to move and shoot elsewhere? If the dollar exchange rate should rise a couple of points, suddenly reducing the sterling equivalent by hundreds of thousands of pounds, what can be cut or trimmed in order to balance the books?

Such decisions are never straightforward and all entail different forms of compromise. For a producer, the considerations are mainly financial, but a director has to bring a different judgement to bear, his prime concern being to preserve the artistic integrity of the finished film.

When producer and director are one and the same – as with *Gandhi* – that person must make such choices all day, every day, throughout the whole of principal photography. And, in order to make the best decision, the right decision, he must have brutally honest and totally accurate information. This is why Dick surrounds himself with people he knows he can trust.

Like me, Terry Clegg started out as a teenage dogsbody at Pinewood Studios. He first encountered Dick in the early sixties when he'd progressed to being a lowly third assistant director. Then, one of his thankless duties was to prise Mr Attenborough away from the phone in his star dressing room, physically if need be, and escort him onto the set. Twenty years later, it is the highly experienced Terry who, as line producer, masterminds this epic juggernaut behind the scenes. Answerable only to Dick, he is in day-to-day charge; practically, financially and logistically. Terry is crazy about golf, ruthlessly efficient and very, very blunt.

Production designer Stuart Craig is a totally different personality. Quiet, determined and ruggedly handsome, his job is to create settings which enhance the scope and mood of the script. Nicknamed 'Give us a Million' by Terry, Stu is always fighting to get his art department a bigger share of the budget. His saving grace, as far as Dick is concerned, is that every penny ends up where it really matters: on the screen. Stu will go on to win an Oscar for *Gandhi*.

Our sound recordist, Simon Kaye, will be Oscar-nominated but lose out to *E.T.*, going on to win for his work on *The Last of the Mohicans* and *Platoon*. His ability to capture dialogue free of extraneous noise in the most challenging of circumstances will save significant amounts of time and money during post-production and add immeasurably to the veracity of the final soundtrack. His quiet but wicked sense of humour is an added bonus in times of stress.

Another of the stalwarts is David Tomblin, our first assistant director. This is a great bull of a man whose head sits on his burly body without any vestige of neck, although his vocal cords could stop a charging army dead in its tracks. Beneath the scary veneer of power and authority, David is the biggest softie on the set. He's the director's enforcer, right-hand man and stentorian voice, who specialises in choreographing the extras for big action scenes, bringing every area of the background to life. It is this skill which makes David the most highly regarded first assistant in the world.

With one week to go before the start of principal photography, David's team is recruiting three hundred skinny and downtrodden-looking Indians to play impoverished mineworkers and fifty European riders to form a troop of mounted police for the first scene of the schedule. Set in South Africa, this shows the young Gandhi as a Westernised lawyer, somewhat fearfully leading a group of indentured Indian strikers on his first protest march. Although no one is yet aware of the irony, the crux of this sequence comes when he persuades the miners to lie motionless on the ground while mounted white police urge their horses to trample them.

It's a tricky visual to pull off successfully and one that will be made even more complicated by Dick's new toy, a small remote-controlled camera, capable of moving almost in a complete circle, attached to the end of a long crane arm. In years to come, the Louma will become a staple piece of equipment, but ours, brought in specially, is pretty much a prototype. And, whether it's due to a freight plane that nearly crashed on landing or the fine Indian dust that seeps inexorably into every crevice, this little gizmo is to prove extremely temperamental.

By now it's becoming public knowledge that the Indian government, led by Mrs Gandhi, is part financing a commercial film to be made by a foreigner. Provocatively, the foreigner in question belongs to the nation which came here at the start of the seventeenth century, merely to trade, and went on to conquer the whole subcontinent, making it the cornerstone of an empire which, at its apogee, controlled 14 million square miles of the earth's surface.

More provocative still, the foreigner's film purports to be about the most heroic and revered figure in contemporary Indian history, the father of the nation and 'great soul', who drove out the British imperialists only thirty-three years ago.

The first of a stream of protests to emanate from the Indian parliament comes from George Fernandes, representing a constituency in troubled Bihar. Not content with tabling a question for the Minister of Information and Broadcasting – as many MPs are doing on a daily basis – Mr Fernandes calls a press conference to announce that Richard Attenborough's Gandhi film is 'a sell-out of the country's honour'. He goes on to denounce the government's investment, patently unaware of how it is structured, and derides whole chunks of the script, obviously never having read it.

Dick, as producer, and I, as the film's publicity director, are in a difficult situation. We are briefing the beleaguered minister's advisers virtually every evening. And we're both very aware of sensitivities in regard to British rule. Dick, as a lifelong socialist, carries more than a trace of post-colonial guilt. I, as the granddaughter of a career soldier who helped administer the Raj, see it somewhat differently.

Whatever our feelings, we are not at liberty to counter Fernandes's wild assertions by making public the actual details of the government's involvement in the film, particularly the significant sums India stands to gain in profit participation should it prove successful. That is the prerogative of the ministry, as are the generous arrangements to benefit indigenous film production which, at Dick's insistence, are also part of the deal.

As to the script, we know full well it would immediately become a political and religious football were it released into the public domain. Even the multitude of scholars who have spent their whole lives chronicling the Mahatma's every action, every meal, every utterance are often at loggerheads. And, among the public at large, the divergence of opinion is greater still, ranging from hatred and pragmatism to admiration and downright worship.

We're still debating how to counter the damage done by George Fernandes when the film comes under further attack from a far more newsworthy opponent. This is Moraji Desai, the right-wing politician reluctantly appointed her deputy by Indira Gandhi in 1967, who took over the premiership when she was briefly deposed a decade later. Mr Desai is an aristocratic Brahmin and an enthusiastic practitioner of the Ayurvedic custom of drinking a medicinal glass of his own urine every morning. He is publicly threatening to fast unto death if the film goes ahead.

Immediately, the Delhi newspapers report that hundreds of protestors are preparing to support Desai by lying down in front of our vehicles as they make their way to the location on the first day of shooting. Such a confrontation, eerily similar to the scene we're going to shoot, must be prevented at all costs. Dick and I decide to call a press conference of our own.

The Fourth Estate in Delhi proves to be very lively. Although eighteen different languages are recognised under the constitution, most newspapers are printed in English, the lingua franca of imperial rule. And we soon discover that many Indians have a greater mastery of our mother tongue than we do, employing words and syntax redolent of a bygone and far more literate age.

Dick enters our crowded press conference and salutes the reporters with a *pranam*. They listen in silence as he explains that we are not here to denigrate Mahatma Gandhi, but to honour him. All seems to be going well, but their body language is disconcerting. Where Europeans would nod agreement, Indians shake their heads from side to side as if negating what they hear. Unfazed, Dick continues, outlining the major events to be depicted in the script, starting with Gandhi's politicisation as a young British-trained attorney in South Africa and ending with his assassination at Birla House, here in Delhi.

The reporters take copious notes throughout. As Dick finishes, a hand shoots up in the front row. 'It is not correct, sir, that your film script is truly about the last viceroy, Lord Mountbatten?'

The question is posed so politely it would be churlish in the extreme to take offence. Dick patiently explains there will be two brief scenes featuring a Lord Mountbatten lookalike who will utter not more than a couple of dozen words. Again the head shakes. Again the pens racing over reporters' pads.

More questions follow in the same vein, all courteous and all totally wide of the mark. Everyone, it seems, has their own idea of what the film is really about.

I can sense Dick's frustration, can see the red tide rising in his face as a young female journalist asks if he is willing to confirm that Ben Kingsley made his screen debut in a pornographic film. This is met with an emphatic and uncharacteristically terse denial. A middle-aged woman is now signalling tentatively from the back of the room. I touch Dick's elbow to bring her to his attention. The woman asks how he intends to show the Mahatma on the screen. Dick visibly relaxes as he enthuses about the acclaimed Shakespearean actor whose meticulous research includes studying Gandhi's voice and gait on old black-and-white newsreel footage.

The woman is unimpressed. This is sacrilege, she says. Sir Attenborough needs to be aware that Gandhiji is a deity in this country, not a mere mortal to be caricatured from newsreels.

Dick is sorry she feels like this. How would she have him portray the Mahatma?

'Not at all. But if you must . . . as a moving light.'

Finally losing patience, Dick ripostes: 'Madam, I am not making a film about bloody Tinkerbell.'

RA— No matter what is happening in his own life, an actor must be able to put himself in his character's shoes. To do this, he requires the ability to excise whole areas of his own existence from his conscious mind and bring about a particular kind of concentration which almost defies logic. It is this obliteration of self which allows him to inhabit another persona.

Over the years, I've taken this ability to compartmentalise – I visualise it as a series of boxes – into every area of my life. If I am chairing one meeting straight after another, I lock everything to do with the first away in its box before I embark on the next. The fact that I don't have a very good memory probably helps. I even need triggers to help me recall the good things in my life, events that have made me laugh or touched me very deeply.

I have to say I never choose to revisit the bad times. I find it so emotionally draining when something awful happens in terms of work that I shut it away completely. As a result, I don't bear grudges and go out of my way to avoid huge screaming rows. I see myself as a sort of ridiculous male Mary Poppins, the eternal optimist whose glass is always half full.

So, when I arrived in India in November 1980, I didn't spend a single moment dwelling on all that had gone before. With childish enthusiasm and every ounce of energy I could muster, I simply immersed myself in the task that lay ahead.

Despite the threats reported in the Delhi press and that extraordinary press conference where, I'm ashamed to say, I did lose my temper, Moraji Desai did not starve himself to death. Neither, to my great relief, was there a single protestor in sight as we drove to the Batra stone works just before dawn on the first day of shooting. There, eighteen years after I first met him and in tribute to the late Moti Kothari, a Hindu priest blessed the camera in a simple *muhurat* ceremony. Then we set to work.

By sunset, under the terms of our severance, Joe Levine had received $750,000 in his New York bank account. In India, I'd completed the first of 126 shooting days which would result in a film lasting three hours and eight minutes, an average of eighty-nine seconds a day.

I have never, before or since, worked so hard or so long. We filmed six days a week from dawn to dusk and often beyond. Back at the hotel, usually after a long car journey, there'd be two or three hours of meetings, both before and after dinner. Exposed film stock, sent to England for processing, came back as biweekly batches of rushes which we viewed late at night in a makeshift cinema we'd built on the hotel roof. If we'd shot a scene with more than one camera – and on one occasion we used as many as eleven – the screening could continue into the early hours. Then we'd grab a little sleep before setting off again in time to reach the next location before first light. On the seventh day, nominally a rest day for the crew, there'd be rehearsals, casting sessions and, inevitably, more meetings.

During our time in Delhi, we also used our rest days to prepare for the re-enactment of Mahatma Gandhi's funeral procession. This was to be filmed on the thirty-third anniversary of the actual event.

Chalky White, our sketch artist, had spent months examining photographs, newsreels and first-hand reports of the huge cortège that had slow-marched the length of Delhi's ceremonial Rajpath following Gandhi's assassination. He'd analysed precisely which regiments made up the military presence and identified the various affiliations of the thousand civilian mourners walking behind. He'd researched the vehicle bearing the Mahatma's body and every detail of the bier on which it lay. He'd counted the uniformed Home Guard and white-clad members of the Gandhi Peace Movement lining the route and could tell us exactly how many there'd been.

What Chalky had been unable to count, because they'd stretched as far as the eye could see, were the people who'd packed Rajpath to pay their last respects. And somehow, long before the advent of computer-generated imagery, we had to recruit a similar mass of citizens, making sure that none was dressed inappropriately.

David Tomblin had commandeered a disused airfield for the rest-day rehearsals and marked out the exact length of the processional route. Here, with the help of our Indian military advisers, we taught modern members of the armed forces the gliding motion of the ceremonial slow march, a pace also to be adopted by the mounted guard of honour and the mourners walking behind.

To retain the mood of the occasion and due to the sheer length of the procession, I was obliged to film the whole sequence during a single mile-long journey from the parliament buildings to Victoria Gate. With the core camera team, I mapped out in great detail the shots we needed, knowing everything must come to a time-consuming halt whenever we changed positions. We were to use the Louma, together with our own first and second cameras, and bring in eight more for this particular day. All eleven crews would maintain contact with David via walkie-talkies.

It was clear from the beginning that I couldn't direct this sequence from a distance. I had to be in the thick of it. This is why a rather portly general with overlong white hair and horn-rimmed glasses makes a fleeting and unintended appearance in the finished film, walking backwards behind the bier.

Having recruited twenty-five thousand 'front-line' extras, all of whom had to be paid in cash and all of whom we'd rehearsed and costumed, there remained the problem of attracting the mass of people needed to throng the borders of our frame. We knew we were taking a risk by shooting this scene on the anniversary of the actual event but believed this particular Saturday offered the best chance of attracting an enormous crowd. Having taken advice from the police, we decided to invite the people of Delhi through advertising and lay on trucks to bring in thousands more from the surrounding countryside.

Meanwhile in London, a completely different drama was being played out. Two weeks into our shooting schedule, Barclays Bank suddenly and without any explanation pulled out of the leasing deal, leaving our budget $8 million short.

I don't remember how I first heard this terrifying news. It's quite possible I've entirely blocked it out. In 1980, it was extremely difficult to communicate within India, let alone between Delhi and London. There were, of course, no mobile phones. Calls via unreliable landlines had to be booked hours, sometimes days, in advance, with very little guarantee of connection and we were obliged to depend, almost exclusively, on telex.

I do know that when Barclays pulled out, Jake immediately went back to the Goldcrest board. He told them they were up to their ears in *Gandhi* and they were stuck. First reports were good and Terry and I had so far remained within budget. But, without a further injection of cash, everything the company had previously invested would be money down the drain.

Quite properly, the institutional investors wanted to be reassured that this was the last time they'd ever be placed in such a position. Jake emphatically gave them that assurance. So, on the strict understanding that negotiations with the Hindujas had been satisfactorily concluded, the Goldcrest board again increased their investment. This small company, formed just three years earlier, had now committed a staggering $7.2 million.

And once again the unassuming Canadian had saved the day. It's extraordinary, when I look back, that Jake never once boasted about his efforts on our behalf or even asked that his name should appear on the finished film. Yet without him, I can honestly say that *Gandhi* would never have been made. I owe him more than I can ever hope to repay.

Back in Delhi, we were re-enacting the moment of Gandhi's death. This was the first time Ben was to be seen in public as the elderly Mahatma every adult Indian would immediately recognise and, due to the skill of a remarkable make-up artist, Tom Smith, the resemblance was uncanny.

The lawn at Birla House where Gandhi had been assassinated was regarded as hallowed ground. For this reason, the whole cast and crew were working barefoot when a very nervous Ben emerged from the building to rehearse. Supported on either side by the two young actresses portraying his nieces, he made his way, unannounced, towards the waiting crowd of extras. When they caught sight of him, several ran forward and stooped to touch his feet – an act of reverence reserved for the Mahatma himself.

Ben was, of course, profoundly moved. This was no longer just an acting assignment, his big screen break. Within living memory, people in this garden had touched the feet of the man he'd been called upon to play, the extraordinary man who'd been shot dead by a fellow Hindu, not a dozen yards from where he stood.

It was then, I believe, it all came together for my leading actor. At my suggestion, he'd been following the Mahatma's simple diet, sleeping on a similar hard bed, becoming adept at spinning cotton, practising yoga – all designed to sublimate himself in order to eat, sleep, breathe and, in so far as it was possible, become Gandhi. Only then would his thought processes be true to the character and it is that truth, those thoughts, revealed by the penetrating lens of the cine camera, that makes for a great performance.

On the evening before we were due to film the funeral procession, David Tomblin and I briefed the unit at the Ashok Hotel. We told them we had no idea how big the crowd would be. It might only be a few hundred or, as we'd put so optimistically on tomorrow's call sheet, as many as a quarter of a million. Whatever the numbers, we only had permission to close Rajpath for a single morning, so we had to press on and do the best we could, regardless.

We also had to point out that there was a very real risk of rioting and advise the crew where to find medical facilities, should the need arise. But, we assured them, no matter what happened, we would leave for Bombay, as planned, the following day. Finally, wishing everyone good luck and goodnight, we retired for a few hours' sleep.

Work started at three in the morning. With one exception, the whole cast was on call that day. By sunrise, the actors in the procession were dressed, made up and gradually moving into their allotted positions. And, I was glad to see, a tide of local people was beginning to pour through the entry points where wardrobe assistants were handing out suitable clothing to cover anything too modern.

I was with the Louma crew, rehearsing the first and all-important master shot which could only be filmed once. The little Arriflex camera, controlled at ground level, was to rise from the catafalque in one smooth movement, pulling back and back, to take in the thousand-strong cortège, the troops, the horses, the honour guard, the massed crowd and finally, through the branches of a tree, the pillars, domes and minarets of the seat of government itself, Rashtrapati Bhavan.

We had just one hour of perfect light. Only five minutes of that hour remained when everything was finally in position and the whole area jam-packed with people as far as the eye could see. Standing next to the Louma operator where I could view what was being filmed on a monitor, I gave the prearranged signal.

David yelled, 'Action!' through his megaphone and the procession began to move. As planned, we turned the camera over thirty seconds before the bier moved into centre frame and began the rise and pull-back at precisely the right moment. My excitement mounted with the crane arm. So far, the shot was perfect. Then, as the Arriflex soared past the branches of the tree on the back of a perfectly placed little Indian boy, he turned, looked directly into the lens and stuck out his tongue.

There was no time to reflect on this disaster, no possibility of repeating the ruined shot. With only three hours remaining before Rajpath was reopened to traffic, we had to press on.

And press on we did, filming the procession for a few minutes, stopping, racing to new camera positions and starting again. There was one moment when the police, seeing the crowd about to burst onto the roadway through sheer pressure of numbers, waded in with their weighted bamboo staves, the dreaded lathis. Fortunately, it came to nothing.

It was about then that I realised the lifelike dummy, representing the dead Mahatma on the bier, would not pass muster when we needed to film it in extreme close up. I asked David to radio a message to the hotel conveying my apologies to Mr Kingsley, who'd been given the day off, and asking if he would kindly get made up and come to the location as soon as possible.

Ben arrived in the nick of time and, taking the place of the dummy for our final shot, lay exposed and motionless, in full view of the public, as he was borne to Victoria Gate.

Back at the Ashok Hotel, we were inundated with calls from newspapers wanting to know how many people had turned up. According to unnamed 'sources' we had attracted only a few thousand. Di and I knew that this was very far from the truth. So we consulted the police who'd manned the entry points. The figure they gave us was four hundred thousand – the biggest crowd in film history.

I was in my room, packing, when a shaken Ben came to see me. On his return to the hotel, he'd been handed an anonymous letter, delivered early that morning. It contained a threat to shoot him if he dared to lie on Mahatma Gandhi's bier.

DH— Taking on board Dick and David's riot warning, on the evening before we filmed the procession, I had put into an envelope everything my daughter would need if she had to travel home alone; passport, air ticket, my parents' contact details and all the money I could muster. Then her Indian nanny, Felicia, had packed up her belongings and taken Kay to stay with Peter and Sheila Lawton, a hospitable English couple I'd barely met, who had a daughter of the same age.

In the event there were no riots on Rajpath. But I was involved in the incident when the police waded into the crowd with their lathis. It was a strange experience; a split second to realise that a solid wall of screaming and yelling people is bearing down on you, another split second to know you have to turn and run with them or be trampled to death and then, after a hundred yards or so, the realisation that the danger has somehow evaporated and people are laughing as they fan out and stroll away.

On the first day of February 1981, happily reunited, Kay and I flew to Bombay, now Mumbai, in a charter aircraft with the rest of the crew. Because there was no seat for Felicia, I'd given her the train fare and, as we walked into the Sea Rock Hotel at Bandra, she was already there, waiting.

Felicia was a middle-aged widow, a devout Indian Catholic, who'd brought up eight children of her own. She was sweet-natured and endlessly patient, never complaining about the long hours I needed her to work. Most important of all, she adored my daughter and took her everywhere, including Mass every morning. Apparently, Kay caused a stir. Passengers on the bus and beggars outside the church, to whom Felicia always gave a few coins, all wanted to touch her white-blonde hair.

During my first weeks in India, I was fearful of the beggars who seemed to accost us at every turn. Unwilling to connect, I refused to give them money and hid behind the story, circulating among the unit, that they were all deployed by rich masterminds who lived off the fat of the land.

The person who helped me confront this fear was one of the film's stars and the greatest president America never had: Martin Sheen. Long before he starred in *The West Wing*, Dick cast Martin as a *New York Times* correspondent who reported from India on Gandhi's first protest march.

We met by the swimming pool at the Sea Rock, overlooking the turgid Arabian Sea. Martin and I were sitting at a table, a tape recorder between us, while our children jumped in and out of the pool. Kay had just turned six and Martin's tow-headed son, Emilio, was the all-American teenager.

I was gathering information for the *Gandhi* press kit and Martin was describing an experience he'd had in Delhi. Hiring a rickshaw to take him to a restaurant, he'd casually tossed a couple of rupees to an emaciated boy, about eight years old, begging outside his hotel. On arrival at his destination, Martin had discovered the boy, who'd followed the rickshaw, had collapsed exhausted, when it came to a halt. He'd talked to him, given him some more money and discovered the child was all alone in the world. Later that night, unable to sleep, Martin had called his wife, Janet, in California. This amazing woman had agreed he could take the boy home with him and the Sheens would adopt him as their third son.

But, although he'd searched and searched, Martin never found him again. As he finished telling me this story, Emilio came running over to the table. 'Dad, there's a dead man in the sea.'

We looked over the parapet. There was indeed a bloated corpse floating past the hotel, an unknown someone who, unlike the people with outstretched hands we saw everywhere, was long past our help. After that, throughout our time in India, I made a point of giving some money to at least one beggar every day and no longer ignoring the others, pretending they didn't exist.

Martin went on to donate the whole of his *Gandhi* fee to Indian charities, the bulk of it going to Mother Teresa's mission among the dying street people of Calcutta.

The journalists we encountered in Bombay were very different from their Delhi counterparts. This was a city of contrasts where hundreds of thousands, maybe a million or more people, lived on streets, beaches and scrapyards in unremitting poverty. It was also the home of Bollywood, renowned for its excess and ostentation. Here, our film was no longer a hot political potato, merely one among many.

This left me free to concentrate on my main function, which was to amass all the publicity material needed to launch *Gandhi* when it was finished. Dick and I were in total agreement about this strategy. There was no point, we believed, in telling the world about the film while we were shooting, since it would all be long forgotten by the time it was shown.

Unusually, I pretty much had carte blanche. Due to the unique nature of our funding, there was no distributor looking over my shoulder and telling me what to do. Neither was there any template for marketing an epic of this kind, since no such film had ever been made. So I was flying by the seat of my pants; facilitating a 'making of' documentary for BBC television, amassing hundreds of photographs, interviewing, researching, reading and, above all, writing. And, because Dick both understood and valued marketing, I finally felt like a fully paid up member of the creative team.

One day, he sent me to Bombay airport on a vital PR mission. The British crew had all been brought out on one-way tickets and Terry Clegg had been trying to persuade Air India to give us a bulk deal to save money on the return journey. He'd been told that IATA, the international regulatory body, would only permit the airline to give us cheap fares in exchange for certain specified services. These included promotion. So Dick and Terry had cooked up the idea that we'd use one of our rest days to film an Air India endorsement, using one of their long-haul jets.

Dick would direct and twist the stars' arms to appear. Terry would put together a small volunteer crew. My mission was to persuade the man in charge to lend us a jumbo.

I took a taxi out to the engineering base at Chatrapati Shivaji airport where the man in charge was not happy. He walked me to a wallchart showing the whereabouts of all the 747s in the Air India fleet. Every one was either in service or scheduled for essential maintenance. That was his job; to ensure there never were any spare jumbos just hanging around.

By now, I'd learned a thing or two about negotiating in India; smile, be patient and polite, stick to your guns and, above all, stay very, very calm. The corrugated-iron office was stifling, the man in charge was friendly but immovable and the worryingly grimy little cups filled with strong black tea kept coming. I sat there, smiling and sipping, for the whole afternoon. In the end, just to get rid of me, the man in charge relented.

I got the plane, John Mills and Candice Bergen agreed to appear in the promotion, Dick directed and Terry entered airfare negotiations which went on and on without ever reaching a satisfactory conclusion.

*

When we left Bombay for Patna in Bihar, it was time for the wives and children to go home. From here on, we'd be staying in smaller hotels and had to travel light. In addition, Bihar was considered a trouble spot. There'd recently been religious riots, resulting in an uneasy curfew.

Kay was to travel to London with Terry Clegg's wife and children and be met there by my parents who'd look after her until I came home. I tried, as mothers do, to make it sound like an adventure. But it was with a very heavy heart that I gathered up her collection of miniature elephants and her paintings from playschool as Felicia begged me to send her to England too.

Nothing would have pleased me more. She'd made it possible for me to go to work every morning, knowing my daughter was happy in safe hands. It would be a long time before I had that luxury again.

Together, we took an excited Kay to the airport. We laughed and joked as we kissed her goodbye and we both cried as she disappeared through passport control. Then we went outside and walked down the long line of waiting Ambassador taxis, seeking one with some vestige of tread on its tyres, and cried again as it took us back to the Sea Rock Hotel. There, Felicia and I parted; she home to Delhi, I to Bihar.

Arriving in Patna the following day, although the state of emergency had been lifted, I could immediately sense a mood of sullen rebellion. No one smiled or looked us in the eye. It took a week to film two complicated scenes, both involving large crowds and steam trains. Then, with some relief, we boarded the unit's charter plane and flew south-west to Pune.

This city was overflowing with Westerners seeking enlightenment, all wearing saffron robes and mystic bead necklaces bearing a picture of their very rich and very strange guru, Bhagwan Rajneesh. Our hotel was full of them too and, as our weary technicians clumped into reception in their work boots, shorts and T-shirts, they found themselves in a sixties time warp of flower power and free love. It was here, at the Blue Diamond, that we faced the biggest crisis of all.

RA— Our main reason for going to Pune was to shoot at the Aga Khan Palace where the British had imprisoned Mahatma Gandhi and his wife during the Second World War. Kasturba Gandhi, who'd entered into this arranged marriage as a child, had died there during their incarceration. For a while, her husband was almost catatonic with grief.

This important and touching sequence was offset by another much lighter scene in which my sweet friend Candice Bergen appeared as the famous *Life* magazine photographer, Margaret Bourke White. Optimistic and opportunistic as always, I'd cast Candy in this part sixteen years earlier when we were both filming *The Sand Pebbles* in Taiwan with my pal Steve McQueen.

Having remained resolutely single throughout the ensuing years as a fashion model, professional photographer and Hollywood star, Candy, now in her mid-thirties, had recently married the French director, Louis Malle, and was fitting *Gandhi* around her honeymoon.

When I got back to the hotel on a Friday evening, after releasing Candy to travel with Louis, Terry Clegg greeted me with the worst possible news: we'd completely run out of money.

Back in London, Terry told me, Jake had gone to the Hindujas' office to sign the final funding contract. Everything in it had been hammered out and fully agreed beforehand. But, to Jake's horror, the brothers had refused to sign. They'd presented him instead with a set of entirely new and inflated demands relating to repayment and profit share which, in Jake's view, were so outrageous as to be totally unacceptable.

That was Terry's bad news. The slightly better news was that Jake had immediately phoned James Lee, chairman of Goldcrest and also CEO of publishers Pearson Longman, which had invested the largest share of British funds committed to *Gandhi*. James, fortuitously as it turned out, had a lunch appointment that same day with the Lords Blakenham, Gibson and Cowdray, who headed his parent company, the powerful Pearson Group.

Lee, then only thirty-seven years old, had been somewhat nervous as he told the venerable peers what had transpired. This was the third time Pearson and Goldcrest had been put on the spot in regard to *Gandhi* and he was expecting a roasting. However, Their Lordships' very evident anger was not directed towards James or Jake, but at the Hindujas.

It was the oldest of the trio, the septuagenarian Lord Cowdray, grandson of the company's founder, who'd been most affronted. He'd said; 'James, we will not be blackmailed. But we must be sure that four million dollars is actually what it's going to take to complete the project.'

The upshot, Terry told me, was that James Lee was flying out to see us. If we could satisfy him we were within budget and would remain so and he, in turn, was able to satisfy the Pearson hierarchy, we'd be able to continue.

We then discussed who should be in the know and decided on Sheila, my partner and executive producer, Mike Stanley-Evans, the film's financial controller, Pat Howell, and the director of publicity, who was of course Di.

Terry was firmly of the opinion that we should be frank with the British crew and ask them to gamble with us by keeping going. Pat Howell was more worried about how we'd get them home, since they still had no return tickets. Mike's main concern, as an officer and a gentleman, was what constituted 'proper behaviour' in a former colony. Di was apprehensive about the public relations fallout should our plight become general knowledge. And we were all aware that, should this happen, the rupee funding would dry up too and we wouldn't even be able to pay our hotel bill.

For the first and only time in my professional life, I was at a complete loss. Had we been in England, I could have mortgaged the house or sold my paintings. But in Pune I knew no one; we might as well have been on another planet.

It was Sheila, Terry and Di who saw me through and bore the brunt of my pig-headed behaviour because, yet again, I elected to take the most monstrous gamble; we'd keep on shooting and tell absolutely no one until we knew the result of James Lee's visit.

He arrived the following day. So too did the former British Prime Minister, James Callaghan, who was on a fact-finding tour of India with his Parliamentary Private Secretary, Jack Cunningham. I knew them both well and had arranged, weeks in advance, that Sheila and I would entertain them to dinner when they reached Pune.

The scene that evening in the restaurant of the Blue Diamond Hotel was surreal. Terry sat with an inscrutable James Lee, going through the budget and cost reports, item by item. Sheila and I were at a table just too far away to eavesdrop and, as she held the fort, chatting away to Jack and Sunny Jim, I craned my neck, trying to read James's poker face. Meanwhile, all around us, dozens of wealthy latter-day hippies in red, orange and yellow robes were laughing and talking sixteen to the dozen as they ploughed their way through the vegetarian option. And, in the adjacent bar, carefree members of our unit were enjoying a raucous Saturday-night booze-up.

After dinner, Terry and I went to his office where James, a neophyte already falling disastrously in love with the film industry, gave me a grilling. Terry had been completely frank with him, explaining what we'd spent, what we owed, what we'd completed and what we yet had to shoot. It was now my turn. Finally James said; 'Dickie, if I go back and advocate putting in these extra funds, are you absolutely confident in your own mind that you can come in on time and on budget?'

I said: 'Short of some inconceivable act of God, James, I will bring this picture in on budget, even if it means I have to compromise. On that I give you my word.'

James left for the UK early the next morning to put his recommendation to the three Pearson peers. He promised to try and give us their decision before cheques needed to be issued the following Friday.

During this nail-biting delay, I received a heart-warming message from a true friend in London. Sydney Samuelson's rental company was hiring out the bulk of our camera and lighting equipment and his most recent invoice, involving a significant sum, was one of those about to fall due. Having heard of our plight, he was now telexing to inform me he was formally waiving all outstanding and future charges until we were in a position to pay. The message ended: 'The clock stops now. Love Sydney.' Needless to say, it reduced me to tears.

The other, eagerly anticipated telex from James Lee arrived in the nick of time, during the early hours of Friday morning. My mental box, labelled ignominy and ruin, could remain firmly closed: the board of Pearson had come to our rescue.

It was to be weeks before I learned that Jake had taken some pleasure in conveying the news that we no longer needed their money to the Hindujas. No doubt anticipating we'd be obliged to accept their last-minute demands, the brothers had, in his words, 'been absolutely apoplectic'.

Having finished our work in Pune and triumphantly paid all our bills, we flew north to the beautiful state of Rajasthan. Here, at the end of our Indian odyssey, we stayed for just three nights at one of the loveliest hotels in the world: the Lake Palace at Udaipur.

*

When Mohandas K. Gandhi had returned to India in 1914 after a self-imposed twenty-six-year exile in England and South Africa, he journeyed the length and breadth of the subcontinent by train, learning about his homeland. It was this travel montage which we were to film, in temperatures well over forty degrees, on a little used railway line to the north of Udaipur.

Throughout the six-month location shoot. I'd been extremely cautious about what I ate and drank, because being ill was out of the question. Now, at the end of the very last day, sitting on the roof of a moving train surrounded by actors and crew, I desperately needed the distant, malodorous and perversely named honey wagon.

Somehow, I managed to hold on until we'd completed the final shot. I remember shouting, 'Cut,' and then, as the train continued along the tracks, entering an oven-like ravine, the ominous rumbling in my bowels miraculously disappeared. Completely cured, I stood up on the roof and did a little dance.

DH— Back in London, everyone had just two days in which to rejoin their families, unpack and catch up on a little sleep. I went down to my parents' house in Berkshire for the joyous, long-anticipated reunion with Kay. Then it was back to work.

We filmed with Ben at Kingsley Hall in the East End of London and with Sir John Gielgud, who played an aloof viceroy, at the Institute of Directors in Pall Mall. We set up at dawn on a Sunday – to be sure the area was free of contemporary traffic – to depict Gandhi arriving at Buckingham Palace to take tea with the King. We also spent a day at Staines Town Hall with Ben and Trevor Howard, portraying the remarkable Judge Broomfield.

Then, mundanely, we assembled for the final time on the familiar backlot of Shepperton Studios, where the art department had recreated the entrance to 10 Downing Street. Dick said, 'Action,' and the exiting Gandhi shook hands with Ramsay MacDonald on the doorstep. Cut, print, check the gate. The film was in the can.

The wrap party which followed in the studio commissary was both celebration and valediction. Somehow we'd not only survived and finished on time but, as Dick had promised James Lee, we were also marginally under budget.

None of us who'd accompanied Dick on his Indian odyssey would ever be the same again. We'd been welcomed, we'd been threatened, we'd come within a hair's breadth of physical and financial disaster, and somehow we'd continued to soldier on, despite the heat, the antimalaria tablets, the ever-present threat of diarrhoea, the lack of sleep and the unbelievably long hours.

Our British production crew, a family of nearly seventy men and a handful of women, who'd loved, laughed, cried, sweated, squabbled, sworn and stuck together through thick and thin, was about to be disbanded. Now it was up to the editor, John Bloom, and his twelve-strong post-production team, together with composers George Fenton, Ravi Shankar and their musicians, to turn half a million feet of exposed stock into the finished film.

At the end of the evening, raising a glass of champagne that was completely full for once, Dick, the eternal optimist, praised and then drank to the crew. He was followed by Mary Mills, wife of Sir John, who raised her glass to Sheila Attenborough: 'And here's to the woman who follows her stubborn old man to the ends of the earth.'

RA— Sheila and I have been married, now, for over sixty years. And beloved, fiery-haired Mary, known irreverently as 'Ginge', had hit the nail on the head. No matter where I've travelled, either to make films or appear in them, Sheila has travelled too. In the early years, she brought the children with her. Latterly, she's come on her own.

When I was so ill at the end of shooting in India, it was Sheila who stayed up all night with me at the Lake Palace Hotel and somehow got me on my feet and out of the door in the morning. On *Jurassic Park*, when I was holed up in a basement while a hurricane ravaged Hawaii, Sheila was right there beside me – as she was in Hollywood, Taiwan, Morocco, Chicago, Zimbabwe, Malta, Arizona, Deventer, New York, Venice and a whole host of other less salubrious locations, including on *Oh! What a Lovely War*, a municipal rubbish tip in Brighton.

My wife and I have many, many things in common, most notably our total dedication to our children and beautiful grandchildren. We are united in our hatred of racism, our enjoyment of old friends, our love of France and football, and our firm belief – contrary to Margaret Thatcher's dictum – that there is such a thing as society.

On political affiliation, we long ago agreed to disagree. People laugh when they see our house in the run-up to a general election. Half the windows, Sheila's half, are dedicated to posters supporting the Liberal Democrats. The remainder, scrupulously apportioned, proclaim my adherence to Labour.

There is, however, one thing on which we never have and never will agree and that is risk-taking. Sheila is averse to any kind of gamble. I think it emanates partly from natural apprehension and partly from motherhood; her determination, at all costs, to protect the children.

I am inherently a gambler. And only once, throughout our marriage, has Sheila gambled with me. It was in 1948, two years after my demob from the RAF. We'd been living with her parents at their flat in Barons Court and, although they couldn't have been more welcoming, we were desperate for a place of our own. Sheila had spotted a very small, bomb-damaged house just off the King's Road in Chelsea. The rent, which seemed enormous, was a couple of pounds a week. Although the workman's two-up two-down needed a great deal of work to make it habitable and we had no furniture, we signed the lease and moved in.

At the time we were both filming *The Guinea Pig*, directed by my friend John Boulting's twin brother, Roy, at the now defunct MGM Studios at Elstree. Bizarrely, at the age of twenty-five I was playing a cockney schoolboy in shorts and a blazer, who'd been catapulted into a public school as an experiment in social engineering. Sheila was co-starring as my housemaster's adult wife. As if this was not fodder enough for mickey-taking on the part of the unit, I was obliged to keep my school cap on whenever possible to hide my incipient bald patch.

It was one of the film crew who told us about a complete outsider which was to run in the Grand National at fifty to one. The name of this unfancied filly was Sheila's Cottage. Of course, we couldn't resist having a bet.

We raided our post office savings account and emptied our pockets, just about managing to rustle up a fiver. On race day, I was dispatched to place the bet at the local newsagent's round the corner. What I didn't tell my wife was that I had a secret five-pound note – big and white with curly black lettering – which was my rainy-day money. I put all ten pounds on Sheila's Cottage to win.

Already passionate Chelsea supporters, we spent the Saturday afternoon watching an away game at Highbury. It was there, just after our team had scored the most fantastic goal, that a fellow football fan announced Sheila's Cottage had been first past the post. We'd won £500; an unbelievable windfall.

I have never, from that day to this, backed another horse, although I have, of course, taken huge gambles professionally and do play the lottery every week. And I have to confess that when things are very risky, I don't always tell Sheila just how risky they are.

She'd known, as she entertained the two visiting politicians over dinner at the Blue Diamond Hotel in Pune, that *Gandhi* was in financial trouble but not that the entire film and with it our lifestyle were hanging by a thread. Neither was she aware, on the last day of shooting, that my entire producing and directing fee was winging its way to Joe Levine in New York. (When she reads this, I hope she can find it in her heart to forgive me.)

The most pressing matter, as we embarked on the lengthy post-production phase, was to sell *Gandhi* to a distributor. Jake's dedication to the project and his extraordinary ability to raise film funding from unusual sources had placed us in a unique and potentially very strong position. For the first and only time in my whole career, I'd made a film which was not owned or controlled by any studio. Up to this point, excluding the rupee element, *Gandhi* had been almost exclusively financed by IFI and Goldcrest, a consortium of British executives and fund managers who'd gone out on a limb to take a massive punt on a dicey project in a notoriously fickle industry.

Now, in order to safeguard their investment, we needed the clout, expertise and deep pockets of a major Hollywood studio, able to book the right American cinemas, pay for hundreds if not thousands of prints and mount a huge marketing campaign. And if that same studio also had both the appetite and the infrastructure to distribute the film throughout the rest of the world, so much the better.

At the end of shooting, I did nothing but sleep and eat for the best part of a week. I then set to work with John Bloom in his suite of cutting rooms at Twickenham Studios. For the next month we worked like lunatics, putting together a rough assembly to which John added a temporary music track. Then, despite my misgivings about the raw state of picture and sound, I invited Marti Baum over from the West Coast to see the result.

At that stage, Marti undoubtedly had mixed feelings about *Gandhi*. He'd ably represented me as an actor for well over twenty years and consistently negotiated top dollar and above-the-title billing in a number of well regarded Hollywood movies. But unlike his other close friends who were also clients – notably Sidney Poitier and Walter Matthau – I'd repeatedly played ducks and drakes with my acting career in order to get *Gandhi* made and, time and time again, Marti had thrown up his hands in despair.

He arrived at the viewing theatre, dapper as always, removed his jacket to avoid creasing it, and sat back as the screening began. Three hours later, the lights came up to the sound of Marti repeatedly blowing his nose.

Having taken several minutes to compose himself, he stood up and said, 'Dickie, I take it all back. This is a wonderful and truly amazing movie. I've never seen anything like it. And I'm going to make you a promise. When you're ready, bring a print to Los Angeles and I'll make sure it's seen by the head of every studio. I don't mean the head of production, I don't mean the head of distribution, I mean the people in control. I will get all of them personally to see this picture. On that I give you my word.'

And he *was* as good as his word. When Jake and I took the rough-dubbed assembly to Hollywood, he'd arranged a series of high-powered private screenings with every one of the majors. Disappointingly, we received an immediate turndown from Fox and Universal. Warners professed interest but never came up with a bid. That left Paramount and Columbia.

Initially I was keen to go with Paramount out of loyalty to their chairman, Charlie Bluhdorn, who'd taken a huge risk by backing *Oh! What a Lovely War*, my first film as a director. There was, however, a major sticking point. Jake was adamant that American television rights had to be sold separately and this Charlie, equally adamantly, was refusing to accept.

Then, at the Columbia screening, I encountered Frank Price, the company's decisive chairman and chief executive, who would be one of the major figures in my professional life for many years to come. Unlike most studio heads, Frank proved to be erudite, witty and very quietly spoken. In addition, although his business instincts were sharply honed, he patently had a social conscience.

After running the footage, he asked Jake, Marti and me to remain in our seats while he consulted with his colleagues. Within ten minutes, he invited us into his office to make an extraordinary offer: Columbia really wanted the film and was prepared to top any other bid we might receive.

It wasn't just the money that swung it for me. What really mattered was Frank's promise that he and his team would really get behind the film and sell it. *Gandhi*, he said, was one of the most powerful and important pictures he'd ever seen. And, if the executives on the East Coast who ran the international side of the company echoed his view, Columbia would wish to acquire distribution rights throughout the entire world.

Jake and I immediately took the footage to New York where, after their viewing, Pat Williamson and David Matalon received us with open arms. To my amazement, nearly two decades after my first meeting with Moti Kothari the essentials of a multimillion-dollar worldwide distribution deal were agreed in Pat's office during a two-minute coast-to-coast conference call just before we left for the airport.

The amount we were to receive up front was relatively small. However, the rising percentage of gross box-office receipts, which would go directly to investors and profit participants should the film prove to be a hit, was phenomenal. And, unlike any other deal in my entire experience, it was to come right off the top from day one.

Equally important to me was Columbia's commitment to spend at least $12 million on prints and advertising. In the event, they spent far more, exceeding the actual cost of making the film by several hundred thousand.

Jake had hoped that the separate sale of American television rights would bring in enough to repay at least 50 per cent of our hard-currency funding. Cannily, while the dollar surged in value, he held out until the film's eleven Oscar nominations were announced in February 1983. Then, in a supremely ironic twist, he sold the rights to Embassy, a company once owned by Joe Levine, for twice the figure he'd originally had in mind. I could hardly believe, as I signed the contract, that virtually all our indebtedness to the Goldcrest consortium was being repaid at the stroke of a pen.

I'd been particularly concerned about the National Coal Board Pension Fund and the Post Office Staff Superannuation Fund whose managers had taken repeated gambles on *Gandhi*. When the box-office returns began to exceed everyone's wildest dreams, it was good to know that they and all our other intrepid backers would reap handsome rewards for their faith and their tenacity.

Embassy didn't do badly either. Within weeks of buying the US television rights, they sold them on to HBO for considerably more than they'd paid. What I didn't know at the time was that Jake's blossoming friendship with one of the partners heading the company would lead eventually to the demise of Goldcrest. Or that, within a matter of months, this same man would also go on to make me an offer I couldn't refuse.

DH— Film technicians are employed on a freelance basis. In exchange for working ridiculously long hours, often in stressful conditions, they're paid extremely well. But, come the end of shooting, they're out of work. And there's the rub. Should you snap up the very next job that comes along? Or dare you hold out for a film you really want to do?

While I was in India, my entire salary had been paid into my English bank account and I'd lived free of charge. On my return, I had a further eight weeks on full pay while I catalogued and captioned the stills and put together a comprehensive press kit.

As my eight weeks were coming to an end, Dick asked me to accompany him to Los Angeles for a marketing meeting with Columbia. Providentially, this three-day trip was scheduled to take place over half-term when Kay could again stay with my parents.

It was the first time I'd been to America. We flew first class, at Columbia's expense, and were met by a ridiculously long limo which wafted us to Sunset Boulevard and the vast pink palace that was Dick's home away from home, the Beverly Hills Hotel. There, the company had reserved a palatial suite for him and a junior suite for me. Both contained exotic flower arrangements – his massive, mine smaller but still impressive – each bearing a note of effusive greetings from Frank Price.

Having unpacked, I went down to Dick's suite where a waiter was delivering a chilled bottle of Dom Perignon, caviar, blinis and a vast basket of fruit, all courtesy of the management. Fighting mid-afternoon jet lag, we sat on either side of a gilded coffee table bearing these gifts.

With the smell of jasmine wafting in from the terrace, Dick surveyed the acres of blond carpet, the Impressionist reproductions on the walls, the wet bar, the signature potted banana tree and the welcoming wink of message lights on both white phones.

Then, this man who'd been rich and famous for years and years and years, who never had to cook an egg, iron a shirt or even refuel his own car, let out a long sigh of satisfaction and said endearingly: 'If only my ma and pa could see me now.'

We opened the envelopes handed to us at reception. They contained identical schedules. That evening we were invited to something called a catered dinner at Frank Price's home. (Thank God I'd brought the little black dress.) The following morning at nine, we were to attend a screening of *Gandhi* for the whole Columbia publicity department. A marketing meeting would take place immediately afterwards.

It was here that my heart plummeted. The first item on the post-screening agenda was a marketing presentation by Diana Hawkins; proof, if it were needed, that there's no such thing as a free first-class trip to Hollywood.

One of Dick's talents, whether he's directing a film, lobbying captains of industry, raising money for charity or organising a new company, is his ability to convince people they can achieve the impossible. Of course I could do it, he said. I knew the film inside out. What was the problem? Then, having bolstered my confidence, he laid it on the line. It was very, very important I got this right.

At the Price residence, which resembled a baronial manor, I was seated with Marti Baum on my right and his friend, Red Buttons, on my left. They were being very kind and making me laugh a great deal when I heard the sonorous voice of Sidney Poitier at the top table over-ride the chatter. 'Dickie,' he said, and then more loudly: 'Dickie . . .'

Dick's eyes were glazed. He didn't appear to have heard. Then, very slowly, to gales of affectionate laughter, his head fell slowly forward into his dinner plate. He wasn't drunk, simply too exhausted, just for once, to exercise that iron will.

We'd worked until ten the night before at the studios, got up at crack of dawn, packed, checked in at Heathrow, flown for twelve hours and gone straight to the hotel, where we'd talked, changed and gone straight out again. In years to come, I was to learn that this was par for the course.

The following morning, having spent a sleepless night rehearsing the dreaded presentation, I was the one who was exhausted. Dick was waiting in the lobby, bright as a button and raring to go.

Our limo took us across Coldwater Canyon to Burbank Studios where we went straight into a screening room. The audience, essentially a fairly cynical and highly paid group of marketing experts, was difficult to read. *Gandhi* was not their picture; they'd bought it ready-made. And we knew that Columbia had a big picture of its own, *Tootsie*, in which they'd invested a great deal of money and effort. Our epic biopic and their cross-dressing comedy were both to be launched, within days of each other, at the end of the year.

Fear ensured I remained alert throughout the running. When it ended, there was complete silence. At such screenings, as with rushes, the most important people sit at the back. Everyone had turned to look at Marvin Antonowsky, the powerful president of Marketing and Research.

Marvin is a man who feels very deeply but is not given to shows of emotion. For years, he scared me rigid. But it's true to say he adores Dick and, on that morning, despite the habitual gravity of his manner, he must have emitted some subtle signal which empowered his staff, after that minuscule pause, to erupt in cheers and applause.

Dick and I were to learn, as we got to know them better, that Hollywood publicists play by a set of strict rules. For instance, they never so much as mention the name, let alone the merits or demerits of any other picture they are launching. And they need to be good at faking enthusiasm. But, deep down, they just love some pictures more. And, without a shadow of a doubt, they loved *Gandhi* that morning.

I've no idea what I said at the hour-long presentation which followed. I do remember it took place around a giant oval table and that Dick and I sat side by side, facing Frank Price, Marvin Antonowsky and more than a dozen other people, all with fancy job titles.

Dick was as thrilled as I was when Columbia hired me to continue working with him on *Gandhi* for the next two years.

4

WE SHALL OVERCOME

DH— MARCH 1982. TRUE to form, having completed a whole year of post-production, Dick has now added a seventh public body to his long list of chairmanships. This time it's the British Film Institute.

With the director, Anthony Smith, this has become a time-consuming crusade to replace old buildings with new, regenerate the archive and transform an elite ivory-tower ethos into a genuine desire to preserve, share and inform. Bizarrely, most of this will be made possible by the reclusive multimillionaire John Paul Getty, now hidden away in the London Clinic, endlessly viewing old black-and-white British films.

Meanwhile, in a surprise move, Columbia Pictures has been taken over by Coca-Cola which they're now obligated to serve on every conceivable occasion. Their soft-drink overlord is Roberto Goizueta, a former Cuban immigrant with a social conscience. Fortunately for us – and our massive marketing budget – he's an admirer of Mahatma Gandhi.

For me, marketing the film has become a full-time occupation. Now bearing the strapline 'A World Event', Gandhi is to have twenty-three premieres in fourteen different countries, including the USSR and China, where Dick and Sheila will be among the first Westerners to see Emperor Qin's vast, recently excavated 2,000-year-old terracotta army.

Having made several lengthy trips to Bombay to supervise the preparation of a Hindi soundtrack for the benefit of the four hundred million Indian cinema-goers who don't speak English, Dick is now selecting the 'voices' to be used in other foreign-language versions. We've also met and briefed Toda San, an enchanting lady reputed to write the best Japanese subtitles. As we shall see when we reach Tokyo, these are actually side-titles, running along the vertical edge of the screen.

We are also heavily involved in a strategy designed to create awareness across America. A million dollars is being spent on high school study guides and more than thirty reprints and new tie-in books about the Mahatma – including *In Search of Gandhi*, which Dick and I have written together – will appear to synchronise with the film's release.

Market research has revealed a generation of college students that is particularly receptive to Gandhi's non-violent credo. Screenings and discussion groups are being set up on every major US campus. Elsewhere, adults best positioned to spread the vital word of mouth – hairdressers, repair men, taxi drivers – are being invited to 'talker screenings' right across Middle America, and another plan, designed to engage the important crossover black audience, will take the two of us to the Deep South.

Since the US has virtually no national newspapers, Hollywood publicists have invented something called the junket. This entails flying up to a hundred far-flung journalists and TV presenters into New York or Los Angeles over a single weekend. The film company puts them all up in a top-notch hotel, taking over another entire floor for interviews.

The whole thing is run with military precision. The press see the film on a Friday evening. Throughout Saturday, the stars and director give non-stop print interviews with only a brief break for lunch. Throughout Sunday, the interviewee sits in a pre-lit room prominently featuring the film's poster, accompanied by a video crew. Each out-of-town television presenter has less than twenty minutes to meet, greet, occupy the vacant chair, mike up and get their interview. On the way out, they're handed a recording of this 'exclusive' encounter before they're shunted back to the boonies.

By now, I've lost count of the times I've been to the States. With the greatest of ease, I've become used to flying first class, to packing swiftly for every eventuality and climate, to chauffeured limos, bouquets, presentations, power breakfasts and haute cuisine. In between, I return to the reality of my housing association flat bearing guilt-laden gifts for Kay, picking up where I left off; frying fish fingers, telling bedtime stories, traipsing to the launderette.

Between grandparents, kind neighbours and a lackadaisical nineteen-year-old girl, plucked idealistically from the dole queue, I've cobbled together a system of childcare that works. Just.

Today, Dick and I have flown to Washington on Concorde and I'm still worrying about Kay as we lunch on lobster in the bowels of the White House. Our host in this subterranean commissary is Morgan Mason, son of the brooding expat British actor, James. Morgan is 'special assistant' to another star, sworn in as President eighteen months ago. It's these wheels within wheels, oiled by Columbia, which have gained us entrée here. The aim of this visit is that Dick should persuade the President to attend – or possibly even host – a *Gandhi* premiere in Washington.

Also at our table is a diminutive elderly man, introduced as Ambassador Terra. He has no foreign posting but, having raised millions for the incumbent's presidential campaign, is designated Ambassador at Large for Cultural Affairs. Lunch over, the ambassador leads us up a nondescript back staircase to a landing where there's a marine on guard with a rifle who, having inspected our passes, raps on a door. It swings open from the other side to reveal, like some pantomime transformation, the full pastel panoply of the Oval Office.

From the threshold, I can see the President sitting at his desk. A man in a suit, bending to whisper a briefing, straightens and beckons us in. Politely, Dick and the ambassador stand back to let me go first.

Ronald Reagan comes bounding over, beaming a megawatt welcome. Because I'm ahead of the men, he takes me for the leader of this little delegation and, totally ignoring Dick, grabs my hand and holds onto it long enough for a photographer, who appears out of the woodwork, to capture our encounter. When the little ambassador shoves Dick forward, two more shots are taken of us all together.

No one yet knows that the President, still recovering from an assassination attempt, is also in the early stages of Alzheimer's. So it comes as a shock that he patently has no idea who on earth we are or why we're here. Dick and I take it in turns to explain. Light dawns briefly. Yes, yes, he knows all about the Mahatma. He's Indira Gandhi's father.

It seems rude to put him right so we press on with our request about the premiere. May we arrange a private screening first? The answer is kind but vague. Someone will get back to us. Audience over. We shake Reagan's hand again, thank him profusely and exit down the back stairs and into the commissary where we compare notes over coffee.

Less than an hour later, as we take our leave of the ambassador, Dick is handed an envelope. Someone incredibly efficient has already developed and printed the colour photographs of us with Reagan. Dick takes one look, snorts and gives them to me. He wants no souvenir of an encounter with this former actor who took part in the Communist witch-hunt which all but destroyed the screen career of his late great friend and mentor, Edward G. Robinson.

(Back in the UK, I will give the photographs to my parents, both to the right of Genghis Khan, who grant them pride of place in Berkshire.)

As we're driven away from the White House, Dick decides he's badly in need of an antidote. He asks our driver to take us to the Lincoln Memorial. There, after he's read aloud the words of the Gettysburg address, we stand on the steps facing the long, straight reflecting pool, imagining the huge crowd which gathered here twenty years earlier to hear Martin Luther King's famous 'I have a dream' speech. Tomorrow, we are to meet his widow.

With time to spare before our flight to Atlanta, we walk to the Vietnam Memorial which, in its eloquent simplicity, has to be one of the world's most powerful testaments to the futility of war; an undulating ribbon of black marble, carved with the names of 58,000 dead American servicemen.

Slowly, we walk its length, talking about the napalmed little Vietnamese girl pictured in Dick's office, until we encounter a middle-aged man in a battered Stetson. He's staring intently at one section of the wall. We stop as he walks towards it, takes a crumpled handkerchief from his jeans pocket and reaches up to polish, oh so gently, one of the engraved names. Then, stepping back, he removes the Stetson, holds it to his heart and salutes, tears coursing unashamedly down his weather-beaten face.

RA— I was seventeen when I volunteered to serve in World War II. Irene and Helga had been with us for a year – a year in which my mother's love had brought about a transformation. They'd both put on some weight and lost the pinched faces and blank eyes so heart-rendingly evident on their arrival. And, hesitantly at first, they'd told us about their lives in Berlin before they came to Leicester.

In 1933, when they were aged five and three, a law was enacted which allowed Jews to sit only on specially marked seats in public places. In 1935, they lost the right of citizenship, marriage with non-Jews was forbidden and many Aryan shopkeepers refused to sell them food or medicine. In 1938, the Nazis smashed their homes and synagogues, forcing members of the Jewish community to pay for the damage and publicly get down on their hands and knees to scrub the streets clean.

Then just before dawn in the summer of 1939, members of the Gestapo had stormed the door of the Bejach family home on which the word *Juden* had been scrawled many months before. They'd dragged Irene and Helga's mother from her bed and bundled her away, never to be seen again.

And all the while I'd been living in blissful ignorance; performing at the Little Theatre, being a self-important ARP messenger, bunking off school and playing endless practical jokes on Dave and Johnny. Hearing what had happened to Irene and Helga, made me face up to the barbarity being perpetrated virtually on our doorstep.

When I told Mary and the Governor I was going to volunteer for the RAF, there was no objection. The first and, I think, the only time I'd ever heard my father swear was when Chamberlain came back from Munich waving his silly bit of paper and boasting he'd secured 'peace in our time'. 'What a fool,' the Governor had said. 'What a bloody fool!'

So I knew, without any shadow of a doubt, when I presented myself to the recruiting officer at the Crusaders' Hall, that this was a war we had to fight. I was told to expect my call-up soon after my eighteenth birthday.

My reasons for choosing to join the Brylcreem boys were, I suppose, typical of a cocky, stage-struck teenager. I thought flying would be romantic and, because we already knew of their heroism in the Battle of Britain, pilots were said to attract the prettiest girls. Banal as it sounds, I also liked the colour of the uniform.

In the event, I was nearly nineteen when my call-up finally came.

By then, I'd spent just over a year studying at RADA, fallen in love with Sheila and was having my first taste of success as Pinkie in the West End stage version of *Brighton Rock* opposite Hermione Baddeley and Dulcie Gray.

The theatre was fully booked during the six-month run, the audience remaining resolutely seated even when the air-raid sirens wailed outside. So the impresarios were not best pleased when I relayed the news that I'd received the long-expected summons to join His Majesty's Armed Forces, and they immediately applied for a short deferment on the grounds that live theatre was good for public morale.

My service life began in a requisitioned block of luxury flats close to the London Zoo. Here I became AC2 1808294 Attenborough R., and, having been issued with boots, kitbag, gas mask and uniform, I quickly mastered the art of anchoring the forage cap at a suitably rakish angle on my shorn scalp.

Next came the medical – no problem there. It was followed by a multiple vaccination which I absolutely dreaded. Determined to keep my cowardice well hidden, I rolled up my left sleeve and stood in line with the others. Come my turn, some great thug shoved a giant needle fit for a horse deep into my arm. Proud that I hadn't made an idiot of myself, I managed to march at least four paces before I fell flat on my face, out cold.

The initial regime was disciplined but bearable. We did our fair share of square-bashing and were required to march everywhere, even to lectures which started with idiotic things like spelling. There were also regular kit inspections, when you had to lay all your belongings out in a precise order on your iron bedstead. I remember having to polish the instep under my clumping boots.

Induction over, we split into different groups. As a future pilot, I was sent to Downing College, Cambridge, where we were taught flight theory and aircraft recognition. In later years – being the only one without a degree – this granted me a modicum of parity with my brainier brothers who both went on to graduate from Clare.

The training was not exactly arduous and I had sufficient free time to join a college drama group for six public performances of Mary Hayley Bell's *Men in Shadow*, playing the part originated by her husband, John Mills. They both attended the dress rehearsal and I remember Johnny was scathing about my ham-fisted Leichner 5 and 9 make-up, insisting I looked like a Red Indian.

From Downing, I was posted to Marshall's Flying School in the nearby village of Bottisham where I spent four weeks under instruction in a Tiger Moth before very nervously making my first solo flight. This I did just once, before being promoted to AC1 and becoming engaged to Sheila. My next posting was to Heaton Park near Manchester. There I hung around, awaiting a troop flight to Canada where I was supposed to complete my pilot training and become an officer.

I never did rise above the ranks. Fate intervened at the end of 1943 when I was propelled into a totally different environment. It began when the fierce Heaton Park commander ordered me into his office. 'You've been seconded to Pinewood Film Studios,' he barked. 'What the hell does that mean?'

'I don't know, sir.'

'Some shower calling itself the RAF Film Unit. You're to report to a Flight Lieutenant Boulting.'

I'd never heard of the flight lieutenant, never been to Pinewood and hadn't a clue why I'd been summoned. On arrival, I discovered the entire studios had been requisitioned and now housed a curious amalgam of aerial reconnaissance, propaganda, moneymaking and insurance. This consisted of the RAF, Crown, Army and Polish Air Force film units, all lumped together with the Royal Mint and Lloyds of London which had been evacuated during the Blitz.

I marched noisily along the echoing concrete walkway flanking the sound stages and turned into a corridor of former dressing rooms where, as instructed, I knocked on the designated door. A surprisingly mild voice politely invited me to enter.

Seeing an officer at a desk, I automatically stamped, saluted and stood to attention. 'AC1 Attenborough. Sir!'

Flight Lieutenant John Boulting was lounging in his chair, tunic unbuttoned, one foot up on the desk, languidly puffing out a cloud of smoke. 'Ah, yes. For God's sake, take off that cap and do please sit down.'

This man, who was to become my lifelong friend, told me I'd been summoned because he'd seen me onstage in *Brighton Rock* and in Noël Coward's film, *In Which We Serve*. He'd been instructed by top brass, in the form of Wing Commanders Derek Twist and Lord Willoughby de Broke, to direct a propaganda film. This full-length feature, intended for showing in public cinemas, was to be made by actors and film technicians serving in the RAF, together with a very special group of flyers, also based at Pinewood.

Flight Lieutenant George Brown was the producer, Sergeant Harry Waxman the cameraman and the eminent playwright Air Gunner Terence Rattigan had written the script. The title of the film was *Journey Together*. Having been selected to play one of the two juvenile leads, I'd be seconded to Pinewood for several months. And, in response to my only question, the Flight Lieutenant assured me I'd be able to resume my flying training afterwards.

Given that assurance, it all seemed too good to be true. I'd be close to Sheila, who'd just landed her first starring role in Michael Powell and Emeric Pressburger's *A Canterbury Tale* which was being completed at nearby Denham Studios. I'd continue to receive an ACi's pay of seven shillings and thruppence and, as Flight Lieutenant Boulting was careful to point out, far from shirking, I'd be making a really important contribution to the war effort. It was heady stuff but what made the prospect even more irresistible was that I'd be working with one of my all-time heroes, the American movie star, Edward G. Robinson.

John Boulting and his identical twin, Roy, a captain with the Army Film Unit, had met Robinson in Hollywood before the war. John had managed to send him a copy of Rattigan's script, asking if he'd be willing to come to England and play the Canadian flying instructor – unusual casting for someone who'd made his name portraying gangsters. I suspect John had also subjected him to the spiel he'd given me about helping the war effort because the reply had been short, emotive and very much to the point: 'Like you, I am a Jew. How can I refuse?'

Eddy G.'s background was not unlike that of Joe Levine. He was born Emmanuel Goldenberg in 1893 and brought from Romania to live in New York's Lower East Side at the age of ten. Like me, he'd won a scholarship to drama school and begun his career as a stage actor on Broadway. Fifteen years later, he'd made his screen debut playing a small part in a silent film and, following the advent of sound, hit the big time with his defining portrait of a murderous thug in *Little Caesar*.

The fascination of Eddy Robinson was the contrast between the actual man and his bad-guy screen persona. In private life he was quiet, cultured and an extensive collector of fine art. Before he could afford to buy paintings, he told me, he'd spent years dreaming up different ways of stealing a particular Renoir from a public gallery in Washington.

Eddy had always been a collector; as a boy it was the labels from cigars. By the time I met him, he'd assembled one of the finest collections of modern art in private hands, including works by Cézanne, Rouault, Modigliani, Degas, Pissarro, Monet and Boudin. They were, of course, worth a fortune. But one of the things Eddy taught me – and he taught me a great deal – was never to buy a picture simply because you believed it would appreciate in value. You bought, he said, only what you had to have because you'd die if you didn't. He denied collecting art, asserting instead that art collected him.

I'd been brought up surrounded by my father's favourite paintings. The reproductions he'd saved up to buy out of the Medici catalogue hung in every room at home. And, like Eddy, the Governor was crazy about the Impressionists.

It was Eddy who gave me the confidence to start buying original paintings simply because I loved them, regardless of price, fashion or investment potential. He was the originator of the one vice which still holds me in its grip more than sixty years later. If things are going well, I'm traipsing from gallery to gallery, looking. But whenever I'm flat broke, I cheer myself up by buying another picture. Irresponsible? Yes, of course. It's an addiction.

Because I've never kept money languishing in a bank, various crises over the years have forced me to sell pictures I absolutely adored. But, as Eddy once said: 'Paintings never belong to any one of us. If we are fortunate, as I have been, we are allowed at most a magical time of custody.'

His own magical time expired during the early 1950s. Ronald Reagan, then president of the Screen Actors' Guild, had testified before the witch-hunting House Un-American Activities Committee in Washington that certain of the Guild's members were Communists. Eddy was among those who came under suspicion and, for a while, his career ground to a halt. The HUAC summoned him to testify three times and threatened him with formal blacklisting before he finally managed to clear his name.

During the same period, Eddy and his first wife, Gladys, were embroiled in a bitter divorce proceedings. Californian community property law dictated that everything acquired during their thirty-year marriage had to be split fifty-fifty and, when the couple were unable to agree on how to divide his magnificent collection, everything had to be sold.

Eddy spent the last sixteen years of his life tracking down and buying back the pictures he missed the most. When some were put up for auction in 1960, he asked one of his friends to bid on his behalf. The friend wrote afterwards: '. . . this afternoon's papers report that the millionaire lady who shot her husband to death because she mistook him for a prowler was the competition I was up against on the Modigliani. This art business can be a very dangerous game.'

The flyers based at Pinewood Studios during the war were also involved in a dangerous game. They were the pilot, navigator and cameraman teams of the RAF Film Unit whose job it was to accompany bomber squadrons over Germany.

I got to know what they did because, between raids, most of them worked on *Journey Together* as technicians or actors. Their operational drill was always the same. When a bomber formation reached enemy territory, a pathfinder would go in first, dropping flares. It would be followed by the Pinewood boys who filmed the target prior to the attack. Then, while they circled above, wave after wave of Lancasters would smash the place to smithereens. Raid over, fires raging, the Pinewood team would go in again to record the devastation. Their exposed stock was brought back to the studios for processing and then sent on to Bomber Command for analysis.

A Lancaster bomber had a crew of seven; average age twenty-three. They flew continuously until they'd completed a tour of thirty operations. In some squadrons no one survived long enough to complete a single tour. Many were volunteers from Commonwealth countries, such as South Africa, and others escapees from occupied Europe. From 1942 onwards, the RAF was joined by the US Air Force and I remember going to one of their bases with Eddy who stood on the tarmac, tears streaming down his face as he saluted the B17s setting off to bomb Nazi Germany.

Working with him on the sound stage at Pinewood was a revelation.

During my time at RADA I'd been obliged to replace my broad Leicester accent with the mandatory upper-class 'received pronunciation'. This was an era when all the vaunting snobbery of the acting profession was vested in theatre. So-called 'legitimate' actors spoke with a plum in their mouths and looked down their noses at anyone reduced to appearing in front of a camera. The flickers, dear boy, were for oiks.

Eddy G. was most certainly not an oik; he was both a gentleman and a great actor who brought every ounce of his very considerable intellect to all of his performances. It was he who patiently taught me the art of acting for the screen.

The technicalities, Eddy believed, needed to be understood, mastered and then sublimated. For instance, in the 1940s, to remain in focus you had to find your key light and 'hit your mark' without being seen to look for either. Today, faster film stock has obviated the need for such precision but back then it was vital.

Many of our most earnest discussions were conducted as Eddy paced the studio floor between one mark and another, over and over again, until the move was so firmly ingrained in muscle memory it became automatic.

'Dickie, above all be real,' he would instruct me. 'Find the truth. Remember, the camera sees what you're thinking. Be your character, know who he is and let his thoughts form the words. And always listen, really listen, to what the other characters are saying. Reaction is very important. It can make or break a performance.' He also famously said: 'The sitting around on the set is soul-destroying. But I always figure that's what they pay me for. The acting I do for free.'

In addition to these one-on-one masterclasses, I was also learning from my other mentor, John Boulting. From him I came to understand that good directors do not shout and stamp around. The crew is an orchestra and the director is their conductor, setting the rhythm, bringing a soloist or a whole section to the fore, each at the appropriate moment, and always remaining firmly in command.

There was another reason I hero-worshipped John. My mama had been a vociferous opponent of Franco at the outset of the Spanish Civil War, marching in Leicester alongside the Communists with their red flags to protest the bombing of Guernica and getting a brick through our front window for her pains. When she and the Governor visited the set at Pinewood, we learned that John had been a volunteer ambulance driver with the International Brigade, narrowly escaping capture.

The third of my role models during this hugely formative period was the brilliant polymath and documentary film-maker, Humphrey Jennings. Crossing the Pinewood car park one day, I heard the sound of film chattering through a Moviola and, having located the source, put my head round an open door in the row of cutting rooms.

Jennings was hunched over his bench, smoking as he spliced two strips of highly inflammable celluloid. He beckoned me inside.

And so began my induction into the twin arts of camerawork and editing. Humphrey was completing probably the most famous of his war documentaries, *Fires Were Started*. He'd developed the idea of telling a story through real people going about their lives during the Blitz and the final result was in large measure to be their creation.

This was revolutionary because British cinema up to that time had mainly aped theatre. Films were all too often like Aldwych farces with a group of actors, known as a 'tight eight', all standing in a row to deliver their lines. No action. Very little editing. Humphrey was the first to show what could be achieved with clever composition, dramatic intercutting and the judicious use of sound effects and music.

Because our filming schedule had to be fitted around the availability of the flyers, it took far longer than anticipated to shoot *Journey Together*. By the end of my secondment, after nine months at Pinewood, I'd grown used to sharing a billet with Jack Watling and George Cole and to the free and easy atmosphere on the set where everyone called each other by their first names and no one ever pulled rank. Awaiting orders to report back to Heaton Park for a flight to Canada for pilot training, I received some pretty lousy news.

The RAF didn't require any more pilots. Unbelievably, they had a glut. So I was to be arbitrarily transferred into the army to serve in the infantry where, it seemed, there was still a shortage of cannon fodder.

I hot-footed it to the office of my Pinewood CO, Wing Commander Baird, known in the film industry as Teddy. He'd been an assistant director before the war and would go on to produce a number of distinguished films including *The Winslow Boy* and *The Browning Version*, both scripted by Terry Rattigan. Teddy said, 'I'm terribly sorry, Dickie, but I can't see any way out.'

'Can't I volunteer to fly with the Film Unit?'

'Not unless you qualify as aircrew and get your brevet. Otherwise, if you come down in enemy territory, you'll be shot as a spy.'

'There must be some way I can get a brevet quickly.'

'Well . . . the air-gunner course is the quickest. Tell you what, I'll look into it and see what I can do.'

So Teddy pulled strings and I was sent on a nine-week course to Bishop's Court on the North–South border in Ireland. My enduring memory is of nipping over at night to buy ham and eggs which weren't rationed in the South and smuggling them back to base. By day I was taught how to clean, mount, load and fire machine guns, mostly Brownings.

My present almost total lack of hearing dates back to my last day on the shooting range. The final test was supervised by a Corporal Wood, nicknamed, of course, Timber. He said airily, 'I don't seem to have any ear protectors with me. Never mind, lad. You'll be deaf for a couple of days but it won't do you any harm.'

So I took and passed my test without them and couldn't hear a thing for several weeks but I didn't care because I was a sergeant with a brevet and I'd never have to fire a bloody Browning again.

Back I went to Pinewood where my friends in the Film Unit – Harry Waxman, Gil Taylor and Skeets Kelly – taught me to use the Eymo, a wind-up camera which used hundred-foot cartridges, each lasting just over a minute. Once I'd mastered that, I became a fully qualified air-gunner cameraman, ready at last, in the words of Winston Churchill, to strike at the evil heart of the Nazi empire.

But by the beginning of 1945, the war in Europe was almost over and I was to fly just a few raids under the command of a Polish skipper who'd escaped to England in order to fight. This wonderful man, who appeared in *Journey Together* as the pilot of an Anson, was Zanni Peremowski. Our plane was a Lancaster in which a camera mount replaced the usual machine gun under the plexiglas dome at the rear. That was my position: arse-end Charlie.

Because it was winter, we'd take off in the dark and, hopefully, return in the dark. I'd get kitted up in long johns, thick sweater, battledress, sheepskin flying jacket, boots and gloves. Then I'd make my way into position, manoeuvring myself over the main spar and along the crawl space to the cramped rear turret, carrying flying rations, the Eymo, my oxygen mask, piss pot and a supply of film cartridges.

We'd roll to the end of the runway where Zanni would put on the brakes and rev up the engines, waiting for the green light to surge forward. As the runway receded beneath us, I'd hear him shout, 'Veels up,' and we were on our way. At a cruising speed of two hundred miles an hour, it took four hours to reach Germany, always in temperatures well below zero.

But it wasn't the cold that bothered me. I spent the whole of every flight fighting airsickness. Whenever I lost the battle, I had an unpleasant choice of either leaving my mask on until I could safely empty it or taking it off and possibly passing out for lack of oxygen.

The targets were towns and factories. During our first pass, I'd film them crouched on my knees in the cramped turret space, then struggle with frozen fingers to reload the Eymo in time for the next run. During the actual raid, Zanni would circle above the bombers until it was time to go down and record the damage. This was more dodgy because, by then, ground anti-aircraft crews had the range and starbursts of shells would be exploding all around us. But mostly the targets were in ruins and there was hardly anyone left to fire at us.

Because I wasn't actually doing the bombing but seeing it through a lens at one remove, I never faced up to what we were doing. I'm ashamed to admit it now, but I didn't look down at the burning buildings and empathise with the dead and dying. I absolutely believed the raids were necessary because what we were opposing was utterly evil. Only years later, when I studied Mahatma Gandhi's writings, did I even consider there might be another way.

Strangely, I wasn't ever conscious of being in danger myself, even when I could see the shells whizzing towards me. I honestly wasn't afraid. The only thing that scared the bejeezus out of me was the airsickness, although I hadn't even felt queasy when I went solo, when I was in control.

After one of our sorties, the wing commander in charge of the bomber squadron didn't come back. I felt like those veterans who are consumed with guilt because they're still alive and kicking and the man who was right next to them is not. For a long time, it just didn't make any sense that I'd made it and a terrific chap like Winco Sutherland hadn't.

DH— On the day following our audience with President Reagan in the Oval Office, Dick and I flew to Atlanta where we were met by the Mayor, Andrew Young, who drove us to the hotel in the delightfully named Peachtree Plaza. There, having ordered coffee and pecan pie, a local speciality, he gave us a potted history of the American civil rights movement. It was an eye-opener.

Andy, as we came to call him, was an ardent follower of Gandhi, as had been his friend and fellow campaigner, Martin Luther King. In the Deep South of the fifties and sixties, they and other black activists had organised a campaign for racial equality on a massive and inspirational scale, employing sit-ins, kneel-ins, boycotts, strikes and marches, all based on the Mahatma's credo of non-violent civil disobedience.

The movement was making tremendous strides when King was shot dead on the balcony of a Memphis hotel, a crime which still remained shrouded in official obfuscation. In the angry aftermath, non-violence had been abandoned for burning, looting and rioting, giving credence to militant Black Power and the aggressive Nation of Islam. At that point, Andy had decided the best way forward lay in mainstream politics.

He'd served three terms as Georgia's first black Congressman before being appointed American Ambassador to the UN, a post he'd been forced to resign, supposedly in disgrace, over an attempt to persuade the PLO to recognise Israel. Within two years, demonstrating their continuing faith in his integrity, Jimmy Carter had awarded him the Presidential Medal of Freedom and the people of Atlanta had elected him Mayor.

Briefing over, Andy took us across the city to the black neighbourhood surrounding Auburn Avenue where we were to have the first of our many meetings with the beautiful and formidable Coretta Scott King.

Here was a widow who'd set out to be a classical singer and instead married a man who was to become both a hate figure and the most charismatic black leader of his generation. While Martin Luther King was raising consciousness around the States, mostly in the South, his young wife had been left alone to face death threats, attacks on their home, the births of four children and an explicit tape recording of her absent husband's dalliance in a bugged hotel room, thoughtfully sent to her by the FBI on the express instructions of J. Edgar Hoover.

Coretta was the most strong-willed, regal and purposeful woman I've ever met. Yet, as she talked about her husband and showed us the gold medal he'd received as the youngest recipient of the Nobel Peace Prize, a softer side was revealed. More than a decade after his death, it was plain she still adored and respected the man, faults and all. Her children were very young when news of King's killing reached her in 1968 but neither their bewilderment nor her own grief had stopped the newly widowed Coretta travelling to Memphis, even before he was buried, to stride out in his place at the head of a pre-planned protest march.

This indomitable crusader went on to tell us how she'd spent the intervening years. Her first priority had been to secure the children's future. Next came a determination to continue her husband's work and build him a memorial. Lastly and most surprisingly, she'd initiated a campaign to free the man serving a ninety-nine-year prison sentence for her husband's murder in an attempt to uncover the truth.

Coretta was convinced James Earl Ray had been used as a fall guy by the FBI. And the way she told it, this sounded eminently plausible. The anomalies surrounding the shooting and the swift disappearance of evidence that pointed in a different direction were suspicious to say the least.

By the time we met, Coretta had already established the King Center, just a few blocks from the Ebenezer Baptist Church where Martin Jr and his father, the now ancient Daddy King, had both preached. But the new complex, dedicated to peace studies and designed eventually to encircle her husband's tomb, remained unfinished due to lack of funds. So, when Columbia Pictures offered the proceeds of the Atlanta premiere of *Gandhi*, Coretta had been happy to accept.

The premiere, several months hence, was to take place on her husband's birthday, a date his widow was determined to commemorate by establishing a national holiday in his name. To her opponents, this was a dream too far. Of the nine existing US federal holidays, only Columbus Day bore the name of a person and even the date honouring George Washington was known simply as President's Day.

Nevertheless, Coretta eventually prevailed. Despite loud senatorial protests, Martin Luther King Day was eventually signed into law by a reluctant Ronald Reagan. It is now celebrated annually on the third Monday in January.

Arriving again at the King Center on the morning of 17 January 1983, we found Coretta surveying her husband's tomb. During the night, it had been covered in foul graffiti, including, in blood red, the chilling initials KKK. Dick, Sheila and I were horrified. But Coretta, the battle-hardened matriarch, was strangely jubilant. 'Honey,' she said to me, 'if this is the worst the Klan can do, we've got them on the run.'

Soon afterwards, we joined a huge peace march through the streets of Atlanta. My abiding image is of Sir Richard and Lady Attenborough, arm in arm with Coretta and Andy – two pale faces in a sea of black – belting out the battle hymn of the civil rights movement: 'We shall overcome.'

That evening, at a reception after the premiere, an elderly white matron with a blue rinse and glittery spectacle frames provided Dick with a comedic line of self-deprecation he was to use over and over again. Patting him on the arm, she gushed; 'When I saw the way you handled those gorillas, I just knew Mr Gandhi was in safe hands.'

RA— No one with twenty-twenty vision could possibly mistake me for my famous brother – he's the tall, thin, clever one with hair.

The shots of Dave bonding with those over-friendly Rwandan gorillas in his *Life on Earth* trilogy made a huge impact on television viewers throughout the world – as have his hundreds of other close encounters with all kinds of wildlife. My own particular favourite is the one where he's in a cave, practically up to his knees in bat shit, while talking to camera as if attending a vicar's tea party. I only wish our pa had been alive to see it; he'd have laughed himself silly.

On occasion, the Governor could be very stern. I had to win a scholar-ship to RADA if I wanted to become an actor and Dave, two years my junior, had to win an open scholarship to Cambridge before he could embark on his natural science tripos.

That sounds, I know, very authoritarian. But the Governor's Achilles heel, as we boys quickly discovered, was his crude sense of humour. This was most manifest at mealtimes when he and our mother insisted that manners were strictly enforced. Any lapse and we'd be ordered to leave the room.

I can see Dave now, aged about nine, sternly dismissed but having the last word in the doorway. 'That wasn't rude,' he's insisting. Then he puffs out his cheeks and blows the most enormous raspberry. 'That's rude!' And the Governor sits at the head of the table, trying desperately to keep a straight face.

Another snapshot comes to mind: I'm chasing David across the lawn in full view of the Governor's study. He slides open the window and shouts that I'm going to get a clout for bullying my brother again but, as he starts to clamber over the sill, the casement comes crashing down on his bald pate and, once again, he can't stop laughing.

People have speculated that Dave and I are locked in some kind of deadly sibling rivalry. Nothing could be further from the truth; I burst with pride over everything he has achieved. The rivalry thing probably stems from an early pact to keep our working lives completely separate and never be interviewed together. In fact, I and both my brothers have followed completely different paths for as long as I can remember. Almost as soon as they could talk, Dave was obsessed with fish, insects and fossils and Johnny was fascinated by anything mechanical, going on, despite his Cambridge degree in French and Italian, to become managing director of the Rolls Royce division of Mann Egerton in Mayfair.

The Governor, being a pedagogue, fostered all these passions by undertaking his own research so that he could converse knowledgably with each of us on our pet subjects. When I returned home after my first term at RADA, I noticed a huge pile of books by his desk, covering the whole history of drama, which he'd assembled – and read – in case I had a question to ask. But of the three of us it was Dave, who he always called Davyth, who inherited our father's love of scholarship.

I took after Mama – the most tactile, energetic and outspoken woman I've ever encountered. I never saw her idle. She would darn socks while she listened to the wireless. She was both a linguist and an accomplished pianist, and if she saw an injustice, she would not only speak out against it but fight to put it right.

As a young suffragette, she'd helped to secure votes for women and gone on to become one of the early female members of the Labour Party. Later, she served as a local JP. As a mother, she was always helping other mothers, poorer than herself. And, as a theatre lover, it was she who introduced me to the stage through the Leicester Drama Society, of which she was chairman.

Despite the different paths our lives have taken, Dave and I are constantly in touch. We speak on the phone at least once a week and, even as octogenarians, still tease each other mercilessly. We both live in Richmond, about a mile apart. My house on the green is Queen Anne, his on the hill is Victorian Gothic. He collects African sculpture; I collect modern, mostly British, paintings and Picasso ceramics. And we're both potty about classical music; the difference being that Dave brings to it the greater academic knowledge.

Only once in my life do I recall my unflappable brother being in a state of near panic. During the early 1970s, I arrived home around midnight to find a message saying it was vital I contact him immediately. Dave picked up the phone on the very first ring. 'Thank God,' said the agnostic. 'Don't go to bed. I'm coming down to see you.'

Never having taken a driving test, Dave had to walk down the hill. My imagination ran wild as I waited for him and I'd conjured up all kinds of horrific possibilities by the time he rang the bell. 'Dick,' he said on the doorstep, 'the most ghastly thing happened today and I don't know what to do.'

By then, Dave had steadily worked his way up the television ladder. He'd started as a producer and gone on to become the presenter of *Zoo Quest* which was followed by *Quest in Paradise* which had taken him to some far-flung places. In 1957, obviously having the time of his life, he'd written from 'Somewhere Blank on the Map, in Unknown New Guinea, Roundabout July/August . . .

Dear Dick,

It occurs to me that sometime in the not too distant future it is your birthday.

As I have not been home for several years now during the month of August, I have not been able to give you a little *cadeau* as I would have wished. This year once again my thoughts are with you but the sum I had put aside to buy you a tiny something will now be spent (after being suitably changed into gold-lip pearl and beads) on a reward to the warrior who, bedecked in bird-of-paradise plumes, is waiting with a cleft stick to carry this note to the nearest patrol post. It's going to take him two days, so you see this is really a rather expensive birthday present.

We are having a particularly arduous time – no food, no shelter and always the fear that the locals ahead will be hostile. To find out what awaits us over the mountain ridge ahead, tune into BBC TV in December. These programmes will make *Ben-Hur* and *Quo Vadis* look like drawing-room comedies. We have (literally) a cast of thousands who swarm into our camp brandishing axes, all of them naked and lots of them ladies!

Unfortunately, however, we are not finding any of the things we have come for. A country more lacking in bird and mammalian life, I have not yet come across. This means we are very short of film subjects but also, and a lot more seriously, short of *food*. Tonight we have had a windfall – we discovered in the bush an egg of the cassowary which will make an omelette for six.

Many happy returns again to you, dear Dick. Give my fondest love to my sweet sister-in-law, my nephew and niece.

Your affec. bro. David.

A few years later, having been sidelined into television management, Dave had become Controller of the new BBC2. There, instead of making his own documentaries it had been his job to commission a whole range of groundbreaking programmes and oversee the changeover from black and white to colour throughout the UK. Promotion had followed and, still unhappily deskbound, he'd become Director of Programmes for BBC1 and BBC2.

Now he was telling me that the chairman, Charles Hill, had that afternoon asked him to become Director General of the entire Corporation. And he didn't know what to do.

I understood his dilemma. This was the most tremendous honour and one that would undoubtedly make our father, then approaching the end of his long life, very proud indeed, since the post was the most influential and prestigious in broadcasting. However, I knew without a shadow of a doubt it would be disastrous for Dave.

'I don't want to do that, do I, Dick?'

'You? Sit on your arse, chairing meetings and making endless policy decisions until you collect a gold watch and a pension? Of course you don't.'

His relief was instant and palpable. 'You're absolutely right. I'll say no first thing in the morning.'

And so began the fruitful, satisfying and wildly successful *Life* series, which has taken Dave, the brilliant presenter, reluctant celebrity and best-selling author, to every corner of the globe. Like me, he relishes his work and has no intention of ever retiring despite the death of his beloved wife, Jane, in 1997 and the need for new knees – which he obstinately ignores.

I've always been fascinated by politics, a career I might have chosen had things turned out differently. Dave, on the other hand, has, until recently, held them in disdain.

For a long time he believed that climate change was cyclical; that it had happened before and was bound to happen again. But, being a voracious reader of scientific texts, he is now convinced that global warming is indeed man-made and, for the first time ever, has entered the political fray, publicly accusing the dreadful George W. Bush of being the worst 'environmental villain' of our era.

In 1932, when Dave and I were aged seven and nine and Johnny was a toddler, the Governor was appointed Principal of Leicester's University College and we moved into a large Victorian house on campus which became the family home. It was, I suppose, a typical professional middle-class household. Although our parents were far from affluent, they employed three live-in staff: a maid, a cook and Mona Pickles, our nanny. Nan, as we called her, was with us for most of her working life. Somewhat butch and far from the cuddly, comforting archetype, she enjoyed nothing more than playing cricket and football.

The Governor also adored soccer and had played for the Corinthians, England's foremost amateur team, only retiring when a badly set broken leg left him with a permanent limp. It was this injury which had kept him out of the First World War and, he told us, had resulted in several white feathers, symbols of cowardice, arriving anonymously in the post.

Our cook produced three meals a day, following menus drawn up by our mama at the start of every week. The maid served at table, answered the front door, accepted visiting cards and showed in the visitors on afternoons when the principal's wife was 'at home' to college staff and their wives. Sometimes, with my mother's connivance, I enlivened these somewhat staid occasions by passing round the cucumber sandwiches wearing the maid's cap and uniform.

Only once did I twist Dave's arm sufficiently to get him into drag.

At the age of twelve, I'd decided to put on a variety show which would have as its centrepiece a comedic skit about two female cleaners, entitled *Lydies Wot Come to Oblige*.

To mount the show, I needed sufficient cash to rent St Barnabas Church Hall. In entrepreneurial mode, I went to Leicester Market and haggled over a job lot of small notebooks. Then, through the simple expedient of attaching pencils to them with ribbon, I resold these indispensable items to every adult I knew, making a quick 100 per cent profit.

Having secured the hall with a payment of ten shillings, I became the director in search of a cast. Boys in my Scout troupe proved very accommodating and, within a short space of time, I'd assembled a number of acts including a singer, a juggler and a conjuror so inept he might have inspired Tommy Cooper.

One problem remained. Naturally, I was to star as one of the 'lydies' but had yet to secure the other. And for once Dave was proving immune to both my bullying and my blandishments. He said he'd rather die than put on a dress.

I briefly considered repeating an earlier strategy. The college had once been the site of a lunatic asylum and, when Dave was younger, I'd locked him into an abandoned padded cell in the cellar of our house. But now, not wanting another of Mary's spankings, I resorted instead to low cunning and made Dave an offer he simply couldn't refuse, telling him every penny of the show's profits would go straight to the RSPCA. He gave in, of course, and I rehearsed him mercilessly over the weeks which followed.

And so it was as the fully-fledged impresario that I was finally able to stand in front of the church-hall curtains, welcoming my paying audience with a suitably gracious and overlong speech. My wary parents sat in the front row, flanking the Lady Mayoress, no less, another RSPCA supporter. Dave, meanwhile, was scowling behind the curtains, clutching his mop. And very pretty he looked.

Our local paper, the *Mercury*, gave him a glowing review:

Variety was promised and rich variety there was. Some of the richest was provided by Richard Attenborough's ten-year-old brother, David, who astounded his parents as a female impersonator. What with rehearsals and his part to learn, David has had hardly a minute to breathe. In fact, he confided to a friend, he was looking forward to a real rest during the last week of the holidays.

Revenge came some years later. When my first film, *In Which We Serve*, finally came to Leicester, my brother was buttonholed by a rookie reporter who wanted to know if we were related.

Dave replied with disdain: 'Only distantly.'

DH— Dick's one of those people who can't sit still in a room with a crooked picture on the wall. Every envelope has to be neatly slit with a paperknife. His breast-pocket handkerchief is always precisely arranged with the 'studied carelessness' prescribed by Noël Coward more than sixty years ago. And his weekly pocket money, used mostly for tips, must consist of crisp, preferably new, five-pound notes folded exactly in half. I could go on and on . . .

This compulsive attention to detail spills over into premieres; it's a way of dealing with first-night nerves. He masterminds the invitations and the seating plan, brochure, presentations, bouquets, wording on the canopy . . . anything and everything. But above all, like most directors, he obsesses about picture and sound.

This was how the two of us came to be carting two heavy aluminium trunks containing a brand-new married print of *Gandhi* across Delhi on a stifling afternoon in November 1982. Our destination was the cinema where the world premiere was to take place the following evening. With the first two reels mounted on projectors and the rehearsal underway, Dick and I moved between different areas of the auditorium, checking the sound. It was not good.

Worse still, when the first reel came to an end, the whole place was plunged into darkness. Dick, of course, was beside himself. Soaked in sweat but doing our best to remain polite, we refused to leave until both picture and sound were just about good enough to receive his grudging approval. Dawn had broken when we arrived back at our hotel.

The premiere passed in a blur of exhaustion, spiked by the fear that the projectionist might again miss the cues and bungle the changeovers. But reel followed reel without any discernible hiatus and, if the track lacked most if not all the subtleties we'd spent weeks achieving in the dubbing theatre, it was at least audible.

Despite fears that objectors might infiltrate the audience, the film was applauded long and loudly enough for Dick and Sheila to leave with their heads held high. There was no time to gauge the reaction in greater depth – we had to go straight to the airport for a night flight to London.

Attending six premieres on three continents within seven consecutive evenings could only be achieved by flying westwards. It was the time gained through this strategy which had made it possible for Dick to attend frequent meetings in the States while maintaining an almost superhuman workload at home, giving rise to my mocking nickname, Chairman of London.

His delight in exploiting the time difference was never more apparent than on the first of our many business trips on Concorde. The plane had left for New York at ten in the morning. I was waiting at Heathrow, having long checked in, when Dick strolled onto the concourse just as the desk was closing, having made umpteen car phone calls en route.

We'd landed at JFK after a flight lasting just three hours and twenty minutes and, as he walked towards the waiting limo, the workaholic had checked the local time. Still only nine thirty. Great. We'd missed the Manhattan rush hour and could still fit in a whole day of back-to-back meetings.

Fourteen and a half hours later and a lifetime since my alarm had gone off in London, we were still working. Coming up to midnight in New York, we were standing in the lobby of a screening room on Broadway, waiting to buttonhole the exiting audience. Utterly drained, I leaned for a brief moment against the wall.

'Anything the matter?'

'It's been rather a long day.'

Immediately he was fierce. 'Never admit you're tired, darling. Ever.'

As he admonished me, the *Gandhi* screening came to an end. The first members of the audience emerged into the lobby where Dick, fresh as a daisy, talked to every one of them. We stayed for over an hour and then went out for a late supper.

The following lunchtime, we again boarded Concorde. Flying eastwards, we lost the five hours we'd gained the previous day. But this didn't bother Dick because it was Saturday; no meetings for him to chair and, being summer, no match at Stamford Bridge.

Conversely, in November 1982, again landing at Heathrow after the world premiere in Delhi, we'd gained five hours which gave us a whole day to prepare for the royal premiere at the Odeon Leicester Square. Here, on home ground, checking the theatre hardly seemed necessary but Dick, of course, insisted. Just as well: the new Dolby sound system had been wrongly installed.

It was put right by the following evening when a nervous Sir Richard waited on the red carpet to greet the guests of honour. The royal car arrived on the dot, as always. From it emerged Prince Charles accompanied by the only member of the royal family as yet unknown to Dick. This was the beautiful, diffident Princess of Wales, whom he would come to know very well indeed.

In London, there was no doubt about the film's reception. As the lights went up at the end of the performance, its originator received tumultuous cheers and a standing ovation.

Flying Concorde to Washington the following morning, we read a stack of cuttings which had been couriered from Delhi. The Indian reviews were astonishing. The very journalists who'd been most aggressive while we were shooting were now the most generous in their apologies and the most lavish with their praise.

They took it all back: the concerns about portraying the living Mahatma on the screen; the accusations about extolling Empire at the expense of India; the anger over government investment. The film was pronounced a masterpiece and Ben Kingsley's performance unbelievably true to life. Three months later, Dick would be awarded one of India's highest honours, the Padma Bhushan, for services to the nation.

The Washington premiere at the Downtown, a strange cinema with an enormous wrap-around screen, was attended by a whole raft of politicians and, despite the absence of Reagan, was deemed a great success although, in our estimation, the reception afterwards was way over the top.

We'd tried to persuade Columbia it would be inappropriate to serve anything but the simplest of refreshments. This was not only out of respect for Gandhi's devotion to frugality, but because Dick had promised the profits from every premiere to UNICEF. His target, eventually achieved, was $1 million.

We were, therefore, more than a little dismayed to be taken to an imposing post-premiere venue dominated by a vast, curving staircase with violinists sawing away on either side of every step, right to the very top. Below were huge displays of oysters, stacked on mountains of ice, and an army of waiters dispensing gallons of vintage champagne. I was so jet-lagged that much of it passed in a blur. So too did the following night's event in Toronto, the next in New York and the last of the six back-to-back premieres in Los Angeles.

In America the success of a film can be foretold by the first weekend's box-office take. But, due to the ballsy release pattern chosen by Columbia, this was not so with *Gandhi*.

They'd elected to platform, opening the film in just a few selected theatres in major cities, waiting for the Oscar nominations to be announced before they went wider and delaying again until the actual ceremony before going wider still. This strategy was not only very risky but hugely expensive. With each new wave of openings they had to revamp, relaunch and increase their ad campaign, adding incrementally to the number of prints in circulation until the film was on two thousand screens throughout the whole of North America.

During the first three months of 1983, after a welcome Christmas break with our families, Dick, Sheila and I attended openings in Hartford, Philadelphia, Atlanta, Montreal, Calgary, Vancouver and San Francisco. Then, accompanied by Ben Kingsley, his wife, baby son and mother-in-law, we travelled to Manila, Tokyo and Hamburg. After two days in London, where Dick of course chaired meetings and also delivered the *Guardian* Lecture, he and I visited Stockholm, Madrid, Paris and Rome, each for a single day, before taking off again with Sheila and the Kingsleys for Sydney and Melbourne with a stopover on the return journey for Dick and Ben to pick up Golden Globe Awards in Los Angeles. Next, it was Paris and Leeds, a flying visit to India for Dick to receive his Padma Bhushan and finally back again to Los Angeles for the Academy Awards ceremony.

Three evenings later, exhausted but triumphant, Dick, Sheila and I stumbled onto a British Airways 747 bound for London. The film's unprecedented success had been headline news in Britain and we'd been told to expect a huge press conference on our arrival at Heathrow.

In order to give the photographers the shot they were bound to want,

Dick was carrying his two Oscars wrapped in newspaper as hand baggage. Once we were airborne, the captain broadcast his congratulations over the intercom and the other passengers responded with cheers and applause.

On landing, Dick was whisked into a conference room jam-packed with journalists, TV crews and photographers. Eerily, there were no cheers or applause here; the press pack greeted him with all the warmth of a lynch mob. Baffled, Dick faced them across a table crowded with microphones, temporarily blinded by a barrage of flash photography. Then came the inquisition.

Was it true he'd agreed to attend a charity premiere of *Gandhi* in Johannesburg?

Yes, next week.

Was he aware it was a whites-only event?

Never normally lost for words, Dick was shocked into silence. Then, as the blood rushed to his face, I knew he was angry.

He said he would never attend any segregated screening. He was going home to discover what had happened and would issue a statement as soon as possible.

After many heated phone calls between Beaver Lodge and our South African distributor, he spoke at the London Press Club the following day.

There, he announced that the distributor had apologised for failing to apply for the mandatory government 'exemption' to hold a multi-racial premiere. He would, therefore, not be going to Johannesburg and wanted to make it clear that, in his opinion, the requirement for such an exemption was a damning indictment of the whole disgusting apartheid system.

This was Dick's first run-in with the administration of Pieter Willem Botha. It would not be his last.

5

SHE'S THE ONE

RA— THERE WERE NO teenagers during the 1930s. As soon as your voice broke, you went straight from short trousers and boyhood to long trousers and manhood. My voice broke in a railway carriage somewhere between Leicester and Birmingham when I was twelve.

Only a month earlier, I'd been the chubby boy soprano singing 'Silver'd is the Raven Hair' in a school production of Gilbert and Sullivan's *Patience*. Spotted by someone connected with the BBC, I was bowled over when asked to appear in a radio drama about the famous band leader, Billy Merrin, playing him as a child and trilling his favourite song.

This was my first professional engagement and it was, of course, hugely important. In the weeks leading up to the live broadcast, I made sure I was word-perfect and practised the song over and over again. Came the great day, my mother put me on a train and off I steamed to BBC Birmingham, just over an hour away.

Finding myself alone in the carriage, I decided to have one final rehearsal. I opened my mouth to sing, 'I'm forever blowing bubbles . . .' and discovered, to my absolute horror, that I'd become a baritone.

On arrival, blushing like mad, I broke the news to the producer and threw him into a panic because there was only one hour to airtime. Although I was still allowed to play the lines, an adorable lady, just four feet ten inches tall, was hurriedly summoned to do the singing.

This was Marjorie Westbury, a founder member of the BBC Repertory Company, who would later find fame as the voice of Paul Temple's wife, Steve.

Even as a small child, I was crazy about women. It started, of course, with my mother and continued at my boys-only junior school where I worshipped my form teacher, Miss Harry. Then, as I approached my fourteenth birthday, hormones raging, I fell totally under the spell of a Spanish beauty called Rosa.

I can still see my first love now, waiting for me in the sunshine at Evington Hall. She can't have been more than fifteen; a small, perfectly proportioned, olive-skinned girl who always wore a rose tucked into her pitch-black hair. And for a few short months, she was my one and only for evermore. Had she but asked, I would have gladly laid down my life for her.

Nearly four thousand children, aged five to fifteen, had been evacuated to Britain from the Basque region of Spain in the summer of 1937 after Hitler's Luftwaffe had rehearsed for the Blitz by bombing the small republican town of Guernica. This devastating raid was undertaken to curry favour with Franco during the Spanish Civil War. The refugee children had all sailed on a single ship, the SS *Habana*, from Bilbao to Southampton, accompanied by adult carers, teachers and priests.

Rosa was one of fifty who came to Leicester. My mother was secretary of the committee formed to look after them and, of course, much, much more. It was she who persuaded local families to sponsor the children by donating ten shillings a week, she who rented the abandoned mansion which was to become their home, she who rolled up her sleeves and scrubbed the floors.

Like Irene and Helga two years later, the youngest of the Basque refugees were traumatised and very homesick. Rosa helped with the little ones and took it all in her stride. At every opportunity, I would cycle up to the Hall to spend hours holding her hand and gazing into those dark brown eyes. As time went by, I came to know all the children and the two sisters in their twenties who looked after them, Marguerita and Mercedes.

We stayed in touch after they went home, but it was not until the 1960s, when I was invited to receive a best actor award at the San

Sebastian Film Festival, that I really understood their plight. After a quarter of a century, the ageing dictator, Generalissimo Franco, was still ruling Spain with a Fascist rod of iron.

My friends from Evington, having read in the local press that I was coming, wrote to say they'd like to meet me. Because state informers were everywhere and it was dangerous for them all to be seen together, they'd come up with a plan.

The festival organisers had booked me into a hotel overlooking the sea in Bilbao. My Basque friends would come up to my room one at a time and, as each left, I was to stand by the window in clear view of the next, waiting at the bus shelter below. This was the signal it was safe for them to enter.

I saw all of them – except Rosa. There was no quarrel, no dramatic bust-up. After Britain shamefully recognised Franco's regime in 1938, she had returned to her parents. And first love – always remembered, never consummated – had simply withered away like the flowers she wore in her hair.

Four years later, I met my future wife.

DH— After *Gandhi* had been well and truly launched, Columbia offered me a permanent job in California. For a while I was tempted but my parents were now in their seventies, I was their only child and Kay was happily settled in our local primary school. Above all, I wanted to continue working with Dick.

He, however, had no new film on the horizon. I was at home, enjoying my first break in three years, when I was asked to publicise *A Passage to India.*

The offer came from two people I'd never met: Dick's friend, Lord Brabourne – known in the industry as John – and his producing partner, Richard Goodwin. They interviewed me at the warehouse in Rotherhithe which Richard and his director wife had turned into a mini film studios. There, the networking behind their approach became clear. *A Passage to India* was to be distributed by Columbia and Richard Goodwin had already recruited as crew some of my Indian friends from *Gandhi.*

Initially, I turned the assignment down. The film was to be shot on location in Bangalore, Ooty and Kashmir with a schedule which would keep me abroad for at least twelve weeks. There was no way I could leave Kay for that length of time. But John and Richard proved very accommodating and it was agreed that I could come and go, alternating two weeks in India with two at home. They had one condition to impose in return: I must never so much as mention Dickie Attenborough's name to their legendary director, David Lean.

Dick and David went back a long way. In 1942, Lean, the conflicted Quaker, had been the unheralded technical wizard behind the wartime propaganda film, *In Which We Serve*, sharing his first directorial credit with the flamboyant Noël Coward. Dick, only eighteen at the time and still a student at RADA, had been the bright-eyed newcomer, eagerly making his debut in a small but telling part which was to bring him great acclaim.

As I was to witness at first hand, David Lean held all actors in contempt, particularly those who were young and, in his eyes, too full of themselves. The only exception was Marlon Brando, whom he greatly admired and had asked to appear in several of his films, without success. And, during the 1950s, another of David's well-known but unrealised ambitions had been to make a film about Mahatma Gandhi.

When he first become involved with Moti Kothari, Dick had honourably gone to see Lean in Madrid in order to make sure he had completely abandoned the project. He was told categorically: 'I am never going to make a film about Gandhi. If you want to take it on, you do so with my blessing.' Reassured, Dick had immediately commissioned his first screenwriter, Gerry Hanley.

However, when Hanley's script failed to attract the necessary funding and Dick was away acting in Hollywood, earning money to keep the project afloat, he was dealt a devastating blow by Moti Kothari. Losing patience with their lack of progress and perhaps sensing that time was running out, his Indian partner approached another writer. This was the eminent Robert Bolt, who immediately accepted the assignment but insisted the film had to be directed by David Lean. Kothari agreed and, with Lean suddenly professing a renewed enthusiasm for the project, a heartbroken Dick felt obliged to withdraw from it completely.

Twelve months passed and, having nothing to show for them, Bolt and Lean soothed the anxious Kothari by explaining they had one 'little picture' to complete before they could turn their full attention to *Gandhi*.

The lead having again been turned down by Brando, this was *Ryan's Daughter*, a troubled epic so long in the making that Moti Kothari succumbed to his final heart attack before it was released.

Dick, meanwhile, had taken a giant step forward, making his hugely successful directorial debut with *Oh! What a Lovely War*.

After he again took command of *Gandhi*, the fickle Bolt and Lean had embarked on their ill-fated *HMS Bounty* project which was destined never to reach fruition.

Only now, in November 1983, after a painful fourteen-year hiatus, was the 75-year-old Lean about to direct his next and last film. His age, together with his famous propensity for going wildly over budget, had made it extremely difficult for the producers, Brabourne and Goodwin, to finance *A Passage to India*. Having succeeded, they were understandably anxious that no mention of Dickie Attenborough or the huge success of his Oscar-laden *Gandhi* should blow the irascible maestro off course.

Initially, having taken a vow of silence, I got on very well with David. Unlike Dick, who encourages the whole unit to attend rushes, he invited only a favoured few. I was flattered to be one of the few and even more flattered when he sought my opinion afterwards.

Everyone on the *Passage to India* crew was thrilled to be working with this legendary auteur. We were all experienced technicians who came to the picture wanting to give of our best and learn. But, in sharp contrast to Dick's all-embracing inclusiveness, the man bringing Forster's classic to the screen proved to be utterly devoid of empathy. He simply wouldn't or couldn't connect.

Had he been able to play all the parts, design and dress the sets, record the sound, operate the camera and make every costume himself, Lean might have been a happier man. Instead, he became so witheringly critical that, by the end of shooting, virtually every head of department had tendered their resignation. I was one of them; *A Passage to India* was the unhappiest experience of my entire film career.

John Brabourne, who'd been seriously injured in the IRA attack which killed his father-in-law, Earl Mountbatten, remained in London. The man at the centre, valiantly trying to hold the picture together and keep Lean in check, was the amiable Richard Goodwin, an old India hand. It was Richard who cajoled and badgered us into rescinding our resignations and, when the demoralised camera crew sent Lean to Coventry, who ordered them at least to wish him good morning.

David had brought with him onto the picture a handful of tried and tested colleagues: his faithful script supervisor, Maggie Unsworth, quadruple Oscar-winning production designer, John Box; phlegmatic sound recordist, John Mitchell; and his particular favourite and fixer par excellence, Eddie Fowlie.

The stories about David and Eddie, his property master, were legion. Most centred around Eddie's willingness to give David whatever he wanted, regardless of inconvenience or cost. I was told, for instance, of one occasion when Lean had decided a magnificent centuries-old tree was wrecking the composition of an otherwise perfect landscape. When the landowner refused to fell it, David had a quiet word with Eddie.

And when he arrived to shoot next morning, lo and behold, no tree. During the night, some vandal had conveniently chopped it down and removed every vestige of log and leaf.

For the first ten days in Bangalore, A Passage to India went incredibly well. Although he gave them little or no direction, Lean seemed content with the young lead players, Nigel Havers and Judy Davis. He also appeared to be establishing some kind of rapport with the crew. Then, one evening after rushes, he told me he loathed the performances and intended to go back to the beginning and reshoot everything. Richard Goodwin was in despair; this was exactly the kind of behaviour the financiers had dreaded. But, as David had correctly calculated, they were too far in to withdraw and he got his way.

Not long afterwards, Goodwin was again in despair. The unit had been due to start work on a new set, Fielding's house, which had been constructed in the grounds of our hotel. But David, having taken one look soon after dawn, had sent everyone packing, maintaining the set was appallingly dressed and the whole damn thing had to be redone before he would shoot a single frame.

I went to see for myself and found the director alone, pacing around, deep in thought. Not wanting to interrupt, I stood on the sidelines. After a while, he beckoned me over and confided the real problem. On arrival that morning, he'd realised he had no idea how to shoot the scene and needed time to work it out.

To be fair, this was the only time I saw David Lean unsure of himself.

Filming *Gandhi*, 1981: One of many crowd scenes

Filming *Gandhi*, 1981: Shooting from the roof of a moving train surrounded by cast and crew

Filming *Gandhi*, 1981: 'Suddenly the ominous rumbling in my bowels disappeared. I stood up and did a little dance.'

1982: In the Oval Office with (*Left to right*) President Reagan, Ambassador Terra and Di.

1982: With Martin Luther King's widow, Coretta Scott King.

April 1983: Arriving at the Oscars with Sheila

April 1983: The Oscar-winning *Gandhi* team: (*Left to right*) Bob Laing and Stuart Craig (Art Direction), Jack Briley (Original Screenplay), RA (Direction and Film), Billy Williams (Cinematography), Ben Kingsley (Best Actor), John Bloom (Editing), Bhanu Attaiya (Costume Design)

1983: With Jake Eberts who stuck his neck out to save *Gandhi* from extinction.

1991: With Di and my stalwart Hollywood agent, Martin Baum

1983: With Hollywood executive Frank Price, one of the major figures in my professional life

Filming *A Chorus Line*, 1984: Onstage at the Mark Hellinger Theatre

Filming *A Chorus Line*, 1984: With Michael Douglas

Filming *A Chorus Line*, 1984: Shooting in the rain with Terrence Mann and cinematographer, Ronnie Taylor

On every other occasion, his 'director's vision' was autocratic and instantaneous, if sometimes surprising. On *Gandhi*, Dick had strived endlessly for authenticity. On *A Passage to India*, David habitually sacrificed authenticity on the altar of dramatic effect. He had the art department create a bazaar that locals considered a pastiche. He turned down actual period costumes in favour of new ones more pleasing to his eye. And he jumbled together contradictory castes and customs to create a mythical, mystical country which, in his view, was more real than the real thing.

With us to gain publicity in glossy magazines was a 'special photographer' brought out from London at great expense – Tony Armstrong-Jones. He came with his daughter, Sarah, a young male assistant and a great deal of expensive equipment. Tony worked long and hard in the heat, mucked in with the film crew and did an excellent job. However, as the former husband of Princess Margaret, this somewhat caustic snapper naturally aroused a great deal of curiosity. Perhaps in the hope he'd let slip some juicy gossip, the camera crew would invite him for a drink with them in the evenings.

David Lean did not socialise with the crew. He spent his evenings savouring imported Scotch on his balcony with Maggie Unsworth, Dame Peggy Ashcroft and his fifth bride, a cool blonde by the name of Sandra Hotz.

In the marriage stakes, David had much in common with Henry VIII. Only one of his official unions lasted more than a decade and the ink on his divorce from Sandy Hotz was long dry before *A Passage to India* was completed. He went on to marry for the sixth time – another Sandra who survived.

In a confiding moment, David told me how he'd split up with actress Ann Todd, the third Mrs Lean. 'I was looking in the mirror one morning, shaving, and could see her in reflection, blathering on about something utterly trivial. I suddenly thought, I don't like you. And I never spoke to her again.'

I've no idea how David found out I'd worked on *Gandhi*. As I'd promised John and Richard, I never breathed a word. But halfway through shooting, when I reappeared on location after one of my agreed absences in England, he looked straight through me and from that moment on as far as he was concerned, I simply didn't exist.

Towards the end of the schedule, the unit flew to Kashmir. The landing was the hairiest ever, worse even than Hong Kong where long-haul jets used to skim the rooftop washing lines. Srinagar airport was on a mountain with the top chopped off. Any plane overshooting the ridiculously short runway was destined to drop into the valley, thousands of feet below.

Kashmir proved both sublime and scary. The lakes full of lotus, the aromatic cedarwood houseboats, the pedlars in punts selling sapphires and carpets were all sublime. The groups of men in Srinagar who surrounded any woman not cloaked in the all-enveloping burka, poking, prodding and jeering, were very scary indeed.

It was there, at the Grand Palace Hotel, that I at last managed to collar Alec Guinness. For weeks, he'd been promising me material for my press kit and, on the morning of his departure, had agreed to meet me over coffee.

Guinness and Lean had a supposed friendship and certainly a professional relationship which extended over forty years and five previous films. However, Guinness's supporting role in A Passage to India was never going to match up to his General in Zhivago, his Prince in Lawrence, his Colonel in Kwai or his incomparable Fagin in Oliver Twist.

Professor Godbole, lecturer and mystic, was an intriguing Forster cameo which Lean originally intended to beef up by having Guinness perform an invented Hindu dance in a shallow pool attached to Fielding's house, the set which had stumped him in Bangalore.

Guinness had arrived in India fully prepared, having spent weeks, as great actors do, taking lessons and rehearsing his dance. No one ever saw it performed. Lean had changed his mind and, without warning or consulting the star, arbitrarily deleted the scene from the script.

I thought, as I waited and waited in the lobby of the hotel, that the cracks had been papered over between them. But something must have happened the previous evening. The mild-mannered Guinness eventually came down the main staircase with a face like thunder. He swept straight past me, out of the doors and into his waiting car. I followed, hoping to rearrange our meeting in London.

As I approached the car, Sir Alec wound down the rear window. 'I do not wish to talk about this film and I certainly don't want to talk about David Lean ever again. Any relationship we had is over.'

The only player who apparently maintained good relations with the director was the sagacious Dame Peggy. But even that turned sour. On the very last day of the schedule, she was filming on a small set at Shepperton Studios. I'd invited her to lunch and, as we sat down in the commissary, Peggy asked for a large gin and tonic. Knowing David disapproved of alcohol during working hours, I warned her he'd booked an adjacent table. The deceptively sweet theatrical dame looked me straight in the eye and delivered her verdict: 'Frankly, my dear, I don't give a damn.'

RA— Vivien Leigh was one of the most beautiful women I've ever encountered but it wasn't Scarlett O'Hara who captured my heart in *Gone with the Wind*. Just short of my seventeenth birthday, in the run-up to the dreaded matric, I'd turned truant and was bunking off Wyggeston Boys' School to earn cash delivering fruit and veg for the local greengrocer. This I spent on covert visits to one of the city's three cinemas during the afternoons. One star in particular made an enormous impression: I fell hook, line and sinker for Leslie Howard's screen wife, the lovely but utterly unattainable Olivia de Havilland.

That was the autumn my father put his foot down: either I won the only drama scholarship in the country which included tuition fees and living expenses or I buckled down to get my matriculation. It was entirely up to me.

The Governor had sent off to the Royal Academy of Dramatic Art for the scholarship application form and given it to me to complete. Immediately, I discovered a major stumbling block: candidates under eighteen were ineligible. But it was now or never; I couldn't wait for another birthday. So, saying nothing to my parents, I falsified my age, signed the form and sent it back.

The summons came at the beginning of December. I had just ten days to rehearse one set audition piece plus another of my own choice. At my mother's suggestion I asked a lady I very much admired, Moyra Haywood, manager and leading light of Leicester's amateur Little Theatre, to coach me. Moyra was very tough, saying over and over: 'I don't believe it, Richard. Do it again.'

A week before Christmas, taking our gas masks, identity cards and a shared suitcase, my mama and I set off for London. We only saw one man on duty in the whole of Midland Station; the rest were away fighting the Germans. I remember this old chap acting as porter at the entrance before rushing away to appear behind the grille as ticket seller and rushing away again, just as the train steamed in, to make his final appearance on the platform, resplendent in a stationmaster's top hat.

London was in the midst of the Blitz; every tube station an air-raid shelter, skies dotted with silver barrage balloons. The windows of the double-decker bus which took us to the Strand were shielded with mesh to prevent injury from flying glass and, through the small aperture in the middle, I could see bombed buildings in some of the side streets. Mary had reserved us a double room at the imposing Strand Palace Hotel, using money saved from her housekeeping.

She insisted on walking me to Gower Street the following morning, allowing, as always, plenty of time. This meant we arrived at RADA far too early and had to hang around for ages on the pavement outside. I was desperate to go in alone, partly due to male pride but mainly for fear she'd discover I'd lied about my age. Eventually, after many hugs and words of encouragement, she left me to my fate. Taking a deep breath, I entered the hallowed portals.

They told me to wait in a room on the ground floor. Term was over and the whole place was echoingly empty. After a long wait, I was escorted down to the Academy's small basement theatre and left in the wings to contemplate, with sheer terror, a brightly lit stage which was completely bare save for a wooden chair.

'Richard Attenborough?' The carefully modulated upper-class voice summoning me into the spotlight was that of the newly knighted Sir Kenneth Barnes, principal of the Royal Academy for the past thirty years and younger brother of the celebrated actresses Violet and Irene Vanbrugh. The latter was about to become Britain's first theatrical dame.

Advancing to centre stage, I peered into the gloom and could just discern the outline of Sir Kenneth, sitting with two other shadowy figures in a box at the back of the stalls. 'And what are you going to perform for us?'

I let go of the chair on which I'd steadied my shaking hands to announce my set piece. This was de Stogumber's last speech from Shaw's *Saint Joan* in which he expresses his horror after seeing her burned at the stake – a golden opportunity to indulge in hysterical rhetoric if ever there was one.

What they made of me, I don't know; a baby-faced schoolboy, wearing his best flannels and tweed sports jacket, playing an elderly fifteenth-century cleric in a broad Leicester accent, screaming, shouting and crying real tears as he thumped his chest and declaimed: 'There was only one Englishman there that disgraced his country; and that was the mad dog, de Stogumber. Let them torture him. Let them burn him. I will go pray among her ashes. I am no better than Judas: I will hang myself!' At which point, supposedly maddened by guilt, I blundered off the stage.

Panting in the wings, I awaited some reaction but none was forthcoming. So I ventured into the spotlight again, took another deep breath, and announced my second piece. Against the advice of Moyra Heywood, I'd chosen broad comedy in the belief that no other scholarship candidate would risk it. The writer this time was J. B. Priestley and the play was the north country farce, *When We Are Married*.

For the next five minutes I staggered about as the drunken photographer, Henry Ormondroyd; squiffy, belching, getting tangled up in my imaginary cloth and tripod, generally making a complete fool of myself. At home, Dave and Johnnie had laughed like drains. At RADA, there wasn't so much as a snigger.

Having delivered the last line, I remained onstage, feeling utterly exposed and foolish, aware of the cold sweat trickling down my spine. After an endless delay, the ogre at the back said tonelessly: 'Thank you very much.'

That was it. I was dismissed. The female registrar came to show me out and bade me farewell without any discernible enthusiasm. 'We shall be writing to you in January.' I walked past the stirrup pumps and sandbags and onto the crowded street, knowing I'd failed. My mama and I went back to Leicester that same afternoon and I spent the whole of Christmas and New Year with a sick feeling in the pit of my stomach.

The letter arrived on 4 January 1940. I remember it so clearly. As an ARP messenger, I'd spent the previous night at the local air-raid lookout post. Come morning, I was pushing my bike up the steep hill in Victoria Park when Dave came running out of our house and down the slope towards me, waving his arms and yelling. Indoors, with the whole family watching, I opened the fateful envelope.

I still have the letter it contained, pasted onto the first page of the handsomely bound cuttings album bearing the initials RSA, which was a celebratory gift from my parents. It reads:

Dear Mr Attenborough,

I have great pleasure in telling you that you have been awarded the Leverhulme Scholarship with Grant. This will be subject, of course, to your continuing to show sufficient promise and to your general good studentship during the course. Your first class will be at 10 a.m. on January 15th.

Yours very truly,

Kenneth Barnes, Principal.

In all truth, RADA proved in many respects a disappointment. I'd expected the Academy to match the rigorous academic standards imposed by my father at University College. What I found instead was an institution where people talked pompously about 'theatah' and which was regarded by some well-to-do Londoners as an 'amusing' finishing school for their debutante daughters.

My bursary of two pounds ten shillings a week wouldn't stretch to the extra guinea a term for French lessons. The rest of the non-stage syllabus consisted of learning to fence, voice production, elocution and poetry appreciation, the last taught by a daunting woman who scared me witless. Worst of all were the plays we were given to perform. There was very little Shakespeare, no Restoration comedy, nothing from any of the great classical European dramatists, just a succession of banal drawing-room comedies.

I joined a class of fifteen girls and three other boys, many of them hugely talented. Boys, of course, were at a premium since so many were already fighting in the services. This worked in my favour because there was less competition for parts and I soon found myself playing Henry Tremayne opposite three different Florence Nightingales. One of them was a girl in the year ahead of me. Her name was Sheila Sim.

Unbeknown to me, our first brief encounter had already taken place in the basement theatre where I'd auditioned. I was down there alone during a lunch break, sitting at the upright piano and showing off as usual. The national anthem was the only tune I knew but somehow I'd mastered the art of playing it with much use of the loud pedal and was singing along at the top of my voice.

Years later I learned that Sheila, having asked someone my name and been told it was Dickie Edinburgh, had crept in unobserved and spent some time listening and watching.

She soon learned that my actual surname was Attenborough. However, on my very first day at the Academy, the registrar had called me into her office to inform me that since she had already enrolled a Richard and a Dick, I was to be known henceforth as Dickie.

That diminutive has continued to dog me ever since. I hated it then and I hate it now. My wife, family and close friends call me Dick, except after I've done something absolutely dreadful when Sheila calls me Richard. But as far as the outside world's concerned, particularly the tabloid press, I'm forever saddled with Dickie.

While we were rehearsing *The Lady with the Lamp*, Sheila and I slowly got to know each other and embarked on an old-fashioned courtship. She was not only stunningly attractive, but sweet-natured and natural, without any snobbish airs or graces. Even today, I can still recall with absolute precision the moment I knew for certain I would marry her.

One early evening in the spring of 1941, I was on my way back to Wimbledon where I lodged with my mother's sister, Aunt Margaret. As I emerged from the Academy, wheeling my bike into a rain-slicked, blacked-out Gower Street, I saw the back view of a girl in a bright pink mackintosh, waiting at the bus stop. Like the child wearing the red coat in *Schindler's List*, that mackintosh sang out in the sea of monochrome. And when the girl turned and I recognised Sheila, I just knew.

At the end of my first term, I came close to being expelled from RADA. Maybe it was because I was part of a group of contemporaries who'd protested about the surfeit of drawing-room comedies. Or maybe, however strange it may seem in retrospect, it really did have something to do with my origins.

Sir Kenneth had summoned me to the principal's den. There, he reminded me, ominously, that my Leverhulme scholarship was subject to my 'general good studentship during the course' before going on bizarrely to cross-question me about my background. Was I perhaps from the Continent? No? Well, from Scotland, maybe? Or even Ireland? I assured him earnestly that both sides of my family were firmly rooted in the English East Midlands.

'Good heavens,' he exclaimed, 'that's a considerable mark against you.' Only later did it occur to me that in Sir Kenneth's world there were two kinds of actors: Londoners with their cut-glass accents and the talented rogues and vagabonds of old, who, he seemed to believe, all sprang from alien stock.

Despite the principal's doubts, I was allowed to stay on. Then, a couple of months later, it was the Luftwaffe's turn to place my studies in jeopardy.

During the Blitz, we boy students took it in turns to fire-watch on the RADA roof, optimistically equipped with a tin hat, stirrup pump and bucket of water. Thankfully, no one was up there when a direct hit from a German bomb completely demolished the rear of the complex containing the main Vanbrugh Theatre.

We all arrived the following morning to find the facade strewn across Malet Street and a gaping hole instead of a stage. Sheila, I and the other students immediately set to work, clearing up what we could of the debris while the governing council held an emergency meeting on the relatively unscathed first floor of the other building which fronted on Gower Street.

Having been warned that the Academy would almost certainly have to close, we finally lay down at the foot of the lobby staircase, gloomy and utterly exhausted, to await the council's verdict. Some time later, waking to the sound of a door opening, I looked up to see a pair of polished brogues, topped by thick socks and tweed plus fours coming down towards me. It was only when the famous face and bushy white beard came into view that I recognised a smiling George Bernard Shaw who, to my huge relief was saying, 'It's all right, children. We're going to carry on.'

Shakespearean plays which would have been put on in the Vanbrugh were now performed for evacuated city children on the outskirts of London. We were transported to these makeshift venues in a charabanc which, for some of us, provided ample opportunity for whispered endearments and a little discreet canoodling.

But true love did not always run smooth. On the first of these excursions, Sheila, having boarded the coach early, saved the adjacent seat for me. I, apparently, was not only the last to arrive, but blithely walked straight past her to sit with a group of other girls, right at the very back. This act of betrayal, she informs me, has continued to rankle to this day.

The play we were performing was *Twelfth Night*. Sheila played Viola and I was her twin brother, Sebastian. The female cast dressed in one room and we boys were strictly confined to another. Anxious to redeem myself, I devised the perfect excuse to flit between the two. It was of course vital that Viola and Sebastian should resemble each other as closely as possible. What more natural, then, that I should keep popping into the girls' dressing room to check my make-up against Sheila's until we achieved the desired effect?

Until I asked my wife recently, I couldn't remember how or when I asked her to marry me. She told me I did not plan it meticulously, as I'd fondly imagined. No down on one knee, violins playing, ring at the ready. In fact, she all but proposed to me.

'While we were at RADA, you asked me every day, first thing in the morning,' Sheila said. 'But we both knew we were playing a game and it was far too early to settle down. Then, later on, when I was appearing in *Landslide*, directed by John Gielgud at the Westminster Theatre, you used to come and watch from the wings. One evening you didn't propose and I became a little anxious. So on my exit I stole over to you in the dark and asked if you still wanted to marry me. A bit puzzled, you gave me to understand that you did. And I said, "Well ask me then!"'

When my prospective bride first met my father, he was completely opposed to our marriage. This was not because he disapproved of Sheila – he fell for her immediately – but in his firmly stated opinion a wedding was out of the question until I was in a position to support her.

During our RADA days I could rarely afford to take Sheila out on a proper date. Much of our courtship took place at the Lyons Corner House close to the Academy where we took it in turns to order one cup of ersatz coffee, served by waitresses known as Nippies. This we sipped very slowly to make it last while we hummed along to the free entertainment provided by Anton and his six-piece Apache Band. If there was an air raid, we'd pop down nearby Tottenham Court Road tube station and stay there, just happy to be together, until we heard the all-clear.

By then, I was lodging with a Mr and Mrs Smith in a tall house just off the Edgware Road. They were a very kind couple who treated me like a son – unlike the friendly ladies living upstairs who received a steady stream of uniformed gentlemen callers throughout the day and night.

During the last of my four terms at RADA, I had a series of extraordinarily lucky breaks. The first came when one of my tutors, the brilliant Ronald Kerr, asked me to make my first professional appearance in *Ah Wilderness* at the Intimate Theatre, Palmers Green. The second was when I was spotted there and taken on as a client by London's foremost theatrical agent, Al Parker. The third was when Al arranged for me to be auditioned by Noël Coward.

Sir Noël was looking for a young unknown to play a small part in the naval propaganda film, *In Which We Serve*, in which he was to star and, for the first time in his career, was also to direct. He was then at the absolute pinnacle of his fame. A friend of the royal family, he spent a great deal of time entertaining the troops and, at the start of the war in Paris, had spied for MI5. Noël was overtly gay long before it was legal; an immensely sophisticated, witty, clever, powerful and wealthy man. He was also a brilliant dramatist, lyricist and composer who sang, performed and directed. Above all, he was probably the kindest, most generous person I have ever encountered.

Noël's thoughtfulness was made apparent at our very first encounter. I was the awestruck teenage nobody, standing in the middle of a huge, empty sound stage at Denham Studios, nervously awaiting the arrival of this famous personage and terrified I'd make a fool of myself. The great man swept in, flanked as always by his two lady associates, and advanced towards me, hand outstretched. 'You won't know me – I'm Noël Coward. You, of course, are Richard Attenborough.'

As he'd known it would, his self-deprecation immediately put me at my ease. After we'd talked for a while, Noël told me I'd landed the part of the young stoker. And so began an enduring friendship during which he would become godfather to our son Michael and only end with his death thirty years later.

Within weeks of our first meeting, I was back on the same Denham sound stage. It now contained a huge tank filled with tepid water, representing the North Sea, in which we shipwrecked sailors were to cling to a life raft awaiting rescue. Noël, as the ship's captain, was in the tank every day, as was another established star, John Mills, also to become a lifelong friend.

It was hardly a glamorous introduction to film-making. The water was covered in oil, supposedly from our sunken destroyer's fuel tanks, which quickly turned rancid in the warm studio environment. This foul-smelling slick, churned by the wind and wave machines, clung to our faces and hair.

On the morning of the very last day, the rest of us lowered ourselves gingerly into the water, holding our noses. The Master's approach was somewhat different. Launching himself from the camera platform, Noël performed a spectacular belly flop and surfaced, covered in slime, to pronounce with hauteur: 'Darlings, there's dysentery in every ripple.'

I don't remember ever being directed by David Lean. I do remember he was responsible for the composition and camera work and that he was a prickly character with whom I never felt completely at ease. All my scenes were directed by Noël.

It was Noël who also gave Sheila her first break, offering her a six-month theatrical tour when she graduated from RADA in July 1942. As a result she was unable to attend the premiere of *In Which We Serve* which took place that September at the Gaumont cinema in the Haymarket. My parents made a special journey from Leicester to witness my screen debut.

I sat between them, my mama gently squeezing my hand whenever I made a fleeting appearance. As the picture came to an end, we all sat forward, waiting for the magic moment when my name would come up on the final cast list. Every single one of the film's participants was credited, including Johnny Mills' six-month-old daughter, Juliet, making her debut as 'Freda's baby'. But, as the names scrolled past, there was no Richard Attenborough.

It was a mistake of course. Nonetheless, as the lights came up on the drum roll which preceded the national anthem, my mother saw my face and, while the whole audience stood to attention, found it necessary to squeeze my hand very hard indeed. Then, as the three of us left the cinema, a young woman accosted me. For the first time ever, someone was asking for my autograph.

One of my great heroes is Winston Churchill, the courageous and dogged man who did more than any other to ensure the future of the democratic process. On becoming Prime Minister in 1940, he had told us: 'I have nothing to offer but blood, toil, tears and sweat. You ask, what is our policy? I can say: It is to wage war by sea, land and air, with all our might and all the strength that God can give us; to wage war against a monstrous tyranny, never surpassed in the dark lamentable catalogue of human crime. That is our policy. You ask, what is our aim? I can answer in one word: It is victory, victory at all costs, victory in spite of all terror, victory however long and hard the road may be.'

War was all Sheila and I had ever known as a couple. Being young and madly in love, we didn't consider ourselves heroic or hard done by. With incendiaries and later the dreaded V2 rockets raining down on London, sudden death was always a heartbeat away and, like everyone else, we simply lived for the day. We'd become officially engaged when I was preparing to leave for pilot training in Canada and now, fourteen months later, with another and more dangerous parting imminent, Sheila wanted us to be married. I'd been put on standby for a new offensive against the Japanese in the Far East.

Our wedding was solemnised on 22 January 1945 at St Mary Abbots Church in Kensington with both our families in attendance. It was the first and only time I knew my father to attend a religious service. Sheila was in a long, blue-grey dress, looking so beautiful, and I wore the RAF sergeant's uniform, which still hangs in my wardrobe today, now somewhat too small. A bomb exploded nearby as we vowed to remain together until death us did part.

The reception afterwards was held at the roof garden of Derry & Toms department store, where, almost forty years later, we would celebrate the marriage of our son Michael to his beloved Karen. I don't remember champagne but we did have an impressive three-tiered wedding cake which couldn't be cut because it was made of cardboard.

This lifted off to reveal a very small fruit cake which had been baked by my sweet mother-in-law, Ida, using precious ration coupons contributed by both the Sim and Attenborough households. I'd been granted two weeks' leave and we spent our longed-for honeymoon at the Norfolk Hotel in Bournemouth, blissfully happy.

Although put on standby to serve in Okinawa, I never went to the Far East. In June, the island finally fell to the Allies and, on 6 August, although we knew nothing about it at the time, the first atom bomb was dropped on Hiroshima. It was followed three days later by a second targeting Nagasaki.

On the late afternoon of 15 August, while Sheila and I were travelling up to the West End by tube, another passenger leaned across to tell us the Japanese Emperor had capitulated and the war was finally over; Atlee and Truman were about to make an official announcement.

We got off the train at Piccadilly Circus and could hear the roar of the crowd as the escalator took us up to the surface. There was hardly room to move. Pieces of torn paper fluttered down from the office windows above us and the whole area was packed with yelling, laughing, dancing, singing and cheering people, all exploding with joy. Some were doing the conga, others the hokey-cokey. Girls were kissing every man wearing an allied uniform.

Sheila and I threw ourselves into the celebrations, safe in the knowledge that, at long last, we could begin to plan for the future.

DH— I wasn't in the least surprised to learn that Dick had clung on to his RAF uniform: this man is a world-class hoarder.

Long ago, the largest room in his office annexe was set aside for meetings. Today, the most prestigious of the many awards he's won – six BAFTAs, two Oscars, six Golden Globes – remain on the Georgian mantelpiece in all their gleaming symmetry but there's hardly a square inch of floor space visible – it's completely covered in stuff.

No art auctioneer's catalogue, no tacky souvenir, trophy, theatre programme, brochure, certificate, photograph, press cutting, script, contract, letter, bank statement or diary ever makes its way from Beaver Lodge to the local council tip.

In recent years, this accretion of ephemera has spilled over into the private cinema at the rear of the Attenborough garden and completely engulfed the adjacent period summer house. And Dick's office, that gracious corner room with the two *oeil-de-boeuf* windows, is now a repository for so many books, pictures, certificates, company minutes, knick-knacks and stacks of new and yellowing correspondence he can barely see over his desk. I've taken to calling him Miss Havisham; not a joke he appreciates.

This is a man who's utterly incapable of discarding or recycling any possession, no matter how worthless or trivial. But, as I am able to attest, he can and does give money away, vast amounts of it, without a moment's regret.

Due to the byzantine Hollywood accounting system, British film-makers who really hit the international jackpot are few and far between and rarely share their good fortune with members of their cast and crew. Two laudable exceptions have been Cubby Broccoli, originator of the hugely profitable *Bond* series, and David, now Lord, Puttnam, producer of the Oscar-winning *Chariots of Fire*. Dick, however, far outstripped both of them.

Having renounced his entire director-producer fee in order to buy out Joe Levine, he had embarked on *Gandhi* with little or no prospect of ever receiving a penny for his services. His contract did, however, award him a significant percentage of hypothetical profits. Against all expectation, this ultimately resulted in a multimillion-dollar payout and, long before he saw any of it, Dick had given well over half away.

Years earlier, he'd set up The Richard Attenborough Charitable Trust to which he'd always tithed, as a matter of principle, part of his acting and directing fees and, unlike most of today's celebrities, every penny he earned from public appearances. Having been allocated a significant proportion of Dick's *Gandhi* profits, the trust went on to donate over £2 million to education, disability, famine relief and the arts.

Further substantial sums went directly to a new charity, the Cine Artists' Welfare Fund, set up in India following the film's release to assist actors and technicians who had fallen on hard times.

On a more personal level, Dick donated generous percentages to Ben Kingsley, the late Moti Kothari's family, Jack Briley, Jake Eberts and his former business partner, Mike Stanley-Evans. A final share, dubbed 'the bucket', he divided equally between a dozen senior technicians.

I was lucky enough to be one of them and used the initial payout to buy my first ever washing machine and, joy of joys, a small car. One of the cameramen bought a holiday apartment on Ibiza, someone else a pied-à-terre in Paris. Dick's lawyer, Claude Fielding, treated himself to a sailing boat, called *The Bucket*, and Jake Eberts added an extension to his Quebec home, known as 'the Gandhi wing'.

Dick's generosity enhanced many lives, not least that of Mike Stanley-Evans, who created his dream retirement home on a plot of land over-looking the sea in Majorca and lived there very happily until his death in 2004.

Conversely, the 40 per cent of his profit share Dick retained for himself made little or no difference to his lifestyle. Still besotted with the ageing Rolls-Royce Corniche he'd acquired during the 1970s, he saw no reason to buy a new car. Two decades and two hundred thousand miles later, 'the old bitch' is still his one and only.

He did pay off his massive overdraft, buy a painting or two and order a couple of the same bespoke business suits he'd worn for many years: grey flannel, single-breasted, three buttons, two vents. He also helped his three children climb the property ladder and undertook to pay for the private education of all seven grandchildren. Everything else remained the same.

He continued to play the football pools and latterly the lottery – same birthday numbers every week – and remained one of Chelsea's most ardent supporters. He and Sheila continued to spend Christmas at Old Friars, Hogmanay on the Isle of Bute and, work permitting, the entire month of August at their holiday home in Provence.

He continued to employ a chauffeur, a team of gardeners, Filipino staff in the house, a young woman to tend his orchids, an accountant, a lawyer, two secretaries and his new PA, Clare Howard. He also continued, doggedly, to rack up one of the longest lists of business and other activities in *Who's Who*. And, above all, he continued to make films.

Immediately after the 1983 Oscar ceremony, as the hottest director in Hollywood, Dick had been showered with lucrative offers, including a bizarre comedy set in a spaceship, which he instantly rejected. There was, however, one proposal – again an unlikely choice for the man who had just made *Gandhi* – which, believing it to be a great career move, his trusty agent, Marti Baum, repeatedly urged him to accept.

When *A Chorus Line* originally opened off-Broadway in May 1975, Clive Barnes, the eminent *New York Times* critic had ended his glowing review: 'This is a show that must dance, jog and whirl its way into the history of musical theatre.'

While the show was still in rehearsal, two of Marti Baum's canny clients, veteran stage producers, Cy Feuer and Ernest Martin, had tried and failed to buy the film rights, offering a mere $150,000. After it transferred to Broadway, becoming a smash hit, the rights were bought by Universal Studios at a cost of $5.5 million, together with an unprecedented profit participation for the copyright holders. Over the next five years, some of Broadway and Hollywood's lesser and greater talents, including the original director/choreographer, Michael Bennett, together with Mike Nichols and Sidney Lumet, had struggled fruitlessly to bring *A Chorus Line* to the screen.

The problems were twofold. First came the question of whether to 'open up' the production. Traditionally, screen adaptations took the cinema audience on a visual journey which far exceeded the limitations of theatre. But the very essence of *A Chorus Line* consisted of bare boards, starkly framed by a proscenium arch within an empty auditorium. It was this very claustrophobia, laced with the psychological striptease performed by the auditioning dancers, which lay at the heart of its immense popularity.

The second problem was cost. Having agreed to pay the show's creators a whopping 20 per cent of the gross as soon as the box-office take exceeded $30 million, Universal had to make an exceptionally successful film or an exceptionally cheap one, if they were ever to see any profit.

Defeated by this twin conundrum, the company finally abandoned the project in early 1980, selling it on for $7.8 million to Polygram where, for two years, it languished under the aegis of producers Peter Guber and his partner, Barbra Streisand's former hairdresser, Jon Peters. With their departure, *A Chorus Line*, still without a viable script and now trailing failed development costs of $8.5 million, became the responsibility of Polygram's president, Gordon Stulberg, a professional executive who'd never made a film in his life.

About to cut his losses by selling the subject on again, Stulberg agreed to listen to a tantalising proposal, devised by Marti Baum and put to him by his tenacious clients, Cy Feuer and Ernest Martin – the same Broadway duo who'd failed to secure the rights for a pittance seven years earlier.

Feuer and Martin persuaded Stulberg to grant them an exclusive six-month window. Within this short space of time, they undertook to produce a completely new script, appoint a director and prepare a bare-bones budget which would not exceed an incredibly low $10 million. The clincher was that none of this would cost Polygram an additional cent. All the duo were asking in return was the freedom to enter into their own finance and distribution deal.

Their writer of choice was Arnold Schulman who came with two previous Oscar nominations. His brief was simple: don't open up the story, keep it in the theatre. Time was so tight that Ernie Martin immediately moved him into his home in the Hamptons, practically chaining him to a desk until, some ten weeks later, gaunt and exhausted, Schulman handed over his screenplay.

Feuer and Martin then put together their budget. Excluding rights and failed development costs, the bottom line came in as promised – well below the average cost of any Hollywood production, let alone a musical. This depended on using an unknown director, no stars and cheap, non-union labour. However, on reading Schulman's script, Stulberg became intoxicated with enthusiasm. Confidently predicting huge profits, he appointed himself the movie's executive producer and, rashly deferring recoupment of Polygram's previous investment, virtually doubled the sum available for production.

Finance and distribution were to be supplied by Embassy, the company formerly owned by Joe Levine and now headed by Jerry Perenchio and Norman Lear, who had purchased American TV rights in *Gandhi*, selling them on instantly to reap a handsome profit. More recently, Perenchio had wooed Jake Eberts, still secretly up to his ears in debt, away from London and into a highly paid non-job in New York. In the long term, this would lead to the tragic demise of Goldcrest and with it City support for the British film industry. In the short term, it was to make Eberts very unhappy indeed.

With production funding for *A Chorus Line* now nudging $20 million, Perenchio and Lear were not prepared to risk hiring any unknown rooky director. They were insisting on a big name and preferably someone with experience of musicals. Unsurprisingly, the name that came to mind was Richard Attenborough, 'hot' double Oscar winner, already the originator of easy money for their company, vouched for by Jake Eberts, director of the highly regarded British cult musical, *Oh! What a Lovely War*, and fortuitously represented by the ubiquitous Marti Baum.

At this point a senior partner at Creative Artists, the most powerful talent agency in Hollywood, Marti had known Feuer and Martin since his formative post-war years in New York when he'd helped cast their original Broadway production of *Guys and Dolls*. In his next incarnation as head of ABC Pictures in Hollywood, he'd engaged Feuer to produce the multiple 1972 Oscar-winning film, *Cabaret*, shot for just $3.4 million, which had gone on to gross $42.7 million at the American box office alone.

Believing *A Chorus Line* could perform just as well, if not better, with Dick as director, Marti now negotiated a sweetheart deal with Embassy, entailing both the highest fee his British client had ever received and, very importantly, the cherished right of final cut.

This meant, provided he did not exceed the contractual running time of 135 minutes, no one could alter the film Dick delivered by so much as a single frame. However, as a director for hire, he would have no control over expenditure during production. With Embassy controlling the overall purse strings, this would remain the prerogative of the producers, sagacious Cy Feuer and quixotic Ernie Martin.

Lack of control was not the only factor which made Dick hesitate. Not only had he never seen the stage production of *A Chorus Line*, but he also had a new film of his own in mind, as yet unscripted, which he fully intended to direct and produce. However, in common with *Gandhi*, this was a politically charged controversial subject about real people and, crucially, one that once again involved a foreign government.

Needing time to weigh up these pros and cons, in January 1984 Dick promised Marti a decision on his return from a two-week reconnaissance trip to the country in question. Although successful in many respects, this did not go as anticipated. Back in London, angry and exhausted after the most dangerous and intimidating journey he had ever undertaken, Dick reluctantly decided to put his own film on hold.

Two days later, he flew Concorde to New York and went straight to a matinee of *A Chorus Line* at the Schubert Theatre where the sheer exuberance and theatricality of the show completely bowled him over. Just to be sure, he saw it again that same evening. Next morning, he phoned Marti and told him he would agree to direct the film on condition he could bring his PA, Clare Howard, and four of his own technicians with him from London. I was one of the four technicians. The others, all former members of the *Gandhi* team, were director of photography, Ronnie Taylor, editor, John Bloom, and sketch artist, Chalky White.

After my unhappy stint with David Lean, I was very keen to work with Dick again. But, facing the prospect of another long separation from Kay, I knew I could no longer rely on a series of ad hoc childcare arrangements. My reluctant solution was to enrol her in boarding school.

RA— In America, they're known as cattle calls. When I started to prepare *A Chorus Line* at the beginning of 1984, they were my first experience of the heartbreak behind the bright smiles and syncopated high kicks of every classic Broadway musical.

At crack of dawn on a February morning, I was driven along Broadway to the Royale Theatre and, as we turned into 45th Street, saw literally hundreds of youngsters in bright clothes with dance bags slung over their shoulders, lined up in the freezing cold, waiting to attend our first open audition. On that day alone, I saw nearly two thousand.

In all, we held more than a dozen such auditions in New York and Los Angeles. The sheer number of young Americans who were prepared to put themselves through this gruelling process was truly amazing. Although many were seasoned professionals, a good proportion were complete amateurs. One teenage boy, I remember, was so determined to stand out in the crowd that he turned up dressed from head to toe in a bear costume.

Echoing the story of *A Chorus Line*, I'd sit in the stalls with Cy and Ernie, two casting directors and our 27-year-old choreographer, Jeffrey Hornaday, fresh from his triumph with *Flashdance*. A group of kids would come onto the stage and tell us a little about themselves before performing the testing 64-bar dance combination they'd been shown on arrival. Straight after they'd finished, we'd confer briefly before announcing who was rejected and who'd been selected for recall. Many were sent away simply because they didn't have the right 'look'. It was that instant, that brutal. And those who didn't make it remained so determinedly upbeat, so incredibly stoical, it was enough to break your heart.

The story may be apocryphal, but I'm told that among the girls I rejected that first day at the Royale was a 26-year-old singer/dancer from Michigan, family name Ciccone, then in the process of recording a debut album called *Madonna*.

Of the thousands we considered, just seventeen kids were chosen for major dance parts in the film, a handful picked to say a few words and a further 350 recruited as dancers. The rest gathered themselves up and drifted away to start all over again.

The first of my many confrontations with Embassy Pictures was over the casting of the shadowy authority figure who sits in the stalls selecting and rejecting the chorus for a forthcoming musical. Although John

Travolta and Mikhail Baryshnikov had previously been interested in the part, to my great joy, word reached me that Michael Douglas was now asking – actually asking – to play Zach.

To secure a star of Michael's magnitude was a huge bonus and I wanted to engage him immediately. However, Jerry Perenchio, mildly described by Jake Eberts as 'volatile', vetoed this casting, claiming ridiculously that Michael couldn't act. He was and is, of course, a terrific actor.

I still don't know the reason behind Perenchio's unpleasant outburst. Despite having just had a huge hit as the producer and star of *Romancing the Stone*, Michael wasn't seeking an exorbitant fee or even demanding above-the-title billing. Indeed, aware that the film was an ensemble piece, he was insisting that his name should appear alphabetically with the rest of the cast. But Perenchio was adamant and the argument raged back and forth until, out of sheer frustration, I threatened to resign, at which point he caved in. Our relationship never recovered.

We quarrelled again, and again I prevailed, over the casting of Cassie, the film's female lead. I was determined that she should be played by Alyson Reed, a sensational 26-year-old actress, singer and dancer who'd played the part on tour and recently won an award playing Monroe in the Broadway show, *Marilyn*.

Unfortunately, a couple of days before we started shooting, exercising his producer's prerogative Ernie Martin took it upon himself to haul Alyson off to some fashionable hair salon without any reference to me. On her return, I was horrified to discover they'd cut off her beautiful long hair, dyed what remained a harsh red and given her a frizzy perm. Proud of his handiwork, Ernie declared she was now 'kooky', whatever that meant. I had a different word for it, but since it was vital to maintain Alyson's confidence, I told her fervently that she looked absolutely gorgeous.

That girl was a dream to direct and she worked her heart out. *A Chorus Line* should have made her a star. Instead, to my everlasting regret, it brought her nothing but heartbreak.

Alyson was to say afterwards: 'The year that followed was the hardest year of my life. I wanted to quit the business. I knew we'd get bad reviews because, for some people, we'd rewritten the Bible.'

Stupidly, I had no idea that, in New York at least, the show was sacrosanct. As far as I was concerned, we were translating a theatrical experience into an alternative medium which would enable it to be enjoyed by a far wider audience than ever before.

To hold that audience, it was not enough to plant a camera in the stalls and simply film what was happening onstage. Somehow I had to devise hundreds of different angles and perspectives which would show each dance to the best advantage, reveal the innermost thoughts of the characters and convey the terrifying nature of the void beyond the footlights.

To further relieve any sense of visual monotony, I decided to incorporate some backstage scenes to illustrate the earlier love affair between Zach and Cassie and to place the theatre in context with some aerial shots of New York.

It was these title shots, filmed from a helicopter, which brought me into conflict with Embassy's Norman Lear. He accused me of stealing the idea from a TV series he'd produced – which I had never seen – and demanded they be removed from the film. I refused and he continued to insist until I trumped him by invoking my right of final cut.

I had another fight on my hands over the casting of the sassy chorus girl who sings about her plastic surgery in the number known as 'Tits and Ass'. I'd already tested a number of totally unsuitable candidates and was beginning to despair when Cy Feuer, for whom I had the most enormous respect, introduced me to Audrey Landers.

I must have been one of very few people in the English-speaking world who'd never watched *Dallas*. So I wasn't aware that Audrey was already hugely famous. What I saw was this bubbly blonde bombshell who, although not a dancer, could deliver the song with tremendous gusto and panache. Again, after a war of words with Embassy, but this time with the support of Cy, Audrey became our Val.

By the time we started shooting, seventeen of America's top dancers had spent the best part of four months rehearsing the energetic and complicated routines devised by Jeffrey Hornaday at the mirrored Minskoff Studios on Broadway. It was there that I came to know them.

They called themselves 'gypsies', a term born of their itinerant show-business lifestyle. Their multiple skills were known as the 'triple threat'. It wasn't enough to be a great dancer. To survive, they also had to have exceptional acting and singing skills and their dedication to all three disciplines was phenomenal. They practised endlessly; warming up before we started shooting, singing scales, rehearsing their lyrics and weight training between shots, attending classes as soon as we finished in the evening. The tragedy was that, like top athletes, their professional lives were so incredibly short.

Handsome Blane Savage, then pushing thirty, who leapt with the effortless grace of a gazelle, showed me his gnarled and bleeding feet one day and confided: 'There's a kind of threshold of pain and tiredness you have to break through. In sport they call it "the wall". You get to it and you have to go past it. Now I'm pretty much in pain all the time.'

They all had a different story. Puerto Rican Yamil Borges had hobbled into her first audition on crutches and in tears, believing she didn't stand a chance. Janet Jones was so incredibly beautiful that I nicknamed her Ugly. Another of the girls was fighting bulimia. Vicki Frederick, who'd danced until the fifth month of her pregnancy, was yearning for her baby. But most inspiring and humbling of all was the story of Chuck McGowan.

Born with a number of severe deformities, Chuck had been abandoned by his mother when a pediatrician told her he'd never walk. The baby had remained at the maternity hospital until one of the Irish nurses 'saw something' in his eyes. She took him home, badgered a surgeon to perform the first of many operations and put the little boy through a gruelling programme of physiotherapy. Almost miraculously, he took his first steps at four. To strengthen his legs, his adoptive mother then put him into a dance class, taking in sewing to pay for the lessons.

I knew none of this when Jeffrey Hornaday insisted Chuck was the only boy in the whole of America who could do justice to 'I Can Do That', the most demanding and acrobatic dance solo of the entire film. I don't remember how many times Chuck repeated the routine before we had it in the can. I do know that, with numerous changes of camera angle, it took us three whole days to complete.

In the beginning, the younger members of the cast respectfully addressed me as Sir Attenborough. At my request, this became Richard. Only when cheeky Matt West started calling me 'Dad' did I realise I wasn't just directing a film but also running a boarding school – in loco parentis to a whole family of fiercely dedicated, hugely talented, highly individualistic and utterly adorable kids.

DH— A *Chorus Line* went into production in the cavernous Mark Hellinger Theatre just after Dick's sixty-first birthday. To mark the occasion, the gorgeous Janet Jones presented him with his first pairs of trainers and jeans. He wore the Levi's until they were threadbare, bought himself some more and, even now in his eighties, still wears them when he's directing.

The theatre was our home for the next four months and it was a phenomenally happy place. For me, the contrast with Lean and A *Passage to India* couldn't have been greater. A quarter of a century later, the trusted technician who was always at Dick's elbow, his remarkable American script supervisor, B. J. Bjorkman, remembers:

'I'd worked with a lot of directors – Coppola, Lumet, et cetera et cetera – but from the moment I met Richard, when he interviewed me for the job, I knew that here was someone completely different.

'From the early rehearsals, sitting in that big rehearsal hall on Broadway with Richard and Cy and all those kids, I knew I was in a special world, a brand-new country. Can you imagine? He looked like he was having the time of his life, although I am sure the problems that surrounded him would have choked most directors.

'Whatever they were, he never pounded them into any of us. He had a plan, obviously, and I think he always knew how he wanted to implement it. But it wasn't screaming, or showing off, or throwing curve balls at anyone. He had been in film long enough to realise the truth about movies: it's the most collaborative business in the world.

'And there was always this glorious sense of adventure, because that's the best word to describe film-making. OK, as the director you've got a script, you've got your actors, you've hired your crew, and you've been huddling with producers and writers for months. But then comes that first day of shooting. How the hell did you ever get here? A bare stage, cameras ready, lights poised, seventeen young kids, probably scared to death – and all eyes staring at you. But Richard never blinked. He absolutely *loved* what he was doing, and because of that, *we* all loved doing it with him.

'Every day seemed better than the one before. Every morning, I'd enter the most wonderful world . . . all music, all singing, all dancing, all acting, all laughing, all bursting with energy. It was as if I had died and gone to heaven.'

RA—It was while we were filming *A Chorus Line* that I met a saint in the making. Two American sisters, Ann and Jeannette Petrie, had devoted five years to a documentary about the life and work of Mother Teresa. When they invited me to view a rough cut in their New York editing suite, I found the work exceptional; they'd captured perfectly this brave, energetic, pragmatic little woman, filled with devotion to God and driven by the unswerving belief that, no matter how hopeless the situation, He would always provide. But it was her humour that did it for me. There was a twinkle in those hooded eyes, so captivating that, even as a non-believer, I couldn't refuse the Petries' request that I should record their narration.

A few weeks later, one of the sisters phoned my PA, Clare Howard. 'Mother' was to about make a brief stopover at JFK airport and had expressed a wish to meet me.

Our encounter took place in a small VIP room. She looked exactly as I had expected; a birdlike figure with wizened face and prayerful Dürer hands, less than five feet tall and clad in her trademark home-spun cotton sari. What I had not anticipated was that this 74-year-old recipient of the Nobel Peace Prize, then well on her way to canonisation, would be the most outrageous flirt.

I of course responded by flirting back and in no time we were holding hands and talking about our mutual love of India. When her onward flight was called, I kissed her on the cheek, expressing the hope that we would meet again soon.

She nodded her agreement and made her way to the door. There she turned to say briskly: 'See you at the feet of Jesus.'

We did meet once more – not, I'm relieved to say, in the celestial circumstances she had so confidently predicted – but a year later when she was invited to address the United Nations General Assembly.

DH— We shot for twenty weeks in the Mark Hellinger Theatre. Kay, soon to be ten, came over for Christmas and we had a wonderful time, putting up a six-foot tree in our hotel room, night skating at the Rockefeller Center and toy shopping at FAO Schwarz.

Then in January 1985, forty years after they'd exchanged their vows in war-torn London, Dick and Sheila celebrated their ruby wedding. He gave her a garnet brooch, she gave him a gold signet ring and they threw a dinner party at which the guests included Dick's adopted German Jewish sisters, Irene and Helga.

The following Saturday, I accompanied Dick to the annual awards ceremony hosted by New York's most influential film critics. I'd been with him at the same function when *Gandhi* had been voted Best Film of 1982 and we both remembered it as a very relaxed and jocular occasion. Tonight, however, Dick was not collecting an award of his own, but standing in for an absent David Lean who had won Best Picture and Best Director awards for *A Passage to India*.

In the yellow cab on our way to Sardi's, we were working out what Dick should say about Lean, when he started to whistle the theme from *The Bridge on the River Kwai*. We agreed that the idea of omitting the words and leaving the audience to sing them in their heads had been a stroke of genius on David's part and that of his composer, Malcolm Arnold. It was a pity the Yanks couldn't have appreciated this subtle subversion because they, of course, wouldn't have known the lyrics.

In a mad moment, believing it could help *A Chorus Line* and dispel some of his rather stuffy British image, I suggested Dick regale our hosts with the vulgar version at the conclusion of his speech. It seemed a hugely funny idea and we both fell about laughing.

Neither of us was laughing on the way back to our hotel. Accepting the awards on Lean's behalf in that most theatrical of Broadway restaurants, Dick had paid eloquent tribute to their absent recipient while our hosts glowed with enthusiasm. Then, to top it off, he'd launched into 'Colonel Bogey.'

As soon as he'd sung, 'Hitler has only got one ball . . .' I'd known that this was a ghastly error. Dick knew it too but had to carry on. By the time he reached, 'But poor old Goebbels has no balls at all,' every critic's face was frozen in shock. It was the worst misjudgement of my entire publicity career and one that would come back to haunt us when we returned to New York for the world premiere of *A Chorus Line* the following year.

RA— Long before that, there was one last battle to fight with Embassy. I was determined *A Chorus Line* should have a truly spectacular finale. My idea was that the whole stage would be filled with mirrors reflecting wave after wave of top-hatted dancers, all wearing identical gold costumes, all dancing in perfect unison to the beat of 'One Singular Sensation'. This was to be my heartfelt tribute to every gypsy who'd ever appeared on the Great White Way.

Cy and Ernie had never envisaged such expenditure while drawing up their budget and, when informed of the additional cost, Perenchio and Lear went ballistic. Yet again the phone lines between New York and LA were sizzling with expletives. And yet again I fought, yelled and insisted until I got the money to shoot the ending as I had wanted: in a blaze of satin and sequins with hundreds of kids singing triumphantly: 'She's the one!'

DH— Monday 9 December 1985. This evening *A Chorus Line* is to have its world premiere at New York's cavernous Radio City Music Hall.

At 6 a.m. Park Avenue is dark and frosty as Dick and I emerge from the Regency Hotel and climb into our chauffeur-driven town car. After a short journey along deserted streets, punctuated by eerie jets of steam, we arrive at the first television station. There's no one else in the hospitality room with its fresh bagels and jugs of jaded coffee. We talk briefly to a researcher before Dick's taken away and I'm left alone to watch his interview on the screen in a corner. The breakfast show's female anchor kicks off by asking if translating America's best-loved stage show into a movie wasn't too daunting a task for an Englishman.

Dick, of course, is charm itself. As always, he's bubbling with enthusiasm and talking up *A Chorus Line* with every fibre of his being. His segment ends. As the anchor elides into an item about the last journey of Amtrak's coast-to-coast sleeper train, he's back at my side saying anxiously: 'How was it, darling?'

'You were great, Dick, really good.'

He's stricken. 'I forgot to mention Cy.'

'And Ernie.'

'Sod Ernie.'

I look at our itinerary; we're due at the next studio in twenty minutes. Here, the coffee smells fresh and there are muffins as well as bagels.

As always, Dick declines make-up and watches the new anchor, a young man this time, on the monitor. He's waffling about cereal. A pretty girl arrives to take Dick away and he comes up on the screen in the corner after the ad break. The anchor tells Dick he's seen the film and, without venturing any opinion, immediately asks why he chose to cast Michael Douglas as Zach. To me there's an implied criticism, but Dick plunges right in, not defending but extolling for all he's worth.

My sense of unease increases. We have one more network breakfast show before we move on to New York's abundance of local radio stations and, although it's barely 7.30 a.m., I put in the call to Lois.

Lois Smith is the doyenne of American press agents, a big, warm generous woman, very astute but totally devoid of cynicism. She acts as personal media adviser to most of the really big stars. Lois and Dick have known each other for years and years and years.

'Hello, my darling. Not good news, I'm afraid.'

It would be a master understatement to say that Lois has contacts. She knows everyone. And here, although it could never happen in London, her contacts have read her the New York critics' reviews for A Chorus Line a day ahead of publication.

'How bad are they?' I ask.

'Bad, bad.' Paraphrasing from memory, she quotes me some damning phrases.

'Surely they can't all be terrible?'

'Every single one.'

I look at the monitor. Dick's been replaced on the screen by a man talking about Halley's Comet. 'Gotta go. Talk to you later.'

Dick bustles in almost before I put the phone down. 'How was it, darling?'

'Terrific. You handled it really well.'

'At least I got in a bit about Cy.'

Back in the town car, Dick's totally relaxed, planning how to inject praise for Alyson Reed into the next interview, while I'm on the horns of a dilemma. Do I tell him now or later?

Above all, I don't want him to make a fool of himself. Equally, with universally bad reviews, the film desperately needs every bit of promotion it can get. I'm still undecided when we pull up outside NBC.

Here, there's a gaggle of autograph hunters waiting on the sidewalk.

I hang back; Dick signs and talks to each of them. We have quite a long wait before his slot and the *Today Show* hospitality room is full of other people; no chance of a quiet chat.

The interview, conducted by Jane Pauley, starts with the question, 'What's this film really all about?' Dick, needing no further prompting, launches into his effervescent four-minute sales pitch: 'It's about kids trying to break into show business . . .' The whole segment, including a great clip of the finale, concludes with a smiling Pauley saying: 'I can't wait to see this movie.'

The girl who brings Dick back is also enthusiastic. 'I just love that British accent,' she tells me, 'and the way he talks in sentences.' Courtly as ever, he kisses her hand.

On our way to the first radio station, we're stuck in rush-hour traffic. Deep breath. 'Dick, I've spoken to Lois.'

'And . . . ?'

'The reviews are bad.'

'What do you mean, darling?'

'They don't like the film.'

Immediately, he wants to know everything: What don't they like? Surely not the performances? Or the choreography? Is it his direction?

'*Time* will snipe but the *New York Times* is probably the worst. Canby says everyone claimed the film couldn't be done and you've proved them right. Apparently, there's a bit which says, "This is no *Gandhi* dances." And he calls Alyson charmless. Lois says almost all of them have a dig at the fact that you're British.'

Dick takes a moment to absorb this and then he's plying me with more questions I can't answer. What about Judith Crist, Rex Reed and Andrew Sarris? Surely one of them had something good to say?

We pull up outside the radio station and he sits still for a moment, eyes closed. Then, having crammed what I've just told him into one of his mental boxes and slammed the lid shut, it's onwards and upwards. In the five radio spots which follow he's more positive and more enthusiastic than I've ever heard him.

Denial, self-belief or acting? I simply don't know.

RA— We went to the world premiere by bus. The idea was that I would travel with the whole of my young cast, all seventeen of them, to create a photo opportunity on our arrival at Radio City.

I was just about to climb aboard when someone handed me a stack of newspapers, saying they were the following morning's early editions. My heart plummeted. By then, I'd spoken to Lois and knew, as Di had warned me, that every review was bad.

So there I was, ensconced at the back of that bus, surrounded by my family of vulnerable, overexcited adopted kids, dolled up in their best bibs and tuckers, all clamouring to hear what the critics said.

It was one of the worst moments I can remember. As we crawled towards the circling klieg lights, past mounted police controlling the sightseeing crowd cramming the Avenue of the Americas, I had to deliver the news that would smash seventeen high hopes to smithereens.

Putting the stack of papers aside, I began: 'The notices aren't very good, I'm afraid.'

Their joyful anticipation evaporated in an instant.

'It isn't you,' I went on as steadily as I could. 'You are all absolutely brilliant, every one of you. It's my fault. They're saying a Brit should never have attempted to make the film, that I completely failed to understand the subject. It's me, not you. I'm the arrogant, ignorant Limey who buggered up their icon.'

Matt West enveloped me in a bear hug as the bus pulled up at the end of the red carpet. 'That's terrible, Dad. How could they say that? You're the best. We all love you.'

With myriad flashbulbs popping and hundreds of fans screaming a welcome, the bus door opened. It was Alyson who rallied the troops, yelling at the top of her voice: 'Screw the fuckin' critics. This is Radio City Music Hall, guys, and this is our night!'

And, unbelievably, she was right. They lined up, bless them, and pinned on great big smiles for the photographers. They made their way, heads held high, through the throng of high-society New Yorkers, each paying $500 a time, to take their seats in the stalls. There, surrounded and cheered on by every other gypsy on Broadway, they whooped, whistled and clapped throughout the entire performance. It was so infectious that the whole audience, numbering well over two thousand, joined in. If I hadn't known otherwise, I'd have believed we had the smash hit of all time.

In our business you learn to take the rough with the smooth. Nevertheless, every actor, every director I know can quote from at least one devastating review which, like a recalcitrant burr, can't be dislodged from the memory. For me it became embedded, word for damning word, when I was twenty-four. An eminent journalist called Leonard Mosley, writing in the *Daily Express*, opined of my first starring role: 'The Boulting Bothers decided to cast the spotty and repellent adolescent Richard Attenborough in *Brighton Rock*. The result, in my opinion, is that the film version of Graham Greene's Pinkie is about as close to the real thing as Donald Duck is to Greta Garbo.'

DH— There was one, just one, journalist in the whole of New York who chose to praise *A Chorus Line*. This was the theatre critic, Clive Barnes who, a decade earlier, had given the original show that rave review in the *New York Times*.

Apparently out of curiosity, Mr Barnes, now writing about dance and drama for the *New York Post*, had paid to see the film a few days after it opened. He went on to write a passionate fifteen-hundred word rebuttal of the film critics' reviews which began:

> It was infinitely better than the disaster I had been led to expect. In fact – you had better not tell a highbrow soul – I actually enjoyed it . . .
>
> At a time when the Hollywood musical is almost a lost art and the cinematic adaptation of a Broadway musical nowadays almost unknown, *A Chorus Line* should surely be greeted with a good deal more than a disdainful chorus damning with faint praise, or at best praising with faint damns.
>
> I liked all of it and loved some of it. It is the best dance film and, for that matter, the best movie musical for years.

6

ASKING FOR TROUBLE

RA— SHEILA AND I never celebrated our diamond wedding. Spearheaded by our beloved Jane, the three children were apparently organising a huge surprise party. The venue was booked and more than a hundred guests, all sworn to secrecy, had agreed to attend.

But prior to this event, Jane, her husband, Beau, his elderly mother and their three teenage children were going away for Christmas. We weren't sure where, but knew it was far away and sunny. Just before their departure, Jane bustled around the family home in Putney, cooking us an early turkey dinner. That was the last time we ever saw her.

On Boxing Day morning 2004, a giant wave crashed onto a Thai beach resort called Khao Lak, instantly killing thousands, among them Jane, her mother-in-law and younger daughter, Lucy. Our other grand-daughter, Alice, was very severely injured. For Sheila and me, both in our early eighties, nothing would ever be the same again. Our sixtieth wedding anniversary on 22 January came and went unnoticed.

Even in my mid-twenties, I was aware of leading a charmed life. I'd managed to win a scholarship to RADA and, unlike so many of my contemporaries, had survived the war unscathed. Through a set of fortuitous circumstances, I'd been demobbed from the RAF with the foundations of a film and stage career already in place. I was married to the most wonderful girl in the world, who was already an established actress, and the two of us were incredibly happy in our little rented home. And, if starting the family we longed for was taking a little longer than we would have wished, we were having a lot of fun trying.

Despite that one damning review in the *Daily Express*, celebrity on a scale I could never have envisaged came in 1948 with the release of *Brighton Rock*, directed by John Boulting and produced by his twin brother, Roy.

It was the Boultings who introduced me to Jack Warrow. He was the first and possibly the greatest of Britain's professional film publicists. And, like Di in later years, Jack was no sycophant, always telling me, discreetly but pulling no punches, exactly where I was going wrong. Knowing how to align the requirements of the post-war press with the film industry's need to attract audiences, he was the originator of what would eventually become known as a photo opportunity.

It was Jack who packed me off with a posse of press photographers, to Stamford Bridge for a kickabout with the late great striker, Tommy Lawton. Under the headline A MAN WITH TWO FREE TICKETS FOR CHELSEA, Ian Mackay wrote in the *News Chronicle*:

Led by Lawton, the team gave Dickie the whole works. They did everything except put him through the mincer. They tripped him, knocked the wind out of him, forgot to catch him when they tossed him in the blanket and, to top the day's devilment off, drenched him with a hose.

Now every Saturday when Chelsea are at home you will find Lawton outside the players' entrance waiting with two grandstand tickets for his pal, Dickie, and his film star wife, Sheila Sim.

Those tickets were the most blissful perk of my new-found fame. Tommy, England's greatest ever centre forward, was then earning the princely sum of £18 a week with a £2 bonus if Chelsea won. Thanks to his generosity, Sheila and I no longer had to spend our Saturday afternoons, armed with a Thermos and packet of sandwiches, shivering on the terraces.

My next film was distributed by Rank and the man in charge of the organisation's nationwide publicity machine was the jolly, cigar-smoking Theo Cowan. He would come to collect me in a chauffeured Austin

Princess, bearing a red carnation for my buttonhole just to make sure everyone knew who was the star. And off we'd go to clubs, pubs, civic receptions, mayoral parlours, ballrooms, bathing beauty contests and a whole host of Odeon cinemas up and down the country.

I've never heard so many screaming women in all my life.

Long before Frank Sinatra and Johnny Rae were rapturously received in Britain and while the Beatles were still little Liverpool lads in shorts, the whole population went crazy over a crop of young film stars who came to the fore during the first years of peacetime.

Among the glamorous girls were Jean Kent, Honor Blackman, Patricia Roc, Diana Dors, Phyllis Calvert, Dinah Sheridan and, of course, Mrs Richard Attenborough, aka Miss Sheila Sim. Fortunately for me, with the exception of Guy Rolfe, I had the field pretty much to myself until a whole clutch of male heart-throbs – Anthony Steel, Roger Moore, Kenneth More and, of course, the hugely popular Dirk Bogarde – came onto the scene in the early 1950s.

Dozens of the handkerchiefs I wore in my breast pocket were snatched as souvenirs. While some women thrust autograph books at me, others proffered their hands, arms and even their breasts for signature, yelling, 'Sign me here, Dickie.'

And all the time, Sheila and I were trying for a baby.

With food, petrol and clothes still rationed, film fans in the late 1940s had had enough of the pious wartime mantras of waste-not-want-not and make-do-and-mend. But, apart from the royal family and particularly the two young princesses, Elizabeth and Margaret Rose, there were no icons. Churchill had been sent packing in the 1945 election, the aristocracy was no longer revered, the reforming Attlee government consisted of men in drab demob suits and, like everyone else, the surviving wartime heroes were back on civvy street.

We just happened to be in the right place at the right time. Forget about acting, forget about talent; what the public wanted from us was an escape from years of austerity and the illusion of glamour. Responding to that need, we toured up and down the country in a caravan of nonsense drummed up by the film companies and breathlessly reported in *Picturegoer*, *Home Chat*, *Photoplay*, *Tit-Bits* and, of course, the tabloids.

I remember Theo put out a story that Maureen Swanson couldn't sleep in ordinary bedlinen and had to travel with her own set of black satin sheets. It was all so vapid, naive and simplistic. We were ordinary young people suddenly transformed into these objects of adulation; openly smoking like chimneys, which was considered sophisticated, but forbidden to be photographed holding a glass or – something I particularly resented – to express a political view.

Heads turned everywhere we went. It reached the point where I literally couldn't venture into the King's Road to buy a pound of potatoes without being mobbed. And I'm ashamed to say that for three or four years I basked in all the attention and revelled in my new-found celebrity.

We were never paid to make personal appearances, judge beauty contests, open shops, make speeches, be photographed or give an interview. It was all part of the job. And, of course, the more publicity you received, the greater the likelihood of being offered another job.

Despite the illusion of wealth fostered by first-class travel, red carpets and hired limousines, we certainly weren't rich. We were, however, carefree and comfortable. In the late forties, when a manual worker was lucky to earn £5, I was being paid £120 a week to play the lead in a film.

To help deal with the mountains of fan mail, I'd persuaded Arthur Goodbourne, a school friend from Leicester, to act as my secretary. He worked at our Chelsea cottage and I remember the only chair we could muster was too low for the desk so he perched on two telephone directories.

It was Arthur who founded the Richard Attenborough Fan Club and produced its quarterly magazine which, at one time, had over 1,500 subscribers. And, like idiots, Sheila and I would pose for these ghastly codded-up pictures of domestic bliss; cooing over the breakfast table, or mugging amazement beside our first car, a Citroën, when I finally passed my driving test.

I began to come to my senses after appearing in two dire films in succession. The first was *The Lost People*, prompting the respected critic C. A. Lejeune to describe my character as 'a sort of village idiot'. The second was *Boys in Brown* in which, together with Jack Warner, Jimmy Hanley and newcomer Dirk Bogarde, I played yet another cheeky cockney chappie, this time banged up in a borstal.

Then, out of the blue, the young impresario Peter Daubeny – later to initiate the ground-breaking World Theatre Season at the Aldwych

– gave me a wonderful opportunity to return to theatre. The play, known in America as *Home of the Brave* and here as *The Way Back*, had been written by the American playwright Arthur Laurents, who would go on to create *West Side Story*.

Although this, his first play, stood no chance of West End commercial success, it was a thoughtful work of real substance which had something important to say. I don't know why Peter chose me as the juvenile lead because physically I was all wrong for the part. I played a Jewish boy, persecuted by anti-Semites, opposite the wonderful Canadian actor, Arthur Hill.

After we opened at the Westminster, I remember Paul Robeson, one of my great heroes, came to a performance and praised it to the skies. That mattered, really mattered, to me. C. B. Cochrane and Gertie Lawrence also came and both wrote me the most extraordinary letters afterwards.

Suddenly I realised I no longer wanted to spend my life going from one lightweight film to another, hoping against hope to be stretched as an actor. Somehow – and I had no idea how this could be achieved at the time – I had to do work in which I could take some real pride.

I was not ashamed of my next film, *Morning Departure*, directed by Roy Baker, although the part I played was pretty much a reprise of *In Which We Serve*. Johnny Mills was the captain with the stiff upper lip and I was again the nervy stoker with the trembling lower lip; this time a claustrophobic trapped in a submarine.

Then came one of the lowest points of my entire acting career, a pointless thriller called *Hell is Sold Out* with Herbert Lom and Mai Zetterling which went out with the inane strapline, 'She invented a husband and he came to life'.

I went reluctantly with Theo to an opening in the provinces and, as the Austin Princess approached the local Odeon, the only person waiting outside was one elderly chap in a cap and muffler. Theo told the chauffeur to drive around for a while to allow more of a crowd to gather but on our return only half a dozen disinterested people were sheltering from the rain. As we drew up at the red carpet, a doddery old commissionaire rushed out of the foyer in his cap and braided uniform. Immediately, sizing up the situation, he flung out his arms as if to fend off a ravening horde. 'Stand back,' he quavered. 'Stand back for the star.' And in I went, sporting my red carnation, tail between my legs.

More eminently forgettable films followed. And then astonishingly, after years of hilarious but fruitless advice from our friends, Sheila was pregnant. With no outside space and no room for a pram in our narrow hallway, we started to house-hunt in earnest.

It was Sheila who found Old Friars. Although the house was massively bigger than we needed and way beyond our means, we fell in love with it immediately. Through the generosity of the owner who dropped the price by £1,000, together with some financial help from parents and friends, we scraped together enough to buy it. So, as Dave, newly released from his national service in the Navy and about to marry his fiancée, Jane, took over our lease in Chelsea, we moved out to Richmond. Not a moment too soon.

Michael John Attenborough was born on 13 February 1950 at a clinic in London. To my great regret, I was not allowed to be present, but throughout Sheila's labour a dozen loyal fans kept vigil on the pavement outside. We still exchange Christmas cards with those who are still alive: Pat, Doreen, David, Ray, Sheila, Susan, Jack, and Robert who lives in the States.

The mentor who finally helped me come to terms with fame and showed how it could be put to good use was Noël Coward. Despite his flamboyant lifestyle, Noël quietly put enormous amounts of his time and energy into the Actors' Orphanage of which he was president. This charity, which cared for boys and girls 'made destitute by the profession', derived most of its income from two annual events: the famous Theatrical Garden Party and *The Night of 100 Stars*.

Initially, Sheila and I were roped in to help with the garden party, an occasion, graced by the Duchess of Kent, which ranked on a social par with Wimbledon and Royal Ascot. I remember that Noël, always immaculately turned out in a cutaway morning coat and grey silk topper, was an extremely persuasive auctioneer and that I, who'd never cooked a meal in my life, put my name to a recipe for chicken risotto in a book called *Our Favourite Dishes*.

Noël subsequently co-opted me to help organise *The Night of 100 Stars* at the London Palladium. This was a massive enterprise which really did bring together over a hundred stars, many of the most celebrated travelling all the way from America at their own expense. This was how I came to know Danny Kaye who had just been appointed UNICEF's first Goodwill Ambassador for the world's children, a post he simply adored and to which he would devote the rest of his life.

Those who appeared with Danny on these occasions included Ivor Novello, Gertie Lawrence, Michael Redgrave, Douglas Fairbanks, Errol Flynn, Marlene Dietrich, Jessie Matthews, Jack Buchanan, Larry Olivier, Frankie Howerd and, of course, the 'Master', Noël himself.

They were each onstage for just a few minutes, and coordinating the whole evening, with no possibility of a complete run-through beforehand, was a logistical nightmare and, of course, the steepest possible learning curve for me.

Then, when Chancellor Stafford Cripps imposed a swingeing supertax of 105 per cent on the very rich, Noël decided to leave the country. His last act before decamping to Switzerland was to persuade me to become chairman of the Actors' Orphanage and, some years later, when Larry Olivier became very ill, to take over as president.

Although the orphanage no longer exists and the organisation is now called TACT, acronym for The Actors' Charitable Trust, Sheila and I still remain very involved. We still provide financial help for the profession's children – no longer in an institution but at home with their parents – and also support a retirement home for actors, with special provision for the various forms of dementia, at Denville Hall in Northwood, Middlesex.

Because I'm simply potty about kids, it's working for children's causes which gives me the most satisfaction. That was the reason I agreed so enthusiastically to join Harry Belafonte and Audrey Hepburn as one of UNICEF's new generation of Goodwill Ambassadors after Danny Kaye's death in 1987.

I also became very involved with the British charity which funds research into a cure for muscular dystrophy. In its most devastating and deadly form, this is a heart-rending genetic condition which mainly affects young boys. Although it was fifty years ago, I can still recall every detail of my first encounter with some of these dying children.

Confronted by the stark contrast with my own son, Michael, running around with his football when I returned to Old Friars, I became determined to give something back, to show my awareness of my own good fortune.

I have, I know, been one of the privileged creatures on this earth, not just slightly but hugely privileged.

DH— A *Chorus Line* was the last time Dick would work as a director for hire. The impetus for his next film, which he'd reluctantly put on hold while he was shooting in New York, was rooted in the parental mantra that it wasn't enough to stand on the sidelines and wring your hands about an injustice, you had to fight to put it right. And, rightly or wrongly, he has always believed that the mass entertainment medium of cinema not only can but should on occasion be used for this purpose.

The spark that eventually became *Cry Freedom* was ignited during the late 1940s. Newly demobbed from the RAF, Dick was appalled that some of the white South Africans who'd accompanied him on bombing raids – young men who'd voluntarily risked their lives to fight Hitler – had returned home afterwards to condone the new and equally vile form of legalised fascism, known as apartheid. His first opportunity to do something about it came in a letter he received in the year he got his knighthood.

In Europe the summer of 1976 had been extraordinary; months and months of brilliant sunshine with hardly a cloud in the sky. While I was holding the fort at Beaver Lodge, in the midst of ugly divorce proceedings, Dick was on location in Holland, filming *A Bridge Too Far*.

This was the story of the disastrous World War II battle of Arnhem. The film's producer and sole financier was Joseph E. Levine who, by giving a solemn undertaking that *Gandhi* would be their next joint project, had inveigled Dick into directing it. Through the crass but effective strategy of brandishing huge amounts of Joe's cash in Hollywood, the two of them had put together a phenomenal all-star cast on a favoured nations basis. Each was to receive $250,000 a week.

On the morning of Wednesday 16 June, Dick was preparing to shoot a scene which would bring together two very disparate personalities.

Dirk Bogarde was playing General 'Boy' Browning. The part was a mere cameo, seriously out of kilter with the star's carefully revised image as one of the leading lights of serious offbeat European cinema. It was, however, two years since his last acting assignment and, still in the throes of doing up his new home in the South of France while writing the first of his five autobiographies, Dirk had allowed himself to succumb to Dick's persuasion.

It was a decision he would bitterly regret. His characterisation would be ferociously attacked by Browning's author widow, Daphne du Maurier, and the resultant establishment fallout, much of it homophobic, wrongly convinced Dirk that the newly ennobled Sir Richard had deliberately contrived to scupper his own chance of a knighthood.

Playing Major General Urquhart, a more substantial role, requiring three weeks' work – and, to Dirk's fury, triple his own fee – was another tax exile, the macho Sean Connery. These two stars had never worked together and, unsurprisingly, did not exactly hit it off. With so many layers of barely concealed animosity, the atmosphere on set that morning was decidedly edgy and the scripted confrontation between Urquhart and Browning would take Dick a very long day to shoot.

Meanwhile, on that same June morning, six thousand miles away in South Africa, an explosive real-life encounter was brewing in the ghetto known as Soweto. There, hidden from the main southerly route out of affluent Johannesburg, a million impoverished black Africans were housed in serried rows of bleak brick huts, most without sanitation or electricity. And while Dick was smoothing the ruffled feathers of his tetchy stars in verdant Apeldoorn, a twelve-year-old boy was slipping out of one of those huts in search of adventure.

Elsewhere in the township, after three months of argument and boycott, twenty thousand angry secondary school pupils had gathered to demand a better education. In particular, they were protesting a new apartheid law that all black children had to be taught in Afrikaans, the language of their oppressors and one they barely understood.

Dressed in shorts, sneakers and his primary school sweater – it was a chilly winter morning on the Highveld – the twelve-year-old made his way towards Orlando Stadium, drawn by the sound of stamping feet and chanting. He was looking for his elder sister, somewhere in the crowd. Approaching her school, Phefeni Senior Secondary, he finally caught up with the mass of teenage marchers, jeering and whistling as they brandished their flimsy placards. They'd been stopped in their tracks by a solid wall of armoured trucks, dog handlers and white police armed with rifles.

Some of the youngsters were singing the Xhosa anthem, *Nkosi Sikelel' iAfrika* – 'God Bless Africa' – while others threw stones. Suddenly, a single shot rang out and they scattered screaming in all directions. The kid caught a glimpse of his sister but that first shot was followed by a volley of rifle fire and she'd ducked down out of sight. Desperately, he also tried to find a hiding place but it was too late – a police bullet found him, killed him and propelled him into history. His name was Hector Pietersen.

The teenager in dungarees who dashed to scoop up Hector's body and rush it to a clinic was Mbuyisa Makhubo. The traumatised girl who ran alongside, hand thrown up in horror, was Hector's sister, Antonette. The local news photographer who captured this shocking image was Sam Nzima.

Dick knew nothing of this as he wrapped up his day's shooting in Holland. But by the following morning, Nzima's picture was appearing all over the world and the murder of this unknown kid – one among several hundred killed that day – was mobilising international opinion as never before. A month later in New York, the UN would declare apartheid a crime against humanity.

On his return from Holland, Dick placed a framed copy of the iconic photograph on his office bookshelf where he could see it while he worked. This was an image he would eventually recreate and animate, down to the very last detail, in *Cry Freedom*.

The letter he received just a few weeks later contained a plea from a friend of his parents: would Sir Richard be willing to use his clout as a celebrity to help bring black children out of the South African townships and educate them at a new school, formed in defiance of apartheid across the border in Swaziland?

The school was the creation of an extraordinary Englishman, Michael Stern. This committed Christian had emigrated to South Africa to become headmaster of a high school for black boys. When the authorities closed it down, reclassifying the area as white, Stern had found donors prepared to fund a new boarding school where pupils of every colour, nationality and religion could live and learn together. The site was donated by a sympathetic Irishman who asked only that the new establishment should bear the name of his birthplace.

From these small beginnings grew the legendary Waterford-Kamhlaba where the offspring of world leaders and the wealthy still live and learn alongside disadvantaged African children. Nelson Mandela's daughters, Zeni and Zindzi, were taught there while their father was serving life imprisonment with hard labour on Robben Island.

Since 1976, as chairman of Waterford's United Kingdom Trustees, Dick has continued to fund-raise for the school and, through their own charitable trust, he and Sheila have financed the education of more than twenty black African children. In their late seventies, they went on to 'adopt' one of them, a fatherless Swazi teenager whose mother was dying of Aids.

RA— I first encountered Donald Woods on a sunny Sunday in the summer of 1982. Sheila and I were hurrying to a late lunch after the cast and crew screening of *Gandhi* at the Odeon Leicester Square, when I found myself buttonholed by a man I barely remembered. He proved to be Norman Spencer, who, forty years earlier, had worked on *In Which We Serve* as a very young third assistant director.

Now a producer, Norman was intent on introducing me to his companion, a grey-haired, bespectacled South African who towered over both of us. After we'd shaken hands, this Donald Woods handed me a book he'd written, saying it was about the dead black South African activist, Steve Biko, and he was trying to get a film made about him. I tucked the slim volume under my arm, saying, somewhat facilely, I would read it and get back to him.

At that point, my knowledge of Biko was minimal. I knew he was the founder of some kind of liberation movement, had read reports of his death in police custody and was aware of accusations of a cover-up on the part of the South African authorities. Only later did I discover that Donald Woods was the chief accuser and the book he'd handed me contained the evidence that Steve had been murdered.

I have to admit it remained unread for nearly a year. This was the year I spent travelling the world in order to promote *Gandhi*.

Then came the row about the Johannesburg premiere on our return from the Oscars. Angry that I'd only learned it was to be a segregated event from the assembled press at Heathrow and sickened by the very idea that black and white South Africans were not allowed to sit in the same cinema without a 'special dispensation', I finally sat down and read *Biko* from cover to cover. It was an amazing piece of work; written in secret, smuggled out of South Africa and published after a penniless Donald, his wife and five kids had been granted refugee status in Britain.

This much I learned when I consulted our mutual friend, Michael Stern, the headmaster-founder of Waterford-Kamhlaba school. If I was contemplating a film about apartheid, Michael said, I really ought to read Donald's more recent autobiography, *Asking for Trouble*. He would get him to send me a copy.

It could not have arrived at a more opportune moment. Sheila and I try to spend the whole month of August at our house in the South of France. Set among olive groves in the hills behind Cannes, it's very simple and rustic, with a telephone number known only to family and close friends; a place to contemplate, listen to music, go blissfully unrecognised and, on this occasion, to read.

In *Asking for Trouble*, Donald writes nostalgically of a childhood spent at a remote trading post in the Transkei, playing with children of the Bonvana tribe and conversing with them in fluent Xhosa. During those years, he later realised with chagrin, he'd also absorbed from his parents the belief that every black African was his inferior.

Then, as a teenage law student, he'd started to question this supposed superiority, going through a period of what he described as 'inner turmoil', before switching careers to take up journalism. In early middle age, as the affluent and respected editor of the *East London Daily Dispatch*, Donald had begun to attack the strong-arm tactics employed by the white minority government against the black majority under the cloak of what was euphemistically known as 'the system'. Priding himself on his even-handedness, he'd also used his editorials to decry the increasingly militant Black Consciousness Movement, headed by a young firebrand named Bantu Stephen Biko.

The South African government had responded with barely veiled threats and ministerial libels. Donald had fought the ministers through the courts and won, flamboyantly splurging the resultant damages on a grand piano and swimming pool.

Biko, however, had responded very differently, challenging the editor to meet him to debate their differences, man to man. Intrigued and scenting a good story, because Biko was a 'banned person' living under house arrest, Donald had agreed.

To his initial discomfort, Steve had proved more than his intellectual equal; able to question, shake and ultimately demolish many of his most sincerely held beliefs. And, although the younger man scorned white liberals who attached themselves to the black cause, he and Donald had forged an unlikely friendship.

Then, four years later, Steve had disappeared, picked up by BOSS, the South African Bureau of State Security. As Donald was to discover, he'd been held in solitary confinement for a month and brutally beaten before being driven hundreds of miles, naked and manacled, to Pretoria where he'd died alone in a cell.

When Steve's wife, Ntsiki, went to identify his body, the editor and one of his photographers had accompanied her to the morgue and covertly photographed his fatal injuries. Within days, the Minister of Justice was announcing that the death was self-inflicted due to a 'hunger strike' and an outraged Donald, possessing clear evidence to the contrary, had started to demand, and vociferously kept on demanding, an inquest.

This time, he'd pushed the apartheid regime too far and he in turn was declared a banned person. The family home was bugged and kept under day and night surveillance and, like Steve before him, Donald was forbidden to be with more than one person at any time, an edict which cruelly included his wife, Wendy, and all five of their young children. He was also effectively deprived of his living and gagged; nothing he said or wrote could be published in any form.

Initially, Donald had treated this as a cat-and-mouse game, taking an almost childish pleasure in staging provocative conversations for hidden microphones and finding amusing hiding places for the manuscript he was secretly writing. But when a small acid-impregnated T-shirt was sent through the post, badly burning Donald and Wendy's six-year-old daughter, this unlikely hero decided he and his whole family had to get out of South Africa.

For reasons that were not yet clear to me, in *Asking for Trouble* Donald had chosen to portray his own escape, involving disguise and a series of extremely close shaves, as a jolly jape undertaken by a naive bungler. Having managed to cross the border into Lesoto, he was joined by his wife and children. From there the family had made their way to London and embarked on a penniless exile in Surbiton.

The sun was beating down on Provence and the cicadas screeching in the olive grove outside as I read the closing pages of *Asking for Trouble* and picked up the telephone . . .

In his third book, *Filming with Attenborough*, Donald would write:

It was precisely at 3:32 pm on August 26th 1983 that I heard by phone from Sir Richard that he was interested. He had some further travelling, reading and research to do himself, after which he would propose a meeting for further discussion about the possibilities. I did a quick caper round the kitchen table . . .

On my return to Old Friars after the holiday, I had a meeting with Donald and Norman Spencer who'd been trying to help him get a film made about Steve. I told them that, in my view, such a film should not be about Steve alone, but about Steve and Donald. What I found fascinating was the story of how they'd formed a real friendship across the racial divide and how Donald had chosen to jeopardise everything he held dear – family, career, home, even his own life – to reveal the truth about Steve's death. If he was prepared to let me tell this story, I would do everything in my power to bring it to the screen.

They asked for some time alone in the garden and when they came back, twenty minutes later, agreed to my proposal. An elated Donald asked: 'What happens now?'

This, I said, was the hard part; I had to find the money.

However, just for once, raising production funding proved ridiculously easy.

Just a fortnight later, I'd been invited to attend a ceremony at which the Queen was to unveil a statute of Earl Mountbatten on Horse Guards Parade. Also present on that occasion was Lord Louis' son-in-law, my friend the film producer, Lord Brabourne. I was saddened to hear that John's wife, Patricia, who'd never fully recovered from the injuries caused by the IRA bomb which had killed her father and one of their sons, was too ill to attend.

'Actually, Dickie,' said John, 'she was going to ask you the most monumental favour.'

'Tell me. Anything.'

The unlikely favour, it emerged, entailed representing the Countess at another formal ceremony, this time a dinner in Calgary, where she was Colonel-in-Chief of a regiment called Princess Patricia's Canadian Light Infantry.

I was devoted to John's wife and, ten days later, was on my way to Calgary via Los Angeles. It was while I was waiting to board my onward flight that I happened to bump into Frank Price, head of Columbia Pictures, and the man who'd so enthusiastically acquired worldwide distribution rights in *Gandhi*.

Frank, it emerged, had just had a bust-up with the company's owners, Coca-Cola, and was about to take up the equivalent post at Universal where he'd be setting up his own slate of new productions. Making the most of this golden opportunity, I proceeded to pitch the story of Donald Woods and Steve Biko. To my utter amazement and joy, Frank immediately offered to finance it.

DH— Having engaged Donald Woods and his wife, Wendy, as the film's consultants, Dick was now itching to start work on *Cry Freedom*. But his screenwriter of choice, Jack Briley – who'd so brilliantly scripted *Gandhi* – would be tied up for many months adapting James Clavell's epic novel, *Tai-Pan*, for De Laurentiis.

With Marti Baum pressing him to direct *A Chorus Line*, Dick elected to defer any decision until after he'd made an initial reconnaissance trip to South Africa. Never having been there, he felt it vital to witness the impact of apartheid at first hand and, with his director's eye, to get a feel for light, architecture and landscape. He also wanted to gauge public opinion, talk to campaigners and activists and, since *Cry Freedom* would inevitably depict real people, to discover if they would consent to be portrayed in the film.

There was also a nagging concern he needed to allay. This was the disquieting disparity between Donald's jokey, laid-back personality and the steely resolve, allied with phenomenal courage, which were such an important element in the story.

Donald and Wendy's first task as consultants was to draw up a list of everyone they believed Dick ought to meet. Having written down every name that came to mind, they presented him with the result, foolishly declaring it would be utterly impossible for him to see even half these people – some of them highly controversial – within the allotted fortnight.

'Impossible' being a red rag to the bullish Dick, he immediately declared his intention of meeting every single one of them. Impressed but daunted, the Woodses retreated to Surbiton to put together the required itinerary.

There, the couple, who had received death threats even in exile, faced up to the difficulties of the proposed journey. Dick and Sheila were to travel over two thousand miles through the Transvaal, Orange Free State, Natal, Transkei, Western and Eastern Capes, talking about a disgraced editor and the dead leader of a proscribed militant movement while consorting with many declared enemies of the state. Moreover, having blithely pooh-poohed the Woodses' warnings about South Africa's secret police, Dick seemed to believe he could accomplish all this without being recognised.

After some thought, Donald picked up the phone and dialled a familiar number in his previous home town of East London. When the call was answered, aware the line might well be tapped, he launched into a string of obscenities in the strange tribal language of his Transkei childhood. Recognising his voice, the white man at the other end of the line responded in the same clicking Xhosa.

The man was Don Card, Donald's staunch friend for nearly thirty years. Now active in anti-apartheid politics, Card had once been a detective with BOSS, the same ruthless organisation which had arrested and bludgeoned Steve Biko to death and later sent the acid impregnated T-shirt to six-year-old Mary Woods.

'Listen, you old so-and-so,' Donald continued in Xhosa, 'a good friend of mine and his wife are flying out for a holiday. Someone will ring to let you know when they're coming. I want you to put them up, show them around and take *very good care of them*. Understand?'

Card understood perfectly. He was later to say: 'I had no idea who the people were but that didn't worry me because I trusted Donald implicitly.'

Woods went on to set up a whole series of meetings through further cryptic phone calls. Some were arranged at one remove through friends of friends, others even more circuitously via a chain of trusted journalists.

Having toyed with the idea of persuading him to adopt some form of disguise, Donald had by now convinced himself that, if he travelled mostly by car, Dick stood a good chance of remaining incognito. The biggest problem was his actual entry into South Africa when he would, of course, be required to present his passport.

RA— It was Donald's idea that we should travel with only two instead of the usual five cases between us. Sheila is a meticulous packer who spends days choosing and folding every garment, using oceans of tissue paper. I rarely pack until the morning of a flight and get the whole job done, usually with dire results, in under half an hour.

Donald had also decreed that our first destination should be Waterford-Kamhlaba school in the tiny landlocked kingdom of Swaziland. Although the most direct route was via Johannesburg, he insisted we fly instead to Nairobi in Kenya where we would transfer to a short-haul flight which would take us on to the tiny airport of Manzini.

The last leg of this journey was not at all comfortable. The small plane was full of children returning to school after the Christmas break. It bucked around the sky, buffeted by strong winds, until we finally made a precarious landing in the middle of a ferocious thunderstorm.

Tired and bedraggled, Sheila and I made our way across the tarmac to be greeted by Athol Jennings, Waterford's new headmaster, and one of the school's co-founders, Christopher Newton-Thompson. Christopher, a South African businessman who would become a close friend, was an extraordinary character. He'd won an MC in Italy during the war, played cricket for Cambridge and rugby for England and, on his return to Cape Town, had become one of apartheid's most vociferous white opponents.

After we had driven for an hour through a torrential downpour, the car reached the top of a hill where I had my very first sight of Waterford: a collection of modern buildings blending seamlessly into the contours of a rocky outcrop. There, we were introduced to Christopher's wife, Philippa, who was to take us into Soweto, and the geography master, Dick Eyeington, and his wife, Enid, who would later be murdered together while working for children in Somalia.

The Eyeingtons became our close friends and were the most intrepid and caring couple Sheila and I have ever encountered.

Waterford was everything I'd hoped and more. It had recently become affiliated with United World Colleges, an international education network based on the work of Kurt Hahn and, as we saw during our all too brief tour the following morning, it was, as Michael Stern had intended, a truly multiracial community.

When the time came to leave that afternoon, the Newton-Thompsons' waterlogged Mercedes refused to start. So, wearing borrowed waders, the four of us edged our way across the raging torrent at the bottom of the hill to reach a hire car on the other side. In old-fashioned safari fashion, we were followed by a column of half-naked Swazi boys balancing our luggage on their heads.

Night had fallen by the time we reached the little used road border with South Africa which Donald had chosen as our point of entry. The frontier proved to be two huts on either side of a line in the road and, as predicted, it was deserted. However, after the Swazis had blithely waved us through, a uniformed South African stepped forward with raised hand to direct us into the second hut.

Christopher and Philippa went to the counter first and the official behind it stifled a yawn as he flipped disinterestedly through their passports, handing them back immediately. He took his time as he looked through ours, particularly, it seemed to me, when he came to the page bearing my photograph. Then, muttering something in Afrikaans, he disappeared into a back room.

My memory – perhaps coloured by what came afterwards – is that Sheila whispered, 'They've rumbled us,' but she maintains it didn't even occur to her. Either way, the official soon emerged to give us back our passports and indicate with a jerk of his head that we were all free to go.

Dawn was breaking by the time we'd driven two hundred miles to the Newton-Thompsons' spacious home on the outskirts of Johannesburg. This was our first taste of the seductive, laid-back luxury lifestyle enjoyed by so many of the white population.

After a short rest, we were on the road again. I wanted to see Tolstoy Farm, close to the town of Lenasia, where the young Gandhi had established his first ashram in the early 1900s and which we'd recreated in India, using archive photographs. I was sad to see that the actual place had fallen into disrepair, although there were moves afoot to restore it.

That afternoon, we went on to meet our first 'banned' person. This was the extraordinary cleric, Beyers Naudé.

Naudé, then seventy-nine, was a former minister of the Dutch Reformed Church who'd embraced and preached apartheid until a single bloody event altered the course of his life. This was the infamous 1960 Sharpeville massacre when government troops had shot sixty-nine black demonstrators and wounded many more. Although destined for high office, a horrified Beyers had quit his own Church to form the ecumenical Christian Institute through which he'd provided covert but invaluable support to the black resistance movement.

Like Donald, Beyers had been made a banned person following the death of Steve Biko. When we met this calm and forgiving man, he'd been living under this punitive form of house arrest for six years.

As an agnostic, I have known very few men of the cloth. But, with the notable exception of Nelson Mandela, of all the extraordinary people I've encountered during my life, the Church leaders I was privileged to meet through *Cry Freedom* – Beyers Naudé, Trevor Huddlestone, Desmond Tutu and David Shepherd – were, without doubt, by far the most inspiring.

That evening, the Newton-Thompsons introduced us to the daughter of the gold and diamond multimillionaire who'd helped to found Waterford. Mary Oppenheimer lived at Brenthurst, a luxurious mansion surrounded by forty-five acres of magnificent gardens, tended by forty-five black gardeners. The contrast with our next destination couldn't have been greater.

The following morning Philippa took us see rows and rows of shanty dwellings stretching as far as the eye could see: Soweto. Visually, it was incredibly bleak and depressing, but the people we met, particularly the women in the crèches Philippa had established, were not sullen or downtrodden as I'd expected, but wonderfully upbeat and welcoming.

Before leaving the township, we drove to Phefeni Senior Secondary School and, recalling the historic photograph on my office bookshelf, I was able to locate the exact spot where it had been taken. We stood there in silence, thinking of Hector Pietersen.

The following day, Sheila and I flew on to Cape Town. Since this was an internal flight and no passports were needed, I kept my hat on and my head down and went unrecognised. On landing, we were met by Tony Hurd, editor of the *Cape Times*, and Jordan Tanner of the US

Information Agency, two of Donald's journalist chums who'd helped to organise our trip.

It was Jordan who took us that same evening to a hellish place I will never forget. Like all South African cities, Cape Town depended on cheap black labour. This was supplied by hungry people who'd flooded in from the surrounding countryside and set up home – if you could call it that – under corrugated iron, plastic sheeting, cardboard, anything they could scavenge, on the wasteland surrounding Cape Flats.

At the time of our visit, the government had started to raze these pitiful shanty towns. Anyone without a work permit, which included most of the women, was being forcibly removed and sent to live more than seven hundred miles away in one of the arid 'tribal reserves' known as Bantustans. Those allowed to remain were to be herded into a specially created township named cynically Khayelitsha or 'new home'.

It was dusk when Jordan drove us to the site. Bulldozers were still at work under floodlights in an area covering eighteen square miles. Incongruously, right in the middle – a beacon of consumerism in a sea of desolation – was the biggest, brashest Coca-Cola sign I'd ever seen. But what really sent shivers down my spine was the high concrete and barbed-wire fence which encircled the whole compound. I'd seen others just like it in newsreel footage of liberated concentration camps at the end of the war. And here it was again, less than forty years later, hidden away on the outskirts of one of the most beautiful cities on earth.

On the drive back, I posed a naive question. Why, I asked Jordan, did the brand-new highway, ending at the gates of Khayelitsha, need to be four lanes wide? What kind of vehicles was it expected to take? He responded with the single chilling word, 'Tanks.'

Sheila and I had dinner that night at the home of the most respected and reviled white woman in the whole of South Africa. The legendary Helen Suzman was then in her mid-sixties. Between 1959 and 1974, she'd been a lone voice in the wilderness; the only woman member of the South African parliament and the only elected politician to oppose, constantly and vociferously, every aspect of apartheid. A previous prime minister, John Vorster, had once asked her in exasperation, 'Where are you heading? What are you and your Communist friends trying to do to South Africa?' And Helen had replied, 'We're trying to stop you.'

Knowing she had fought to improve conditions for political prisoners, we asked Helen about Nelson Mandela, recently transferred from the infamous Robben Island to another prison on the mainland. How had eighteen years of hard labour affected him? She said they'd made him into the strongest person – physically, morally, intellectually – she'd ever encountered. Would he ever be released? She said she desperately needed to believe he would, adding ruefully: 'But almost certainly not in my lifetime.'

We also talked about Steve Biko. Was it true that after his death in custody Helen had warned the Justice Minister: 'The world is not going to forget the Biko affair and we will not forget it either'? And did he actually have the gall to reply: 'His death leaves me cold'?

When she confirmed the conversation, I asked her permission to include it in the film and this she gave me. She also kindly agreed that I could depict her attending Steve's funeral as the only white person who'd been invited to take part in the service.

The following day, Tony Hurd drove us through beautiful wine country to Stellenbosch. There, in a secret location, we met Peter Jones, co-founder of the all-black South African Students' Organisation, who'd been with Steve Biko on the night of his arrest. I asked Peter to describe what had happened. He said he'd driven Steve way outside his banning zone to attend an important meeting to discuss the unification of all the disparate black liberation groups, a move the government dreaded. On the way back, Peter had rounded a bend and driven straight into a police roadblock. He and Steve were taken to a local jail, summarily charged under the Terrorism Act and moved to the prison at Port Elizabeth where they were placed in separate cells.

Peter had never seen Steve again. He described how he himself was stripped, beaten with fists and metal pipes, kicked and humiliated during interrogation. This continued until, a year and a half later, still without access to a lawyer or any form of trial, he was suddenly released. Before we parted, Peter gave me his permission to depict him in the film.

So far, all our meetings in South Africa had taken place away from the public gaze. But on our return from Stellenbosch, we'd been invited to dine with Helen Suzman's colleague in the Progressive Federal Party, Frederik van Zyl Slabbert, parliamentary leader of the opposition.

Zyl had booked a table at one of Cape Town's best-known restaurants. He proved to be an excellent host and the meal was very convivial.

The only depressing note came when I again asked about the pace of change. He'd begun to doubt, Zyl said, that the democratic process would ever solve South Africa's problems. The whites were too entrenched in their racism and too scared even to contemplate any form of dialogue with the black majority leaders. Less than eighteen months later, having resigned from parliament, he would set up the first such dialogue in distant Senegal.

Early the following morning we were due to fly to Donald Woods' former home town of East London. As arranged, Tony Hurd had phoned ahead to advise Don Card that the couple his friend had told him about were on their way. No names were mentioned; Don was to recognise us by the clothes we'd be wearing.

At our Cape Town hotel, when Sheila and I were packed and ready to go, I phoned down to the concierge and asked if someone could come and collect our luggage. It was as I was tipping the departing bellboy that I spotted it in the corridor. Lying on the floor outside the room opposite, was an Afrikaans newspaper with the word ATTENBOROUGH screaming at me from the front-page headline. Knowing I wouldn't understand a word of the accompanying story, I scooped it up and took it with me.

During the flight to East London, I scoured all the English-language dailies; nothing. On our arrival, Don Card and his lovely wife, Hetty, were visibly taken aback as they greeted us. As soon as we were in the privacy of his car, Don said he'd recognised me immediately.

I handed him the Afrikaans newspaper and asked him to translate the story. It said Sheila and I had been seen dining with a well-known politician and went on to speculate, wholly inaccurately, about the reason for our visit.

I have to admit I was shaken. It was nearly a decade since I'd appeared on the screen in any meaningful role and I'd sincerely believed I'd be able to travel around South Africa without attracting any attention.

Fortuitously, our next destination was the remote and sparsely populated Wild Coast where Donald's sister, Joan, had a holiday home. We stayed with her for three days, talking about Donald, beachcombing, drinking sensational wine.

By the time we left, any doubts I'd harboured about Donald had been well and truly dispelled. Yes, his family and close friends regarded him as a golf-mad prankster who made light of everything, but there was no doubting his sincerity, his probity or the depth of his loyalty to Steve Biko.

Both Beyers Naudé and Helen Suzman had praised Donald's courage; Tony Hurd and Jordan Tanner had vouched for his journalistic integrity; and Don Card, it emerged, had willingly risked his own life to help him escape. But it was Donald's sister, not herself overtly anti-apartheid, who finally made me understand the magnitude of her brother's moral journey.

Having inherited my own code of behaviour from my parents, I'd never had cause to doubt it and had always strived, as best I could, to uphold their principles. Donald, on the other hand, had not only faced up to the realisation that his parents' racism was inherently immoral, but had jeopardised everything he held dear to bring it to an end.

Back in East London, Don Card sat me down and delivered a lecture. As a former BOSS detective, he was warning that the people I was going on to meet would be watched round the clock and their homes would almost certainly contain hidden microphones. This meant I had to be very careful indeed because the security police were quite capable of arresting me on some trumped-up charge. Worst-case scenario, Sheila and I could simply disappear.

Given his experience and the gravity of his manner, I knew Don was not exaggerating. He ended by assuring me he'd do everything he could to help if we did find ourselves in difficulties and made me promise to check in with him every day by telephone until we left the country.

Next morning, Don handed us over to the next person in Donald's chain of contacts. This was Rob Amato, a legal columnist for the *Sunday Independent*. Following instructions, Rob drove us to a hotel near King William's Town, escorting us in through the front entrance and straight out again through the back to where another car was waiting.

The new driver – we never knew his name – first took us to a deserted stretch of road. There, he drew up briefly beside a parked car, pausing just long enough for us to see and be seen by the two black ladies sitting in the back, before he pulled away.

After a long drive we reached another hotel, this time large and very busy. I don't remember its name but retain an impression of a casino and people gambling. There, in a public lounge, we finally came face to face with the women in the other car: Steve's wife, Ntsiki, and elderly mother, Nokuzola Biko.

Ntsiki and Steve were born in the same year which made her thirty-eight at the time of our meeting. I remember a shy, dignified and quietly spoken woman. I knew she'd given Steve two sons and had worked as a domestic in an Anglican mission to keep the family afloat financially after he was banned.

Steve's mother, also a devout Christian, was then in her mid-sixties. Her husband had died when Steve was four and she'd brought up three children single handed, working as a domestic and then as a hospital cook. Now, she, Ntsiki and the two little boys, Nkosinathi and Samora, all lived together in Ginsberg, a black township on the outskirts of King William's Town.

The four of us sat at a small round table as I talked about the film. Both women listened intently. I told them this would not be Steve's biography. That was a film which should and hopefully would eventually be made by black South Africans. As a white man, what I wanted to do was open the eyes of other white people all over the world to the terrible injustices of apartheid. I also hoped, by depicting the friendship between Steve and Donald Woods, to show that change was possible. Most important of all as far as they were concerned, I wanted to demonstrate what was known about Steve's death in the hope that this might bring his killers to justice.

After I'd finished, the two women spoke to each other in a language I didn't understand and then, reverting to English, asked if they might have some time alone.

Sheila and I retreated to another table out of earshot and waited until Ntsiki beckoned us back. 'Ma-Biko and I would like you to make your film,' she said formally. 'You came all this way to ask our permission and for that we thank you. We ask only one thing.'

I waited to hear what it was. This time they spoke in unison: 'Make it strong.'

Two days later, we flew into Bloemfontein. My heart sank as we entered the airport concourse to be greeted by a barrage of flashbulbs and a crowd of reporters, all shouting questions. Thankfully, Don Card had arranged for the manager of our hotel to meet us and he was able to hustle Sheila and me into a waiting car which immediately sped away, taking us into the hotel's underground garage where there was a lift which allowed us to go straight up to our room.

Feeling somewhat besieged, with all incoming phone calls blocked by the switchboard, we had a room-service dinner followed by an early night to prepare for the long drive ahead. Our next destination was the remote town of Brandfort and this time we were to drive ourselves.

The following morning, still unseen, we took the lift down to the garage where a hire car was waiting, fuelled up and provided with a map. Like an idiot, I hadn't thought to bring my driving licence, so Sheila took the wheel. During the whole of the journey, I kept a weather eye on the rear-view mirror, making sure no one was following.

Brandfort was in sheep country and at mid-morning on a weekday we found it hot, dusty and deserted. The town itself was designated whites only and here, for the first time, I saw shops with separate entrances for the two races. Black people were obliged to live some distance away in the township of Majwemasweu.

Following our written instructions, Sheila pulled into a large and virtually empty parking area which boasted a single public telephone kiosk. Being early for our rendezvous, we settled down to wait. We didn't have to wait long.

Suddenly, a black car containing two white men in dark suits and glasses pulled in on the opposite side of the parking area. This was followed by another car, exactly the same, which stopped at right angles to the first. Then came a third, containing two more men, which took up the remaining position, effectively boxing us in.

No one got out of the cars and, thoroughly spooked, we remained in ours. Within minutes, a Volkswagen van arrived. A black woman I can only describe as an empress clad in purple robes descended from it and made her stately way to the exact centre of the car park where she stood immobile in the blazing sun. We recognised her immediately. This was Winnie Mandela, wife of the imprisoned Nelson, then known as Mother of the Nation.

We knew that, as a banned person, Winnie was only ever allowed to be with one person, so Sheila remained in our car while I went to greet her. Up close, this woman of nearly fifty still had the complexion of a young girl. She was also engagingly light-hearted, with no sign of the violent and sadistic streak – triggered, I believe, by the cruelty inflicted on her during the seventeen months she spent in solitary confinement – which would eventually bring about her downfall.

I thanked her for coming and, indicating the three black cars, asked if there was somewhere we could talk.

Winnie said we were welcome to visit her home but warned that a crew from the state-run South African Broadcasting Corporation was waiting outside. They had already filmed her and told her they knew we were coming. When I was back in our car, Sheila went to greet Winnie, returning to tell me we were on our way to the township. The Volkswagen led, we followed and the three black cars followed us.

Winnie's house – I'd call it a hut – was a small brick-built box with a corrugated roof, a patch of vegetation and an outside tap. The television crew, armed with a single camera and microphone, was waiting outside. The interviewer told me Mrs Mandela had already spoken to him and he hoped I would do the same. I said I would consider it but wanted to spend some time with her first.

While Sheila sat in a patch of shade outside, Winnie showed me into a room – I think there were three in all – about ten feet square. It was comfortably if somewhat over-furnished, with pictures of Nelson and her two daughters, Zeni and Zindzi, taking pride of place.

We talked for a while about the girls, Winnie telling me how difficult it had been when they were younger to find any school that would accept the children of a convicted 'terrorist'. She was grateful for the years they'd been able to spend at Waterford-Kamhlaba.

I mentioned the shop I'd seen with separate black and white entrances. Winnie laughed, saying she'd made a point of using the white door and had been arrested and fined for doing so.

Why, I asked, had the government chosen to send her to Brandfort? She had no idea, except that it was completely cut off from everything and everyone she knew. The telephone kiosk in the town car park was her only means of communication and the line was, of course, tapped by 'the system'. She'd been here, under house arrest, for almost seven years since the police raided her Soweto home at dawn and spirited her and her belongings away. She laughed again, remembering how, when she arrived, her furniture wouldn't fit in and much of it had to be stored at the local police station.

We moved on to the film. When I'd outlined the story and what I hoped to achieve, Winnie asked how soon I would make it. 'If all goes according to plan,' I said, 'shooting will start in October.'

Aware that Sheila was still sitting alone outside, I asked if we might exchange places. 'The SABC are waiting,' Winnie reminded me. 'Will you talk to them?'

I considered. They'd already filmed me and, as Winnie had already given them an interview, it seemed churlish to refuse. She led the way out of the house and paused on the doorstep for me to catch up. Incorrigibly tactile, I took her hand as we walked over to Sheila. Then, while the two women retreated inside, I gave the man from SABC the most bland interview of my life.

The drive back to Bloemfontein was uneventful. We slept well that night and the following afternoon flew unrecognised to Johannesburg to be met by yet another of Donald's friends, a man whose kindness I will never forget. This was Robert Gosende, then working for the US Information Agency and later President Clinton's ambassador and special envoy to Somalia.

On the drive to his house in Pretoria, Bob told us he wanted to get back in time for the SABC evening news. They'd been trailing pictures of me and Winnie all day, promising sensational revelations about our meeting. I brushed it off, telling Bob what I'd said during the interview: nothing, absolutely nothing sensational, just plain boring.

But boring it wasn't. The white anchorman's name, I remember, was Schwartz. He gave a rundown of my film credentials over a shot of me and Winnie entering her house. A little of my uninformative interview followed. Then Mr Schwartz posed a rhetorical question: what was I *really* doing in South Africa?

This he proceeded to answer with a whole series of preposterous and inflammatory accusations. I'd come as a Communist agitator, he said, financed by Moscow to bring about armed insurrection. I'd even informed Mrs Mandela, the banned wife of a terrorist, now serving life imprisonment, when the revolution was due to begin. This is what I'd told her. And here, over a long shot of the hut, they'd superimposed my voice saying, 'If all goes according to plan, shooting will start in October.'

They then showed me and Winnie leaving her hut, hand in hand. Mr Schwartz ranted on some more and ended by demanding the authorities take immediate action. I must be thrown out of the country and never allowed to return.

When Bob Gosende turned off the television, I started to explode with apoplectic steam. He stopped me in mid-flow, putting a finger to his lips and jerking his head in the direction of the French windows leading onto the garden.

My head was reeling. This was an accredited diplomat, representing the American State Department, and he was telling me his house was bugged. And I'd just seen a totally rigged piece of reportage being broadcast to the whole of South Africa by the state television service. This in a country where children were shot, freedom fighters secretly beaten to death, men and women herded into latter-day concentration camps.

While we strolled in his garden, Bob explained how I'd been duped. There was no way the SABC could have broadcast their interview with Winnie. As a banned person, nothing she said could be published in any form. And if the security police wanted to arrest me, they certainly had cause: I'd been filmed touching her – holding her hand – which was also forbidden. He asked how close the television team had been to the house while we were inside.

I told him they'd been about twenty feet away; Sheila had been far closer. That worried Bob. It almost certainly meant, he said, that my voice had been picked up by microphones planted in Winnie's home. And that meant . . .

The enormity of it suddenly dawned on me. '. . . It was the police who supplied the recording of what I said inside.'

Bob was of the opinion that Sheila and I ought to leave the country now, tonight, if there was a flight available. But I had one more important person to see. And, because I was buggered if I was going to let people like Mr Schwartz determine what I did or didn't do, I stubbornly refused to accept Bob's excellent advice.

Our guide the following day was Diana Taylor, Donald's former secretary. There wasn't a single sinister black car in sight as she took us to the subtropical town of Tzaneen, close to the great Limpopo River, where we were to lunch with Steve Biko's remarkable partner and closest associate, Mamphela Ramphele.

This feminist powerhouse of a woman was one of the few black female doctors in the whole of South Africa. She and Steve had met as students when both had become involved in anti-apartheid activism and, with others, founded the Black Consciousness Movement, contemporary of the 'black is beautiful' campaign in America.

Both passionate in their beliefs and ferociously intelligent, they'd fallen in love and then drifted apart. Mamphela had then entered into a short-lived marriage with someone else and, by the time it ended, Steve was married to Ntsiki.

Mamphela and Steve came together again after he was banned and she went to live near him in King William's Town, taking over part of his political role and setting up her own clinic to serve the local black community. Shortly after Steve's death, Mamphela herself had been banned and sent to live here, in a township just outside Tzaneen, where she was now running another community health programme.

Mamphela had not come to meet us alone. The handsome child sitting on her lap was the third son Steve had never lived to see. This was six-year-old Hlumelo, meaning, his mother told us, 'the shoot that sprouts from the dead tree'.

Again I described the film I intended to make. Again I asked permission to depict my listener on the screen. Mamphela did not give this readily because she did not wish to upset Ntsiki. Neither did she want the important work that she and Steve had done together to be dismissed as some lightweight tale of star-crossed lovers.

I said that was not my intention and promised she would have an opportunity to see the part of the script in which she appeared before I started filming. On that we shook hands.

Mamphela's banning order was lifted a few months later. The last time I saw her was when she came to lunch with us at Old Friars. The distinguished Dr Ramphele, by then in her mid-fifties, had recently stepped down as vice chancellor of Cape Town University and was about to take up the post of Managing Director of Human Development at the World Bank in Washington.

When we drove away from Tzaneen after that first meeting in February 1984, Sheila was in the back of the car and I was sitting next to Diana Taylor, again keeping a weather eye on the rear-view mirror. Halfway through the journey, Diana had to stop for petrol and, while the tank was being filled, I went to the Gents.

Standing at the urinal, I was joined by two beefy white men, both rather drunk, who took up position on either side of me. Sensing one of them staring, I gave him a friendly grin.

I didn't catch what he said at first, partly because of the thick Afrikaner accent and partly because his voice was so slurred. Then he said it again: 'Commie bastard nigger fucker ... you bin asking for trouble ... now you gonna geddit.'

As both men turned, zipping up as they made to back me against the urinal, my brain went into overdrive. It was two against one and they were younger and fitter than me. But I was sober and, even at sixty, hopefully quicker on my feet.

As the first meaty fist began to descend, I quickly feinted to one side before making a dash for the exit. This consisted of two chest-high saloon-type doors which swung in both directions. After I burst through, I heard them hit the first of my would-be assailants on the rebound.

Having gained valuable seconds, I pelted towards the car, shouting at Diana to start the engine. She did and, with great presence of mind, leaned across to open the passenger door. I piled in and off we sped, tyres screaming.

Diana took us to the Newton-Thompsons' home in Johannesburg. Three black cars, each containing two impassive white men in the now familiar dark suits and glasses, were already stationed at the end of Christopher and Philippa's drive. They were surrounded by a pack of reporters and cameramen. Our hosts were effectively under siege.

I phoned Don Card, Helen Suzman and the British Ambassador to seek their advice. All believed I should talk to the press to deny the allegations contained in the SABC television report. This I did before Nelson and Winnie's youngest daughter, Zindzi, and the white South African novelist, Nadine Gordimer, came to the house to meet us, both having run the gauntlet outside.

In the end it was an apologetic but insistent Christopher who convinced us we had to leave. Embarrassed at having placed him and his wife in such a difficult position, we managed to get seats on the next flight home.

The three security police vehicles followed us all the way to the airport, the lead car dangerously tailgating us and continually nudging the bumper of Christopher's Mercedes.

I have never in my entire life been so glad to board a British Airways jumbo. As the plane lumbered into the sky, I heaved a huge sigh of relief. Then, as the lush city of Johannesburg began to recede beneath us, I had a glimpse of that barren ghetto, Soweto, once home to the murdered twelve-year-old Hector Pietersen. I knew then, with absolute certainty, I had to make *Cry Freedom*.

I was equally certain it couldn't be made in South Africa.

7

CLOUD CUCKOO LAND

RA— AS 1950 DREW to a close, I'd been out of work for nearly for six months. Then, for the first time since we were at RADA, Sheila and I were asked to appear onstage together. *To Dorothy a Son* was a frothy drawing room comedy about a struggling composer with a very pregnant bride who takes to her bed to await the happy event. I played the harassed husband, the bubbly American actress, Yolande Donlan, was my first wife and Sheila, heard but not seen until she took her curtain call with a twin in each arm, was the expectant mother.

We started with a tour of the provinces which, trading on our film-star celebrity, did tremendous business. However, convinced this success would not be replicated in front of a more sophisticated West End audience, Sheila and I decided against taking the play into London, committing instead to John Boulting's new film, *The Magic Box*.

Immediately we were approached by an impresario friend, Stanley French. Stanley was in a mess, stuck with an expensive lease on a dark London theatre, having gambled everything he possessed on a total flop which had closed almost as soon as it had opened. Now he was begging us to save him from ruin by taking *Dorothy* into the Savoy for a limited four-week run, giving him just enough time to line up another production. On the understanding that the playwright, Roger MacDougall, would rework the first and second acts, we agreed to help Stanley out.

The Magic Box was the film industry's Festival of Britain tribute to the cinematographer William Friese-Greene. It was an ensemble piece with a huge all-star cast which brought together such diverse talents as Robert Donat, Thora Hird, Stanley Holloway, Bessie Love, A. E. Matthews, Laurence Olivier, Sid James, Dennis Price, Michael Redgrave and Sybil Thorndike.

More was not better; although I absolutely adored him, I have to record in all honesty that this odd roster of household names did not result in one of John Boulting's finer directorial achievements.

To Dorothy a Son opened at the Savoy with very little fanfare and almost no advance bookings. To say we were apprehensive would be a huge understatement. But, to my total amazement, when I delivered the first of the new lines, just minutes after curtain up, the whole place exploded with laughter. The notices were phenomenal and we immediately sold out for the whole of the four-week run.

Buoyed by this unexpected success and with no other work on the horizon, Sheila and I agreed to stay on until Stanley's lease expired and then, still with nothing else on offer, transferred to the Garrick on Charing Cross Road. Amazingly, we were still playing to packed houses the following summer and, by the first anniversary of the London opening, *Dorothy* had been seen by half a million people.

When you deliver the same lines night after night, your mind starts to wander. What will you have for supper after the show? Do you need a new toothbrush? Then, terrifyingly, you suddenly snap out of autopilot with no idea of where the hell you are in the play or how on earth you got there.

As my grandchildren would say, I don't do exercise. My principal recreations, as listed in *Who's Who*, are sedentary: collecting paintings and sculpture, listening to music and watching football. I have been known to splash around a bit in the small pool at our French house when it's very hot during the summer and, on rare occasions, might be persuaded to take a leisurely stroll in Richmond Park.

Only during the eighteen-month run of *To Dorothy a Son* have I ever been tempted to take up a sport.

Persuaded by fanatical fellow actors, I joined the Stage Golfing Society, kitted myself out with a wardrobe of suitable clothes, bought a madly expensive set of clubs and took lessons from a professional. After several frustrating weeks, when I seemed to be making no progress at all, my coach suddenly pronounced me ready to tackle the full eighteen holes.

He took me onto the course at Moor Park where I made a total hash of the first two. Teeing off for the short third, I gritted my teeth and, after three or four practice swings, managed to connect with the ball and watched open-mouthed as it soared straight down the fairway to land miraculously on the green, where it bounced, once, twice, before trickling towards the flag and vanishing. 'Hole in one,' said the pro. 'Congratulations.'

As a performer, you know there are some things you will never top, no matter how hard you try. At my insistence, the pro and I went straight from the third to the nineteenth hole. There I gave him my complete set of clubs, bought drinks for everyone in sight and drove home. That was the last time I ever set foot on a golf course.

Unusually for me, I was depressed. A year and a half in the theatre and I hadn't been offered any decent film. Then, with a single phone call, came the chance of a lifetime.

The caller was Ronald Neame, who'd produced *The Magic Box* and was about to direct *The Card*. Ronnie was asking if I'd be willing to replace Alec Guinness who, having agreed to play the lead, had suddenly pulled out.

The wonderful part Alec had abandoned was Arnold Bennett's social-climbing, romantic Staffordshire chancer, Denry Machin. This was not only the kind of multilayered oddball character I dreamed of playing, but a heaven-sent opportunity to put my flagging film career on a whole new footing. I said yes immediately.

Alec had turned his back on cinema to realise his own dream. He'd already played Hamlet in a highly successful, modern-dress production by Tyrone Guthrie. Now he had the opportunity to establish a reputation as a Shakespearean actor-director by recreating the part in his own production at the New Theatre. Sadly for him – and for me – he failed.

Described as an 'intellectualised renaissance production' and fiercely savaged by the London critics, *Hamlet* opened and closed in rapid succession.

Almost immediately, Ronnie Neame rang me again, full of apologies, to say a chastened Alec had returned to the fold and would be playing Denry Machin after all. I managed to tell him it didn't matter and of course I understood perfectly before I put the phone down. If I'd had a gun I'd have shot myself.

By January 1952, still playing in *Dorothy*, I became so desperate to break the routine that I stupidly agreed to double my workload by playing the lead in an equally vapid film. Worse still, this hopefully forgotten comedy, *Father's Doing Fine*, echoed what I was doing onstage. I played a daft son-in-law with a pregnant wife in a cast that included a newly graduated drama student, the young Virginia McKenna.

It was the avant-garde impresario, Jack de Leon, who finally came to the rescue by casting me in another play, *Sweet Madness*, opposite Geraldine McEwan, Laurence Naismith and Martin Miller. This sophisticated piece by Peter Jones had a short out-of-town try-out, followed by an enjoyable four-month London run. This was perfect; long enough to explore the character fully, short enough to keep the performance fresh.

Then, at the end of 1952, with my film career still in the doldrums, Sheila and I were again asked to appear together, this time in a whodunit to be presented by a relative newcomer to the world of theatre.

Our long association with Peter Saunders, which would develop into a deep and abiding friendship, started with a teasing put-down which, at that low point in my life, I really could have done without. During our preliminary discussions, he chose to confide that the distinguished lady playwright had primarily wanted Sheila and I'd been engaged as part of a job lot.

Originally a short radio drama called *Three Blind Mice*, commissioned by the BBC to celebrate Queen Mary's sixtieth birthday, the play was *The Mousetrap* and the authoress who'd eventually accepted me as the male lead, was, of course, the redoubtable Agatha Christie.

We took the piece to the provinces for a two-month try-out and the first performance in Nottingham was anything but a triumph. Late that evening, Peter was officiating at an exceedingly gloomy post-mortem in the lobby of our hotel. Agatha, I remember, sat there, absorbing our pessimism but saying nothing until she decided to repair to her room for the night. Halfway up the stairs, this deceptively mild little old lady stopped to lean over the banisters and deliver one of the greatest under-statements in theatrical history. 'Don't worry, my dears. I'm sure we shall get a nice little run out of it.'

For the move into London, Peter had put reserves on two very different theatres. Convinced the play worked best in an intimate setting, I begged him to settle for the smaller of the two, the Ambassadors. It was at this juncture, as I began to believe we might indeed have a minor success on our hands, that I told Peter Sheila and I would like to take a 10 per cent stake in the production. Not unnaturally, he enquired how soon I could come up with the money.

'Oh,' I said cheekily, 'we don't have any cash. We'll put in part of our salaries.'

It proved to be the wisest business decision I've ever made. *The Mousetrap* opened in November 1952 and, having broken all previous box office records by its seventh week, remained at the Ambassadors for the next twenty-one years. It then transferred to the larger St Martin's, where, having become the world's longest running stage play, it's still going strong today.

Our 10 per cent stake should have made us comfortable for the rest of our lives. But foolishly I sold some of my share to open a short-lived Mayfair restaurant called the Little Elephant and, later still, disposed of the remainder in order to keep *Gandhi* afloat.

For the first year of *The Moustrap*, Sheila and I appeared together. Again, after the initial excitement, the weekly routine of six evening performances and two matinees soon began to pall and then, frankly, became totally stultifying.

Sheila was onstage from curtain up. However, much to her annoyance, I'd negotiated an unusual clause in my contract stipulating the Saturday matinee would never start before 5 p.m. While she held the fort, this allowed me to attend Chelsea's home games at Stamford Bridge before driving at speed through a series of carefully calculated back doubles to arrive at the Ambassadors just in time for my own first appearance, eighteen minutes into the first act.

By the summer of 1953, Sheila was desperate to leave the cast; Michael was an active and affectionate three-year-old and he was missing her dreadfully. The opportunity came when she was asked to star opposite Anthony Steel in *West of Zanzibar*, a film about ivory smuggling. Following a short location in East Africa, this was to be shot at Ealing Studios, a mere fifteen-minute drive from Old Friars. So she left *The Mousetrap* and I slogged on alone for another six months.

To add some variety to my life, late on Saturday evenings I became a BBC radio hit-parade presenter, alternating on the Light Programme with the legendary 'dean of deejays', Jack Jackson. My programme was called *Record Rendezvous* and the eager record pluggers from nearby Tin Pan Alley who congregated in my dressing room to push their wares taught me a great deal about the music industry. This was to prove invaluable in later years when I headed the consortium which set up Capital Radio.

Soon after the coronation in 1953, I was finally offered another film. *Eight O'Clock Walk* was a low-budget production and the fee on offer was negligible. However, the subject – an examination of the death penalty – was for once meaningful and, doing two jobs at once, I embarked on eight weeks of seventeen-hour days.

It was with enormous relief that I finally left *The Mousetrap* in the summer of 1954. Basil Dearden, a director I very much admired, had cast me as a satisfyingly odious villain in an Ealing film, *The Ship that Died of Shame*. George Baker was the hero, with Virginia McKenna as his wife, but the real star of the production was the ship, a former wartime MTB. The climax of the story came when the ship, used ignominiously for smuggling, finally rebelled, washing my character overboard and killing him.

We were due to shoot this tricky special-effects shot, involving a huge hopper of water whooshing down a twenty-foot chute, at the end of the working day. Knowing we were running behind schedule, I was happy to go along with Basil's suggestion that we should dispense with any rehearsal. All I remembered afterwards was hearing him shout, 'Action!' and then nothing until I regained consciousness in hospital. Having recuperated – although I still bear the scars – I was out of work for the next eight months.

Then it was back to the Boulting brothers for *Private's Progress* in which I reverted to type as a wily army regular opposite Ian Carmichael's twittish upper-class recruit. British audiences having tired of the cult of the stiff upper lip, this witty send-up of service life became one of the decade's big successes. Unable to finance the crusading dramas of their early years, John and Roy had found their new métier in satire.

John in particular was fiercely critical of the fifties film industry, raging there were 'too many banquets, too many champagne-soaked conventions, too many luxurious offices, too many ornate brochures, too much tasteless advertising and too much undiluted, unprofitable and unproductive nonsense'.

My luck changed in September 1955 just as Sheila gave birth to our longed-for first daughter, Jane Mary, and decided to give up work and devote herself to the family. Soon afterwards, I was asked to star opposite my old friend Johnny Mills in *The Baby and the Battleship*.

British Lion flew me out to the Malta location in the company of another actor I'd never met before. During the journey it emerged that, in addition to being cast as a rather posh national serviceman, this Bryan Forbes was responsible for all the witty lines in the script which had made me laugh so much. Forbsie, as I came to call him, also had a genius for storytelling and an extraordinary ability to create naturalistic dialogue. By the time we met, he had written, rewritten or 'doctored' eighteen scripts but only received a screen credit for three of them.

Having arrived on the island and checked into our hotel, my new friend and I decided on a leisurely stroll along Valetta's main street. Eventually we came to a sweet shop and, being a chocoholic, I stopped to admire a particularly fine window display of Walnut Whips.

'I can't resist them,' I said. 'How about you?'

Forbsie declined and I went inside and bought half a dozen. Emerging, I offered him the bag which he grandly waved away as we resumed our saunter under the colonnades. Ten minutes later, he changed his mind. 'I think I will have one after all.'

'Oh! I'm sorry, there's none left.'

'You're not seriously telling me you've scoffed the lot?'

Shamefaced, I admitted my gluttony. 'You bleeding Billy Bunter,' he said. And Bunter I have remained ever since.

Forbsie was to become my closest friend and, for many years, my professional partner. We were both ambitious and roughly the same age. But what really bound us together was a shared sense of humour, a fondness for flash cars and our joint passion for thought-provoking cinema.

I've never had so much fun on location as I did on the battleship moored at Malta's evocatively named Abbatoir Quay. Johnny Mills was at that time Britain's most popular screen hero. The joy of *The Baby and the Battleship* was that it gave full rein, for once, to his amazing gift for comedy. We must have driven the director, Jay Lewis, insane because we constantly ruined his shots by corpsing.

At the end of the shooting day, while the rest of the cast toured the bars of Valetta, Johnny, Forbsie and I would share a leisurely evening meal. Endless teasing apart, we invariably talked shop, bemoaning the entrenched complacency of the British film industry and its appalling lack of originality.

Like me, Bryan was desperately keen to do something worthwhile and, as our friendship deepened, we came up with a plan to form our own production company as soon as we could find the right subject. This proved more difficult than we had anticipated, and over the next two years, as we discussed and discarded any number of ideas, my film acting career continued to decline.

I appeared in *Brothers in Law* for the Boultings, again with Ian Carmichael. Then came the schmaltzy *Strange Affection*, also known as *The Scamp*, which was stolen by a brilliant ten-year-old, Colin Peterson.

Next was *Dunkirk*, sadly one of the last Ealing films, superbly directed by Leslie Norman, father of Barry, the film critic. Immediately afterwards, I appeared for a token fee in *The Man Upstairs*, a thought-provoking low-budget drama made by ACT, the film technicians' union.

Then, for the remainder of 1957, nothing. Eventually, in the spring of the following year, Guy Green, asked me to join the all-male cast of *Sea of Sand* which he was directing in Libya. This was yet another staple of wartime derring-do, featuring a group of Desert Rats sent behind enemy lines to blow up a Nazi ammunition dump. And yet again I was cast as a minor variation on the same bloody character I seemed condemned to play forever.

The location was both long and arduous, lasting from May to August. From our hotel in Tripoli, we went out into the Sahara every day to do battle with heat rash, blinding sandstorms known as *ghiblis* and a single chemical convenience housed in a stifling tent. I was so determined to avoid this reeking apology for a lavatory I developed crippling constipation.

On one particular day, when the *ghibli* was approaching and all the actors had taken shelter under a groundsheet until it passed, I launched into my favourite career gripe. John Gregson, Michael Craig and the Aussie actor, Vince Ball, listened patiently as I moaned that I'd rather do anything than remain typecast for the rest of my life. I went on to tell them about my great pal who was a wonderful writer, adding that, even if it meant giving up acting completely, we were determined to make our own films.

With typical Antipodean directness, Vince asked what the hell was stopping us. When I said we hadn't yet found the right storyline, Michael Craig chipped in to say he and his brother had a synopsis they'd written together, entitled *God is a Bad Policeman*. It was about a factory hand who, having refused to join a wildcat strike, crosses a picket line and is sent to Coventry by his workmates.

I was immediately interested. Despite being a passionate supporter of the Labour Party, I was against the infiltration of the socialist movement by the extreme left. And real-life intimidation, such as the situation Mike had described, was very prevalent at the time. I told him I thought his idea had great potential and asked if Bryan and I could have a go at it. 'It's all yours,' he replied wearily. 'We've tried everything and we can't get it made.'

Although he loathed the title *God is a Bad Policeman*, Forbsie shared my enthusiasm and went on to write the gritty script which would turn our lives around. He called it *The Angry Silence*.

DH— April 1986. Two years have passed since Dick and Sheila made their hasty departure from Johannesburg. Now, with *Cry Freedom* fully financed and shortly due to start shooting, he and I are on our way to Lusaka.

We're hoping to find a young African who can take on the role of Steve Biko. In his heart of hearts, Dick knows this will require an experienced actor, almost certainly English or American. But honour dictates that, if at all possible, Steve ought to be played by one of his fellow countrymen. This is just one of the reasons we're flying to Zambia. Our other, more delicate mission has not yet been fully revealed to me.

The plane takes off in the early evening. With my companion unable to phone anyone for the next fourteen hours, I'm planning an in-depth discussion about marketing. No such luck. Having spent the day chairing umpteen meetings in London, as soon as the seat-belt sign goes off Dick twinkles at the hostess, waves away her offer of dinner and announces: 'I think I'll have a little nap.'

Producing an ultra-soft first-class blanket, she tenderly tucks him in. Back goes the seat. He closes his eyes and is instantly asleep. It's maddening. The man can nap anywhere and, what's more, he has some kind of inner alarm clock which allows him to state with absolute precision when he'll wake up again.

He makes no such prediction this evening and remains out for the count as the plane lumbers through the night, lands somewhere called Libreville, refuels, takes off again and lumbers on again for another eighteen hundred miles. Only when the pilot announces the final approach to Lusaka does he open his eyes and sit up – instantly on the ball and brimming with energy.

I'd expected Africa to be hot and sunny. Instead, it's decidedly chilly and very, very wet. Dick bounds down the aircraft steps, arms outstretched to embrace the leader of the small delegation waiting below to greet him. I trail behind in a soggy, sleep-deprived haze.

As the saying goes, one man's terrorist is another man's freedom fighter. Here, the small bespectacled black man clasped to Dick's bosom is a hero in hiding. Not far away, across the South African border, he's a target of undercover murder squads and an enemy of the state. Neither description seems to fit the soberly suited 69-year-old who gravely shakes my hand. This is Oliver Tambo, former law partner of Nelson Mandela and now President in exile of the African National Congress, the oldest, largest and most powerful of all the anti-apartheid organisations.

Dick is hoping to find his South African Biko among the young émigré guerrillas living in hidden ANC training camps scattered around Lusaka. Our casting director, Susie Figgis, has travelled ahead to make a preliminary selection, assisted by Oliver Tambo's son, Dali. This Oxford-accented former public schoolboy is keen to find a niche in show business. Under the pseudonym Daly Campbell, he will be under my wing, attached to the publicity department while we are filming.

Dali and Susie have found eight potential Bikos. Dick is to interview them at our hotel, a modern sore thumb towering over the crumbling colonial rooftops of the surrounding city. On the morning following our arrival, the four of us rendezvous in a small top-floor conference room and Susie starts to take Dick through her list.

Suddenly an alarm bell starts to ring very loudly. Susie, Dali and

I look at each other and then at Dick who's stirring saccharine into his coffee, completely unconcerned. While Susie continues to brief him and the bell continues to ring, I attempt to call the hotel switchboard. No reply. I go into the corridor. Fifty or more diminutive Japanese businessmen are leaving the large conference room opposite and making their orderly way, two abreast, down the emergency staircase.

Back in our room, I tell Dick the hotel is being evacuated. 'Only a fire drill, darling,' he murmurs, studying a Polaroid of one of the would-be actors. I go to the window. There's a huge crowd milling about in the car park below. The bell rings on and still there's no reply from the switchboard.

'Susie,' I say, 'we've got to get out. Now.'

Her enormous eyes widen as I take hold of Dick's arm, ready to prise him out of his chair. And then, suddenly, silence. 'What is it, de-ah?' he asks testily.

'The bell. It's stopped.'

'What bell?'

Only now do I realise the full extent of his deafness.

All the would-be Bikos are a disappointment. Even Dick, who, according to the trusty Terry Clegg, can extract a performance from a block of wood, is defeated. But honour is satisfied; at least he tried.

Only when the last of the eight has departed does the underlying reason for this trip finally become clear to me. Another unannounced visitor appears and Dali, somewhat in awe, confides this is his father's closest aide. The bearded new arrival, who addresses him as 'Comrade', is another South African exile in his mid-forties. He's head of the ANC's Information Department and their foreign affairs spokesman.

The name of this jovial pipe smoker is Thabo, Thabo Mbeki. He starts by telling Dick that Mahatma Gandhi was one of his childhood heroes, the other Karl Marx. The son of teacher activists, he joined the ANC as a teenager. In his early twenties, when the net was closing in on Nelson Mandela, he and a group of other promising young men were smuggled out of South Africa, posing as a football team. Two years after their escape, Mandela and seven others, including Mbeki's father, Govan, were sentenced to life imprisonment on Robben Island.

Meanwhile, the young Thabo had made his way to England to prepare himself as one of the next generation of leaders by studying at Sussex University – of which Dick now happens to be pro-chancellor – gaining an MA in Economics before going on to train in guerrilla warfare behind the Iron Curtain.

At this point, the Cold War is not yet over and, as a Conservative voter, I'm having difficulty adjusting to this surreal conversation with a charming revolutionary who is funded, as are all the activities of the ANC, by the Soviet Union. But, despite his own left-wing views, Dick is not here to debate the merits or demerits of Marxism. What he is seeking from Thabo Mbeki is an undertaking.

From the discussion which follows, I learn that Steve Biko's aims and philosophies are anathema to the ANC. Black Consciousness, in their view, is an inherently racist movement which denounces their allegiance to the Soviet bloc, utterly rejects Nelson Mandela's dream of establishing a 'rainbow nation' and aspires, ultimately, to expel every white from the whole of Africa.

Thabo tells us he has read Jack Briley's script twice and thought long and hard about its impact. He has reached the pragmatic conclusion that the film's potential to change hearts and minds among white South Africans has to outweigh the bitter internecine feud between the two liberation movements. The ANC, he finally pronounces, will not publicly endorse the making of *Cry Freedom*; neither will it speak out against it.

Mission accomplished, we fly back to London.

Less than a month later, alarm bells were ringing again in Lusaka.

The BBC reported: 'South African troops have launched raids on three neighbouring countries in an effort to destroy bases purportedly used by the anti-apartheid organisation, the African National Congress. At least three people are reported dead after this morning's coordinated attacks on cities in Zambia, Zimbabwe and Botswana by South African warplanes, helicopters and commandos.'

RA— Marti's elbow jerked me awake again; Hamlet was about to make an entrance, stage left.

I'd flown into New York late that afternoon. My American agent, who was helping to cast *Cry Freedom*, had met me at JFK and brought me straight to this off-Broadway theatre to see the one actor, in his estimation, who would make the perfect Donald Woods. And, whether it was due to the mental leap required to transpose an American-accented Prince of Denmark into the South African Donald or the stuffiness of the small auditorium, I repeatedly found myself nodding off.

The actor knew we were out front, and since we were sitting in full view of the stage, Marti had taken to jabbing me in the ribs whenever he spied him in the wings. But, in fact, I'd already reached my decision.

As this quirky Yankee Hamlet had reached the end of his first marvellously layered soliloquy, saying: 'But break, my heart, for I must hold my tongue,' I'd known that he could do it.

While he was onstage, you simply didn't want to look at anybody else. He was also tall and somewhat gangly, with an ability to convey the underlying intellect combined with an endearing absence of guile which were so much part and parcel of Donald's character. When we went backstage after the curtain, I immediately offered Kevin Kline the part and he immediately accepted.

The following day, Marti and I flew on to Los Angeles where, on the Monday morning, we were to have a meeting with Frank Price, now the president of Universal Pictures. Riding the crest of a wave with his hugely successful slate of new productions, Frank was, as always, polite and reserved but very welcoming. He was impressed with Jack Briley's script, he told me, and greatly looked forward to seeing *Cry Freedom*.

Then, to my complete surprise, he went on to make me a proposition. He was keen, he said, that he and I should go on working together when this film was finished. What were my plans? Did I have another movie in mind?

I told him that many years earlier, while I was still in my teens, my father had given me a copy of Thomas Paine's visionary pamphlet, *The Rights of Man*. My greatest ambition was to make a film about this radical eighteenth-century Englishman who'd been at the heart of both the American and the French Revolution and had written –

'– *Crisis*; "These are the times that try men's souls",' Frank chipped in. 'Yes, I know all about Tom Paine and I'm a fan. You don't have to pitch him to me.'

And, being a scholar, Frank did know and evidently shared my enthusiasm. 'Dickie,' he said, 'Would you be interested in entering into a first-look deal?'

Under such an arrangement, he explained, the studio would have right of first refusal on any feature film I chose to develop. My own expenses would be defrayed and, in addition, Universal would underwrite the fees of any agreed screenwriter and put Di under contract, enabling her to work with me full time.

This was manna from heaven. Going for English understatement, I said: 'Yes, Frank, I would be interested.'

'That's great. We'll leave it to Marti, shall we, to work out the details with our legal department?'

DH— For me, the first-look deal proved to be a major milestone. Being paid by Universal meant I no longer worked *for* Dick but *with* him. Once I was established in a new office at Twickenham Studios, backed by two able assistants, Alison Webb and Judy Wasdell, he proceeded to involve me in every area of production until, two years later, I became his producing partner.

Donald Woods observed in the book he wrote about *Cry Freedom*:

> It was clear that Attenborough relied heavily on Diana's judgement, not only about public statements and replies to queries about the film but on a wide range of general matters. As a problem came to mind he would turn from his position at the camera and look around for her ... 'Di, darling ...' he would begin, and in time I formed the impression that if Sir Richard were ever confronted at the pearly gates by Saint Peter with a range of awkward questions he would turn around and call: 'Di, darling ...'

Dick has never called anyone 'luvvie' but everyone drawn into his aura is a darling. His son, now nearly sixty, whom he still kisses wherever they meet, is Michael Darling. Bill, his endearing, extreme right-wing cockney chauffeur, is Bill Darling. Sheila is Sheila when he's irritable, Poppy when he's loving and Poppy Darling when he's exuberant.

The most unlikely darling was Margaret Thatcher, who Dick loathed for her policies but reluctantly admired for her acumen when he led a film delegation to an emergency seminar she'd convened in Downing Street. After he'd formally thanked her for taking on board the industry's problems, the Iron Lady asked: 'Why on earth didn't you come and see me before, Sir Richard?' He riposted: 'Because you never invited me, darling.'

I've heard him address Gordon Brown as Gordon Darling and his predecessor was decidedly Tony Darling. Whenever Dick encounters a woman whose name he can't remember, she also becomes a darling. Men with forgotten names can also be darlings – but only if they're theatrical.

RA— Following our extraordinary meeting with Frank Price, Marti had arranged for me to see a young American television actor who might be right for Steve Biko. One of my greatest regrets was that I had never met Steve, although I'd read a great deal, seen every available photograph and talked to his closest colleagues and family. In my mind's eye, there were two absolute prerequisites for any actor who set out to portray him. He had to have the stature of my screen Donald in order they could confront each other, eyeball to eyeball. And, above all, he had to be charismatic.

Denzel Washington was thirty-two when he came to see me; just a year older than Steve at the time of his death. He was exceptionally hand-some, well above average height and his magnetism was immediately apparent. Although he knew little about him, as I related Steve's story I could see that he was also an attentive listener. That was important too.

Denzel's biggest concern was his ability to capture Steve's accent. Rightly so; the South African vowels and cadences are among the most difficult for any English-speaking actor to replicate. I reassured him that Donald and Wendy Woods would always be on hand to help and then showed him the pictures of Steve I'd brought with me. The resemblance was remarkably good, with one major exception: like many African men, Steve had had a large gap between his front teeth.

When I commented on this, Denzel broke into a grin, revealing his own perfectly aligned incisors. That wouldn't be a problem, he said. He also had a gap and, were I to offer him the part, he'd have his dentist remove the caps that disguised it. He added, 'My ancestors didn't come here on a cruise ship, you know.'

We both laughed and that, I think, relaxed him. He got up from his chair and started to move around. Finally he came to a halt by the mantelpiece, on which he rested an elbow. In that moment it all came together for me. There – engaging, loose-limbed and totally confident – was my perfect Biko.

DH— In May 1986, I issued a press release stating that Kevin Kline, Denzel Washington, Penelope Wilton, John Thaw and Josette Simon had all been signed to star in Richard Attenborough's new $23 million film, *Cry Freedom*, which was to be shot in Zimbabwe.

This was the country Dick and our production designer, Stuart Craig, had finally selected to stand in for the neighbouring apartheid state. When their choice became public knowledge, a South African producer issued a furious counterblast, attacking Dick for declining to shoot in his 'free' country and announcing his own rival film – bigger, better, more authentic – to be called *Biko, the True Story*. Not long afterwards, his offices were closed down by the South African security police.

Meanwhile, Terry Clegg, whose newly enhanced title was Executive Producer in Charge of Production, was worrying about Dick's safety. On the advice of his friend Don Card, the redoubtable former BOSS detective, Donald Woods was warning that the same security police would stop at nothing to halt our production. Card had predicted their most likely course of action would be to infiltrate the 200-mile shared border with Zimbabwe in a covert attempt to 'eliminate Attenborough'.

When Terry put this to Dick, the response was: 'Absolute bollocks, darling. Forget it.' But Terry, also responsible for protecting Universal's multimillion-dollar investment, couldn't forget it. He felt obligated to inform our insurers and, when the additional cost was agreed, engaged Control Risks, a British company specialising in protection.

This was how I came to know John and Brian, adding mercenaries to my list of unlikely new acquaintances. We never knew their other names. Both former SAS, they were tough, impassive and prepared to take a bullet for the man who, for security purposes, was simply listed on our call sheets as SRA, aka Sir Richard Attenborough, code name 'Sirrah'.

John and Brian travelled with him to Harare – Sirrah in first class, 'the boys', as he came to call them, keeping a watchful eye from business. They came armed with discreetly holstered Browning automatics, and on landing, by prior arrangement with Zimbabwean 'contacts', walked straight through customs and immigration to be ready and waiting when Dick emerged with his luggage.

There were always two cars. Dick would travel in the back of the first with one of the boys as the driver. The other took the wheel of the second vehicle which followed closely behind. I learned the reason for this arrangement when they allowed me to accompany them to the open-air shooting range where they went for their mandatory weekly workout.

There, after a session of unarmed combat, John and Brian practised firing at static and moving targets. They then took the cars onto the perimeter road to rehearse an ambush. It was the job of the lead driver to stay put during an attack, buying time for his passenger to escape while drawing the assailants' fire. His partner's role was to bundle Sirrah into the second car and drive him to safety.

John and Brian never needed to put this drill into practice but they certainly earned their money. Even at the end of a long day's filming, they remained on duty whenever Dick elected to dine in one Harare's restaurants. Having completed an advance reconnoitre, the boys would nominate where Sirrah should sit and, posing as diners at an adjacent table, maintain surveillance throughout his meal.

Only when Dick and Sheila finally retired for the night did John and Brian hand over to a member of the local police who stood outside the door with his rifle until they took over again in the morning.

RA— 'The boys' were not best pleased when Sheila and I went to take afternoon tea with Robert Mugabe. It was the only time I refused point-blank to let them accompany me; perhaps, in view of horrific recent events, not the wisest decision I ever made.

The Zimbabwean Prime Minister and his first wife, known throughout the country as Comrade Sally, resided in a spacious home set in manicured gardens. They couldn't have been more gracious as a uniformed flunkey showed us into their drawing room. Bizarrely, as I look back, the four of us sat in chintz armchairs, sipping tea from bone china and eating fish-paste sandwiches while our host spoke admiringly of the world's most famous proponent of non-violence, Mahatma Gandhi.

Having welcomed us all to Zimbabwe, the Prime Minister moved on to the possibility of establishing a local film industry, asking how much influence did I think it could exert. I said the potential was infinite, but it would be a mistake to impose Hollywood criteria. If the medium was to succeed, it had to be truly indigenous and, in order to help achieve this, our film would be employing and training a great many local people.

I have to say in all honesty that I took to Robert Mugabe. To me in 1986, beautiful, fertile Zimbabwe, newly independent under a black majority government, appeared to be the Dark Continent's brightest beacon of hope. Black and white were working, side by side, without any apparent acrimony. The country was settled, virtually self-sufficient, and beginning to earn significant amounts of hard currency from its burgeoning tourist industry.

What I didn't know – and neither did the rest of world at the time – was that the ancient tribal rancour between the Ndebele people in the south and his own more numerous Shona in the north, had already prompted Mugabe into a vicious act of genocide. Nor was it then conceivable that my solicitous host, who told me he had no less than eight university degrees, most of them gained in prison, would become a murderous, land-grabbing despot, presiding over a starving nation while boasting he held a ninth degree in violence.

When we said goodbye at the end of the afternoon, I clearly remember him saying, 'Do please keep in touch. Whenever you are in Africa, always come to Harare to see us. It's very important that we have friends in the West who understand what we're trying to do here.'

DH— So near and yet so far. It was more than seven years since Donald and Wendy Woods had last set foot in Africa. Now they were back – on the 'wrong' side of the Limpopo River, yet standing outside their luxurious old home on South Africa's Eastern Cape. The house, disqui-etingly, was merely a facade, recreated by Stuart Craig's art department in an affluent residential area of Harare.

Eager, starry-eyed and profoundly homesick, the Woods were about to be inducted into the mysteries of movie-making Attenborough-style. Both were by now accustomed to being addressed as 'darling' or, when Dick was irate, as 'dee-ah', but hadn't yet been subjected to his full-on, steely dedication.

Film-making wasn't nearly as glamorous as they'd anticipated. Donald would write:

> These workaholics required everyone to rise at cock crow, spend every moment physically present on the set within listening distance of the action, concentrate on everything, know every-thing and stay through blistering heat or nightly chill until the last cry of 'It's a wrap!' Then after viewing rushes and tumbling into bed, to wake what felt like ten minutes later to do the same thing again. Every day for four months.

Dick had engaged the Woodses as consultants. They would discover that, in addition to monitoring the actors' accents and being able to demonstrate a Xhosa tribal war dance, this also entailed pronouncing, instantly and authoritatively, on such abstruse subjects as the precise number of buttons on a South African policeman's uniform. But first, they had to master the rigid but unwritten rules of filming; not least the protocol of the chairs.

Dick was always provided with a collapsible wood-and-canvas chair, bearing his name. Props also set out similar chairs for the exclusive use of the producers and stars. It was a golden rule that no one else ever occupied these prime ringside seats – not even two weary consultants – and an absolute given that 63-year-old Dick, leading from the front, never sat down at all.

Second unwritten rule: no one but Dick was allowed to do or say anything that might in any way influence an actor's performance. He had to be their sole point of reference, whether silently egging them on beside the camera or coaxing them to do better in a whispered huddle afterwards. If Donald and Wendy felt it necessary to correct a

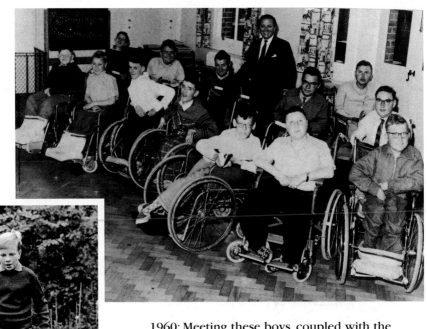

1960: Meeting these boys, coupled with the image of my son Michael (*left*), playing football, marked the start of my involvement with the Muscular Dystrophy Campaign.

1988: As a Goodwill Ambassador for UNICEF, I visited many countries. Pictured with Sheila and a group of rural African children.

Filming *A Bridge Too Far*, 1976: With Joseph E Levine and Dirk Bogarde.

Filming *A Bridge Too Far*, 1976: With Sean Connery

Filming *A Bridge Too Far*, 1976: Directing a river crossing

Filming *Cry Freedom*, 1986:
With Denzel Washington

Filming *Cry Freedom*, 1986:
Kevin Kline chest deep in the
River Zambezi

Filming *Cry Freedom*, 1986:
Cast and crew in Zimbabwe

Filming *Cry Freedom*, 1986:
(*left to right front*) Dali Tambo, Donald
Woods, Zimbabwean assistant director,
Steve Chigorimbo and Wendy Woods
rehearse a group of chanting students

Cry Freedom, 1987: Recreation
of the death of Hector Petersen

Cry Freedom, 1987: The scene in which South African riot police
open fire on Soweto schoolchildren

Filming *Cry Freedom*, 1986:
On location in Zimbabwe
with Donald Woods and Di

1984: 'Illegally' holding the hand
of Winnie Mandela

1989, *Cry Freedom*: Zimbabwean despot, Robert Mugabe,
attends the Harare premiere.

1987: Greeted by the Thatchers at a
Downing Street reception

1995: A party in London to celebrate Nelson Mandela's release.
Signed by Oliver Tambo and Nelson Mandela. (*Left to right*) With Sheila,
Oliver Tambo, Adelaide Tambo, Nelson Mandela and Di

Best wishes.
so profound Love as always.
OO Tambo

Compliments and best wishes
N Mandela 25 4-91

2007: Remembering the late Oliver Tambo, Nelson Mandela is overcome with emotion during the unveiling of his statue in Parliament Square. (*Left to right*) Gordon Brown, Nelson Mandela, RA and Nelson Mandela's wife, Dame Graça Machel.

pronunciation, they first had to seek his permission and woe betide them if they so much as hinted at a different interpretation.

Third unwritten rule: what Dick expected of his crew was the four Es – exactitude, expertise, energy and, most important of all, unbounded enthusiasm. Nothing less was acceptable.

Last unwritten rule: Dick had eyes in the back of his head. During a particularly arduous all-night shoot, Donald made the mistake of sloping off to Kevin Kline's star camper van for an illicit kip in the early hours of the morning. No one noticed his absence except our director, who immediately dispatched a lowly third assistant to track him down. When the bleary consultant finally reported for duty, Dick greeted him, oozing bonhomie: 'Ah, there you are, Donald, dee-ah,' and proceeded to justify his unnecessary summons with a completely spurious question.

When stars play real people they usually do an enormous amount of research but are rarely, if ever, required to perform under the scrutiny of their assumed alter ego. Fortunately, Donald and Kevin Kline hit it off straight away and, indeed, became lifelong friends. Together, they whiled away the interminable waiting between shots discussing classical music – a shared passion – and playing a complicated word game of Donald's devising.

Donald also took delight in telling Kevin about the various life-threatening diseases endemic in Southern Africa. Among them was bilharzia, transmitted via river water, in which worms make their way to the veins supplying the human liver where they remain in a constant state of copulation, producing thousands of eggs and eventually killing their host.

Kevin had yet to play a scene which required him to wade chest-deep into the Zambezi River and, not unnaturally, this information preyed on his mind. The sequence, depicting part of Donald's escape from South Africa, was to be shot just above Victoria Falls towards the end of our schedule.

The worried Kevin had a little chat with Dick who instructed Terry Clegg to find some way of reassuring him. Terry dispatched a bilharzia expert to the Zambezi to take water samples. On learning the test was negative, Kevin was fine for a while but the mental image of those little worms kept returning to haunt him.

After another heart-to-heart, Dick instructed the wardrobe department to order a wetsuit that Kevin could wear unseen under his Donald costume. The weeks went by, regular water tests remained negative, the wetsuit was delivered and Kevin was still unhappy.

Finally, sensing he'd exhausted Dick's patience, he came to me with a cunning plan. Could someone build him a special tank? This would constantly be filled to overflowing with sterilised water supplied by a hidden hose. He'd play the scene inside the tank and, just to be on the safe side, wear his wetsuit as well.

I promised to pass on the idea but said I doubted it was feasible since, according to the script, Kevin had to wade forward until he was almost up to his neck in river water before deciding to turn back. There was no way a tank could move at a convincing pace, let alone remain invisible to the camera. Dick, of course, agreed and, being unable to risk telling Kevin it was entirely up to him, darling, delivered instead another of his bracing pep talks.

Finally, the day dawned and we all congregated on the banks of the mighty river, shouting to make ourselves heard over the roar of the nearby Falls. With camera and unit ready to shoot, an extremely apprehensive Kevin appeared, wetsuit under his Donald costume. When Dick yelled, 'Action!' he entered the water and, mustering all his acting skills, waded manfully until water was lapping at his chest.

Knowing how hard it would be to psych him up for more than a single take, the first was fortunately good enough for Dick to yell, 'Cut and print. Well done, Kev, darling. Check the gate.'

Emerging dripping, Kevin made a beeline for me. 'The guys in the boats over there,' he said, pointing upstream, 'why the rifles?'

Put on the spot, I could only reply: 'Crocodiles.'

RA— At the end of *Cry Freedom*, the Woods family make their escape from South Africa aboard a small plane. In a scene, reflecting my own hasty departure from Johannesburg, Donald looks down at his homeland receding beneath him and conjures up, in flashback, the Soweto massacre of 1976.

We filmed this sequence in a township on the outskirts of Bulawayo. As in Soweto, here again were the bleak rows of identical huts marching across the skyline, the dried reddish earth, the almost complete absence of vegetation. Only the country and the Ndebele people – then all too briefly free of hunger and oppression – were different.

Filming started with the master shot of a dirt road packed with hundreds of jubilant secondary pupils advancing towards camera, singing, whistling and dancing as they brandished their home-made placards, more pouring in to join them from every side street. Then, from their point of view, the confrontation; camera tilting up to reveal a chilling line of police marksmen backed by a phalanx of armoured trucks. An officer shouting: 'Stop right there. This is an illegal gathering. I'm giving you three minutes to disperse. Go home. Go home, I'm warning you.'

Throughout the morning and most of the afternoon we continued to cover the ensuing mayhem; the tear gas, the young demonstrators scattering in every direction, the nervous young policeman mistakenly letting off the first wild bullet, his companions joining in, aiming deliberately at the crowd. Then images of their targets: thirteen-, fourteen- and fifteen-year-old kids; injured, dying, dead . . .

And finally, just before we lost the light for the day, I brought to life the image which had stood on my office bookshelf for the previous ten years.

In setting it up, I had no need to consult the famous photograph that the wardrobe department had used as reference to dress the young man in the correct dungarees, the teenage girl in her neat Phefeni Senior Secondary uniform and the twelve-year-old African boy in his shorts, sneakers and primary school sweater.

The clapper went in; I said, 'Action.' With Antonette at his side, her hand thrown up in horror, Mbuyisa ran towards camera carrying the dead Hector Pietersen. In a single take, it was in the can. Five seconds of screen time encapsulating forty years of apartheid.

Originally, I had intended that *Cry Freedom* should end as the little plane carrying the Woods family disappeared into the distance. However, during post-production, I came up with the idea of finishing on a caption followed by a list of seventy-nine names.

The caption read: 'By Act of Parliament in 1962 the South African government legalized imprisonment without trial. Since that time, the following are the official explanations for all known deaths in detention.'

The monstrous cynicism of those explanations included 'slipped in shower', 'fell ten floors', 'self-strangulation'.

First on the list was L. Ngudle, 'suicide by hanging'. Forty-third was S. Biko, 'hunger strike'.

And, to my horror, even while we'd been recreating the Soweto massacre in Zimbabwe, the seventy-fifth victim had been dying in a South African police cell, allegedly due to an 'asthma attack'.

DH— On our return from Zimbabwe, we received some unwelcome news. Less than three years after he'd taken charge of production at Universal Studios, our friend and champion, Frank Price, was out.

One of his more expensive projects, *Howard the Duck*, had proved to be a giant turkey. This came at the end of a disastrous summer season when two of Frank's other movies had also failed at the American box office. Suddenly, his triumphs of the previous year, the multiple Oscar-winning *Out of Africa* and hugely profitable *Back to the Future*, counted for nothing. Such is the nature of Hollywood.

Headed by Sid Sheinberg – the man who'd been so bitter about *Gandhi* beating *E.T.* at the Oscars – Universal's parent company, MCA, reacted with ruthless speed. News of Frank's departure was announced on a Wednesday and his successor, Tom Pollock, an entertainment lawyer who'd never held any executive studio post, was named the following Friday.

Cry Freedom was one of Frank's pet projects. Knowing it would not be a cheap or an easy picture to launch – particularly in the United States – Dick and I became concerned that it would not be well supported under the new regime, despite the fact it had come in $1 million under budget. However, while we were shooting some final interior scenes at Shepperton, both Sid Sheinberg and Marvin Antonowsky, who had stayed on as Universal's president of marketing, took the trouble to come over and reassure us.

They were as good as their word. *Cry Freedom* was first screened publicly for members of the United Nations Assembly on the day Dick joined Harry Belafonte and Audrey Hepburn to follow in the late Danny Kaye's footsteps as UNICEF's fourth Goodwill Ambassador, a post which allowed him to dispense with his British passport and travel on an impressive ambassadorial laissez-passer.

Our world premiere, which took place two evenings later in

Washington, was followed by a charity reception at Hickory Hill hosted by Ethel Kennedy, widow of Robert, the assassinated former Attorney General.

Connection made, Dick and I were subsequently invited to a private dinner at Ethel's New York brownstone. The narrow house was filled to overflowing with highly articulate, cookie-cutter Kennedy offspring and one other guest. This was Bobby's biographer, Arthur Schlesinger, who was at pains to remind us that the Senator had been the first American politician to visit South Africa and speak out against apartheid.

Over the meal, it became clear this branch of the Kennedys believed JFK's glamorous and much publicised presidency had unfairly eclipsed his younger brother, denying him his rightful place in history. They were asking Dick to set the record straight by making a Bobby biopic, a proposal the new ambassador – about to announce Thomas Paine as the subject of his next film – diplomatically declined.

As the date of our London premiere approached, Margaret Thatcher infuriated Commonwealth leaders by again refusing to impose full economic sanctions on South Africa. And when a journalist dared to suggest the ANC might some day occupy a position of power, her closest aide, Bernard Ingham, memorably replied: 'It is cloud cuckoo land for anyone to believe that could be done.'

Cloud cuckoo land, however, lay closer to home. Attending a reception at 10 Downing Street, Dick was greeted at the door by a jovial Denis Thatcher, who asked: 'And what have you been up to lately?' On hearing he'd been filming in Zimbabwe, the Prime Minister's consort came up with the unbelievably reactionary rebuke: 'In this house it is still referred to as Southern Rhodesia.'

Dick riposted by inviting a large number of MPs to the premiere. He was angered but not surprised when Labour members turned up in droves while the Tories, without exception, declared themselves otherwise engaged.

Although Universal had mounted an excellent marketing campaign, *Cry Freedom* did not do well in America, even among black audiences, which was disappointing. But elsewhere in the world it was a success; particularly in Sweden, Japan and West Germany, where ministers told Dick it had resulted in even tighter sanctions being brought to bear on the increasingly beleaguered President P.W. Botha.

We waited a long time to find out if his government would dare to allow the film to be screened in South Africa. Finally, Tom Pollock, the new production chief at Universal Studios – a man of conscience who was vehemently anti-apartheid – issued a challenge.

His company would undertake to donate all local profits from *Cry Freedom* to a UNICEF fund for Southern African children on two conditions: first, the film must not be censored in any way; second, it had to be shown in fully integrated cinemas.

The censors, known as the Publications Committee, first viewed the film in November 1987. To our amazement, they announced it could be screened without any cuts. The head of the committee declared: 'This decision is an indication of our objectivity.'

But by January 1988, when quote ads began to appear in South African newspapers, the authorities were beginning to clamp down. The Witwatersrand Attorney General decreed that the quotes – words put into the mouths of characters by screenwriter, Jack Briley – 'freely promoted the views of a banned person to the general public' and threatened prosecution.

The row rumbled on until, just days before the film was due to open, the Minister of Home Affairs, in a blame-shifting exercise, ordered the censors to review their decision. The committee defiantly stood its ground, delaying at first and then, less than an hour before the first performance in thirty cities and towns across South Africa, again announcing the film could be shown in its entirety.

Soon afterwards, bombs exploded at two cinemas, one in Durban, the other near Johannesburg, and others had to be evacuated after receiving threats. Everywhere else, the police stormed in. What happened next was described in a typical report from the Woodses' home town of East London: '*Cry Freedom*, the controversial film about the relationship between Steve Biko and former editor of the *Daily Dispatch*, Donald Woods, was seized by plain-clothes policemen minutes before it was due to be screened here yesterday. The policemen said they were acting under orders from the Commissioner of Police.'

Two momentous years were to pass before *Cry Freedom* would be released again in South Africa. Meanwhile, although the security police kept the seized prints under lock and key, pirate videos were circulating throughout the country.

RA— April 1991. Sheila, Di and I are on our way to a celebration hosted by Oliver Tambo and his wife, Adelaide, at their north London home. When we stop at traffic lights, Sheila becomes aware that the passenger in the rear of the minicab alongside is smiling and waving at me. There's something familiar about him but, before I can put a name to the face, the lights turn green and we pull away.

I'm still racking my brains when we stop at the next set of lights and there he is again. He opens his window; I open mine. 'Richard!' he exclaims. 'You do not know me, but I know you. We shall talk at the party.'

And then it hits me: he is Nelson Mandela.

This is the man who strode out of prison just fifteen months ago after twenty-seven years of incarceration. This is the man who turned his prison into a university and his jailer into a friend. This is the man who ended apartheid.

Mahatma Gandhi said: 'My life is my message.' Mandela said: 'The struggle is my life.'

Our cars arrive at the Tambos' brightly lit house – no longer bugged but still with the bulletproof windows. On the pavement, I hug Nelson; he hugs me. And before we both hug Oliver, he takes me to one side and says: 'I want to thank you, Richard. And I want you to know your film had more impact on the white population than any speech I ever made in my life.'

I am, of course, completely overwhelmed by his generosity. Is it true? Of course not. But I like to think *Cry Freedom* did help the struggle.

DH— Two of the other guests that evening were Donald and Wendy Woods. During his fourteen-year exile, Donald had fought ceaselessly to bring about political change in South Africa. He had written seven books, become the first private citizen to address the UN Security Council, undertaken thirty-six lecture tours in America and raised sufficient funds to send more than a hundred young victims of apartheid to British and American universities.

Following the release of Nelson Mandela, Donald's banning order was rescinded and he resumed writing for the *East London Daily Dispatch*, characteristically beginning his first article: 'As I was saying when I was so rudely interrupted . . .'

He was again interrupted before he could achieve his final goal. In August 2001, two years after Thabo Mbeki had succeeded Nelson Mandela to become President of South Africa, Dick received an urgent phone call from Wendy at his holiday home in France.

He immediately flew to London where he found the 'lion in sheep's clothing' terminally ill in hospital but still cracking jokes. Between quips, Donald had one last request to make. He had recently commissioned a statue of Nelson Mandela and started campaigning to have it erected in Trafalgar Square, close to South Africa House, scene of the world's longest anti-apartheid vigil. Would Dick see this through for him?

Donald Woods CBE died three days later and Dick, having given his word, embarked on the mission which would take him six years to achieve. He and Wendy established a fund to have Ian Walters' nine-foot sculpture cast in bronze and, with the backing of Mayor Ken Livingstone, fought long and hard to secure it the position Donald had set his heart on. When permission was denied by an intransigent Westminster Council, he continued to fight until the Mandela statue was finally granted a plinth in Parliament Square.

The unveiling, attended by former President Mandela and his new Mozambiquan wife, Graça Machel, was performed by Gordon Brown, Ken Livingstone and Wendy Woods on Dick's eighty-fourth birthday in August 2007.

8

DEVELOPMENT HELL

DH— I gained my first tenuous toehold in the film industry through sheer nepotism. From the age of fifteen, I'd worked as a freelance broadcaster, presenting a radio show called *The Younger Generation*. On leaving school I won a place at RADA, but quickly realised I wasn't cut out to be an actress.

There followed three happy-go-lucky years as an Air France ground hostess until one particularly frustrated passenger, who'd missed the last flight to Paris, hit me over the head with his umbrella. On learning I'd resigned, my film-production designer father decided it was high time I buckled down to a proper job and proceeded to pull a few strings at Pinewood Studios.

During all the time I spent with the Rank Organisation, I never encountered our chief executive, the faceless ogre known as 'JD'. Sir John Davis reigned supreme from Mayfair where, having taken control of the avuncular J. Arthur Rank's debt-ridden empire, he embarked on a process announced as 'rationalisation', which I soon learned was accountant-speak for a sacking spree.

Every weekday morning, it later transpired, JD travelled up to London by train. And every morning he shared his first-class carriage with a man called Norman. After months of merely nodding, the two of them got talking. On learning that his fellow traveller was a Fleet Street executive, JD sought his opinion of the Pinewood publicity department which then consisted of the controller, Theo Cowan, his deputy, six unit publicists, seven stills photographers, three PR specialists, eight secretaries and one newly recruited dogsbody.

Norman, an unassuming individual, diffidently agreed this did seem rather a lot of people. Before he knew it, he later told me, JD had hired him; ostensibly to run the department, but in effect to run it down.

I was the newly recruited dogsbody, engaged as a favour to my father by the cigar-smoking Theo to help organise the Rank Organisation's lavish twenty-first birthday celebrations. Only weeks after he'd hired me, my new boss flew off to the South of France for his annual holiday and, on checking into his hotel, was informed he'd been fired.

I found Norman Hardy installed in Theo's office the following Monday morning. His predecessor had been much loved and, since Norman patently knew nothing about films or publicity, he was cold-shouldered by the entire department. I became his reluctant confidante.

It took him several weeks to decide who should stay and who should go. Came the fateful Friday, the whole department was summoned, one by one. Some emerged from his office shell-shocked, others effing and blinding, a few looking relieved but guilty. Finally, it was my turn. A speechless Norman sat at his desk, face ashen, tears rolling down his cheeks. To put the poor man out of his misery, I told him I perfectly understood; last in, first out. He didn't have to tell me: I knew I was going.

Quite the contrary, he said. With so many leaving, there remained a whole collection of odd jobs that JD still required to be done: organising the twenty-first birthday party, conducting studio tours for his VIP guests, preparing detailed graphs of the editorial space devoted to Rank films for his monthly board meetings and, finally, taking charge of the studio's extensive photographic library. All these tasks were now mine.

The photo library was housed in a large corner office and I was sitting there, still shell-shocked and surveying my new domain, when a star from one of the nearby sound stages materialised in the doorway. Although he was in costume – unshaven, seedy and wearing a filthy blazer – I recognised him immediately. This was the glamorous Richard Attenborough in his less salubrious incarnation as 'one of the screen's great slimeballs', in the eminently forgettable SOS Pacific.

Laying on the charm, this celebrity spiv on the scrounge explained that he needed a few black-and-white stills. Would I kindly allow him to look through the Rank collection and maybe purloin one or two to add to his own archive? Star-struck and gullible, I said of course he could.

As he rifled through file after file of expensive glossies, Mr Attenborough distracted me by confiding the shocking news that he planned to give up acting to become a producer. He explained that he and his partner, Bryan Forbes, owned this terrific subject, *The Angry Silence*, but – a refrain that would become all too familiar – they were experiencing enormous problems in raising the money to make it.

This was the first time anyone had talked to me about film finance and I was fascinated – so fascinated and busy trying to come up with helpful suggestions, I barely noticed when he made off with a huge pile of stills.

RA— At the beginning of 1959, when Forbsie had finished the *Angry Silence* script, we'd cemented our partnership with the formation of a limited company. Our wives having teased us about our eagerness, we named it Beaver Films. To further bolster our shaky credibility, we commissioned a handsome but wildly extravagant letterhead from the master engraver, Reynolds Stone.

For the first time ever in Britain, two actors in their thirties, both lacking any relevant experience, were spending their own money, hand over fist, in an attempt to set up their own production. But, even when we'd hocked everything in sight and were fending off the bailiffs, there was no sense of doom and gloom. We were buccaneers, kids let loose in a sweet factory, prepared to roll up our sleeves and work like lunatics. And, although no one was willing to finance us – a state known in the industry as development hell – a mixture of blind faith and enthusiasm kept us going.

Forbsie and I were well matched; his spiky scepticism the necessary foil to my emollient optimism. And we talked, God how we talked, morning, noon and night, sharing what I can only call a grossly insulting smutty sense of humour and a burning sense of common purpose, enlivened by our wildly divergent political views. In addition, we were both married to actresses and both were very pregnant; Sheila with our third child, Charlotte, and Bryan's Nanette with their first daughter, Sarah.

Having only the vaguest idea of how to prepare a detailed break-down, schedule and budget, we'd had the sense to engage someone highly experienced. Jack Rix, a rock-like figure recommended by trusted friends, would become the associate producer of all four films that Forbsie and I would make together.

We then approached Guy Green, the perceptive director I'd met on *Sea of Sand*, and, having secured his services, set about casting the three main parts. Kenneth More, then one of the biggest stars in the country, agreed to play Tom Curtis, the decent factory hand sent to Coventry by his workmates for crossing an unofficial picket line. The beautiful Pier Angeli, whom I'd met on *SOS Pacific*, was to portray Tom's Italian wife and Michael Craig, joint creator of the film's original storyline, signed up as his best mate, Joe. This was the package I took to British Lion in search of funding.

There, my mentors, the Boultings, both directors of the company, had expressed the depressing view that, although Forbsie's script was terrific, at a cost of £138,000, the production was far, far too expensive. Two other directors, Frank Launder and Sidney Gilliat, deemed it an extremely risky political subject, lacking the necessary safety net of any commercial ingredient. British Lion's chairman and deputy chairman – the eminent lawyer, Arnold Goodman, and developer-philanthropist, Max Rayne – could see no possibility of any profit. However, after lengthy discussions and a great deal of pleading on my part, the board grudgingly admitted they might agree to back us if we could limit their exposure to £100,000.

Maybe they believed I'd go away and forget it. Instead, Forbsie and I spent weeks chipping away at the budget. But even when we'd pared everything to the bone – cutting crowd scenes and sets, reducing crew numbers, increasing the speed of shooting – the bottom line remained too high.

We were having another go, trawling the script for even more savings, when I suddenly saw the light. I told Forbsie, 'We're being a couple of complete idiots. If we go on stripping out production values, we're eroding any chance of success. If we are to make this film the way it deserves to be made, there's only one thing to do.'

He raised a sardonic eyebrow. 'Oh yeah? You tell me, Bunter, what is it?'

'We have to persuade people to work for nothing.'

'You raving, bleeding idiot. Who the hell's going to do that?'

'We are for a start. You'll defer your writer's fee and we'll both defer our producers' fees. If we do that, I think there's a good chance Guy will join us. Then we have to persuade the actors.'

When Guy Green had very generously agreed, we approached Mike Craig who immediately said yes. So did Pier Angeli and Kenny More, although we knew he was strapped for cash.

I didn't stop there. Somehow, I also managed to persuade our costumiers, lawyers, accountants and laboratories to defer their charges in exchange for a share of any future profits. As a result, I was able to go back to British Lion and tell them I'd taken them at their word, handing in a final budget that came in at an amazing £96,000. The board succumbed to this blatant arm-twisting and, having emerged from development hell triumphant, we immediately started to spend their money – hiring the crew, renting stage space and building sets at Shepperton.

Then, two weeks before we were due to start shooting, disaster struck. With money going out at an alarming rate, a devastated Kenny More rang to say he had to pull out; he'd been offered real money to star in the prestigious Fox film, *Sink the Bismarck!*.

We had to cast someone else in double-quick time and the only actor I knew for certain was available and wouldn't cost us a penny was me. This was not part of the game plan. However, I was the right age to play Tom Curtis and, of course, I knew the script inside out. The grand irony, totally lost on me at the time, was that Kenny's last-minute withdrawal would turn out to be the most monumental blessing in disguise.

The Angry Silence opened in the UK in the industrially troubled spring of 1960 and, although enjoying great success at the box office, it immediately caused a furore among left-wing activists. Then stories began to emerge of people who had suffered the same fate as Tom Curtis. One man sent to Coventry for strike-breaking said, 'I have seen my workmates, grown men, standing still and doffing their caps as I passed by to tell me that, as far as they were concerned, I was dead.' And elsewhere, a train driver had gassed himself after living in silence for a whole year.

Meanwhile, militant trade unions up and down the country were mounting mass demonstrations, demanding the film be banned. In the

Welsh valleys, where miners' halls doubled as local cinemas, the National Union of Mineworkers voted overwhelmingly to deny *The Angry Silence* a public showing. I decided to drive to Aberdare and tackle this head on.

Never have I faced such an overtly hostile audience. But they were, at least, prepared to give me a hearing and, after I had talked for half an hour, explaining why we had made the film and what it was trying to say on a human level, pronounced themselves willing to sit through it. To my utter astonishment, at the end of the running they all stood up and cheered. Before I drove home, they presented me with the miner's lamp which still occupies pride of place in our drawing room.

Forbsie and I were over the moon when *The Angry Silence* went into profit in the UK, allowing us to repay all the deferments, and going on to produce a small but regular income for everyone who had agreed to gamble with us. Then, towards the end of 1960, the film was bought for US distribution – at that time a terrific coup for any independent British production – and the company concerned invited us to America, all expenses paid, to attend the East and West Coast openings.

Wildly excited, in the run-up to Christmas, Brian, Nan, Sheila and I boarded a Pan Am Clipper for our very first transatlantic flight. We landed in the middle of a blizzard to discover the whole of New York under a deadening blanket of snow; streets deserted, our premiere cancelled. Even the critics were staying at home. As a bitterly disappointed Sheila travelled back to London and the children, the Forbeses and I flew on to Los Angeles where our distributor had booked us into the ultra glamorous Beverly Hills Hotel.

The phone rang before I'd even finished unpacking. Since he was the only person I knew in Hollywood, I picked up the receiver, half expecting to hear the gravelly voice of my friend, Eddy Robinson. But the female caller proved to be the legendary Merle Oberon – someone I'd never met – who stunned me by announcing she was hosting a party in my honour at which she planned to introduce me to a few of her friends who'd attended a private screening of *The Angry Silence*. To this day, I have no idea how she knew I was there.

Miss Oberon lived on one of the wide, tree-lined streets that run between Sunset and Wilshire Boulevards, an area of grandiose star residences. Having greeted me with a kiss on the cheek at the door of her mansion, my hostess – still an exceptional beauty – took me by the arm and escorted me from room to room, revealing a series of jaw-dropping tableaux straight out of a fan magazine.

Katharine Hepburn and one of my great heroes, Spencer Tracy, were there. So were Jack Lemmon, James Stewart and Bette Davis. The familiar giant who took my hand in a bone-crunching grip really was John Wayne. And so it went on, Merle introducing me to an incredible roster of Hollywood greats: Gregory Peck, Walter Matthau, Henry Fonda, Audrey Hepburn, the young Shirley MacLaine, George Cukor, Billy Wilder, William Wyler . . .

Finally she took me across to a balding figure with horn-rimmed glasses who, she said, particularly wanted to meet me. This was John Sturges, who had just produced and directed *The Magnificent Seven*, catapulting a young maverick actor called Steve McQueen to instant stardom.

Mr Sturges was very complimentary about *The Angry Silence*, adding – as I supposed was only polite in those circles – he very much hoped he and I would have the opportunity of working together in the not too distant future. Less than two years later, John would cast me opposite Steve in *The Great Escape*, the massive break which was to elevate my own recently abandoned acting career into a whole new dimension.

My substantial fee and above-title star billing on that movie would be negotiated by my new Hollywood agent. Following Merle's party, I'd managed to arrange a meeting with a dapper, red-headed New Yorker, who headed the impressively named motion-picture talent department at General Artists Corporation. The two of us hit it off immediately and, after we'd chatted for a while, Mr Baum said he'd be happy to represent me. I said I'd be happy too. On that, fifty years ago, Marti and I shook hands, sealing the only contract that's ever existed between us.

Back in England, we learned that Forbsie had received a well-deserved Oscar nomination for his *Angry Silence* screenplay. Meanwhile, the two of us had joined a new producers' cooperative to make our next film, *The League of Gentlemen*. The script was one that Bryan had originally been commissioned to write as a vehicle for Cary Grant by the black-listed American film-maker, Carl Foreman. Grant had turned it down and, after a two-year hiatus, the rights had been purchased by Michael Relph and his partner, Basil Dearden, the director who'd so nearly killed me on *The Ship that Died of Shame*.

Until recently, Basil and Michael had worked at Ealing Studios under the aegis of Sir Michael Balcon. Now based at Pinewood, they were proposing that Forbsie and I should team up with them to film his script; hopefully the first in a whole series of independent productions under the cooperative banner of a new company, Allied Film Makers. Jack Hawkins, due to play the lead in *The League of Gentlemen*, was to be chairman, Bryan and I roped in Guy Green and each of the six directors put up £5,000 as working capital. Importantly, though the choice of future subjects had to be approved unanimously, those actually involved were to be granted total artistic freedom.

At that time, although Rank had been running down the production side of its empire, Pinewood remained the biggest and best-equipped studios in the country, boasting excellent, if pricey, facilities and a large permanent staff of highly qualified technicians. In addition, the company owned a chain of six hundred hungry cinemas which, as the newly incorporated Allied Film Makers were well aware, required a constant supply of new product. With this in mind, we took our proposal to the Rank Organisation's chairman, John Davis, the autocratic former accountant famous for saying: 'When want I your opinion, I'll give it to you.'

Having heard us out, Davis struck an immediate deal. We would shoot our films at Pinewood, providing employment for his in-house technicians and, in return for distribution rights, Rank would supply a revolving fund of £1 million from which, providing we came up with the remainder, we could draw 75 per cent of any agreed budget.

DH— Having laid waste to the publicity department, Norman Hardy had abandoned Pinewood for the relative sanity of Fleet Street. But then, as now, film-making was a cyclical business and, almost inevitably, less than a year after his departure, the studios experienced a sudden upsurge in production. With too few unit publicists available, I found myself promoted by my new bosses, John Behr and Derek Coyte.

My first film was the Norman Wisdom vehicle, *Follow a Star*, mostly shot at the Old Met, a disused music hall on the Edgware Road. Mindful of the attention JD paid to his graphs showing the amount of publicity achieved, I was anxious to gain as much editorial space as possible. Egged on by Wisdom's manager-minder, a former policeman called Al, I took to phoning the tabloid gossip columns, posing as a cockney member of the public and managed to plant whole series of stories and pictures.

As a reward, I was assigned to a bigger film. This was *The Singer Not the Song*, a curious saga of good versus evil set in Mexico and filmed in the hinterland of the then undeveloped Costa del Sol. John Mills starred as the good priest in a cassock and Dirk Bogarde was the evil bandito in skintight black leather trousers. It would be an exaggeration to say that Dirk hated me on sight, although I was well aware that his favourite middle-aged publicist was one of those Norman had fired. As a naive greenhorn, clueless that there was such a thing as homosexuality, I was never going to be Dirk's favourite person.

Our female star was the Brigitte Bardot lookalike, Mylene Demongeot. She came to Spain accompanied by her photographer husband, Henri Coste, an intensely proprietary Svengali to her Trilby. Henri was determined that no shot of Mylene should ever be published in which the tousled hair, the pout or the all-important embonpoint were in any way lacking. To this end, he had demanded and received 'kill' rights over every still photograph in which she appeared.

Rolls of exposed black-and-white film shot by our unit photographer went back to England for processing and returned to Malaga in the form of contact sheets. I would then select the frames I considered good enough to be enlarged. Early in the shooting schedule, Henri and Mylene saw me glancing through a new batch of contacts in the hotel lobby and asked if they could see them too. It was this tableau – the three of us poring over the pictures – that greeted Dirk on his return from location, prompting his demand that I be fired on the spot.

With the benefit of hindsight, I can see the production team were in an almighty fix. Their star, outraged that a lesser player had seen the contacts before he did, was threatening to walk out if I remained. As the youngest and most inexperienced member of the unit, it would have been easy to pack me home, bringing my fledgling career to a premature end. But this was a Pinewood crew and, since many of its most senior members were good friends of my father, they decided to hide me instead.

Initially, I was told only that I'd managed to put Dirk's nose out of joint and it would be wise to stay out of his sight for a while. I spent the next week away from the set learning about the jobs of three people I'd known since childhood: costume designer, Yvonne Caffin, production designer, Alex Vetchinsky, and the associate producer, Jack Hanbury.

At the end of the week, when Dirk had calmed down, I went back on location. I steered clear of him as much as possible and the matter was never mentioned again until, much later, I was asked to work on another of his films. Older, wiser and a great deal more confident, I bearded him in his dressing room, saying I would stand down if we couldn't resolve our differences. To give him his due, Dirk responded well and, although never exactly friends, we went on to establish a reasonable working relationship.

Meanwhile, back at Pinewood after my adventures in Spain, my next assignment was *The League of Gentlemen*. One of the stars – and someone, to my certain knowledge, who also took a keen interest in photographs – was Richard Attenborough.

RA— Our unit publicist was the blonde who used to be in charge of the Pinewood stills library, the girl who'd insisted on giving me all those pictures for my archive.

On the first day of shooting, this Diana Carter came up with what seemed like a really silly stunt. She wanted the eight 'gentlemen' – Jack Hawkins, Nigel Patrick, Roger Livesey, Kieron Moore, Terence Alexander, Norman Bird, Forbsie and me – to line up for a group photograph. Fair enough; but, in an ominous foretaste of things to come, we all had to jump when this slip of a girl said 'jump'.

She earnestly explained this was called jumpology, a new craze, originally invented by a *Life* photographer to enliven a formal portrait session with the formidable Mrs Henry Ford. Intrigued with the result, the cameraman had gone on to ask all his famous subjects to jump – JFK, Elizabeth Taylor, Salvador Dali, Richard Nixon, Marilyn Monroe, even the Duke and Duchess of Windsor. These unusual pictures were causing a stir and Diana was convinced that a similar shot of our cast, all jumping together, would achieve major space in the following morning's newspapers. Would I help her to persuade them?

I couldn't say no; the one thing I can never resist is enthusiasm. Together we rounded up the other actors and, despite giving me some funny looks, they all agreed to jump. The following morning, as our publicist had correctly predicted, that image of joyous male camaraderie – the film's main selling point – got our marketing off to a great start. A framed enlargement, a reminder of those far-off happy days, decorated my office wall for many years afterwards.

Making a movie is unbelievably difficult, and I don't just mean raising the finance and shooting it. Equally important is setting it up under the right circumstances and gaining the maximum amount of attention in order to attract an audience. To justify the expenditure, the time and the effort, publicity is absolutely vital. It can, of course, be banal and crude but, in the right hands, it has a definite style and substance.

There are producers, directors and stars who disdain publicists but, from the moment I started working with Di, she was never a servant to the production but part of the overall plan, her contribution being as important as that of the production designer or cameraman.

On *Gandhi*, she became my sounding board and I would insist she sat close enough to confer during rushes. Even then, she was performing a producer's function over and over and over again in all sorts of areas. Nine times out of ten she wasn't seeking publicity but deftly keeping us out of the media. Whether she was dealing with politics, elements of racism, financial crises, international public relations or the management of one or two actors and financiers who were not exactly easy, her skill and diplomacy were phenomenal.

When it came to promoting the finished film, Marvin Antonowsky, Sue Barton and the rest of the marketing team at Columbia were bowled over by the breadth of her expertise. By keeping her on, they gave her the opportunity to learn about international distribution and exhibition, gross and net receipts, trailers, foreign versions, ad campaigns, release patterns, talker and test screenings . . . a whole other side of the business.

Later still, as our professional partnership developed, I was to realise that Di was also a script editor of a calibre that I had never encountered before. Nobody I had worked with was better at analysing a screenplay and pinpointing the advantages, the disadvantages, the good passages and those that were merely mundane. She was and is the best script editor I have come across.

The danger of having any kind of entourage is that you surround yourself with people who kowtow to you, who tell you what you want to hear because their jobs depend on it. The great thing about Di is that she has never allowed me to get away with anything. She doesn't make any bones about it, never humiliates me, but always tells me straight what she believes is right. Her creativity and loyalty are second to none, as is the depth of my gratitude to her.

Over the years, Di and I have had tremendous differences of opinion – mostly about party politics. She is a dyed-in-the-wool stand-on-your-own-two-feet Conservative, who sees me as the archetypal champagne socialist, cushioned from what she likes to call 'real life' in my elite ivory tower. We had one of our biggest rows when I was electioneering at the request of Neil Kinnock and Peter Mandelson in a very deprived area of the Midlands during the run-up to the 1987 general election.

Having accompanied me on other business in the area, Di was horrified to hear that I intended turning up at the local Labour HQ in my chauffeured Rolls-Royce. What was I thinking? Couldn't I see that this showed an appalling lack of empathy?

I countered that this was my usual mode of transport and it would be dishonest of me to pretend otherwise. What would she have me do? Turn up in some rusty old banger?

Eventually, we drew up in this bleak street full of boarded-up shopfronts. Emerging from the Rolls, I immediately registered a local press photographer crouching by the bonnet to frame a telling shot of me which included the distinctive Spirit of Ecstasy mascot. Looking over my shoulder, I also saw the infuriating I-told-you-so expression on Di's face.

Nothing more was said until, visit over, we returned to the Rolls where the argument raged – unabated, unresolved – all the way back to London.

DH— A few weeks later, Dick was in mourning; Labour had lost the election. Possibly out of frustration, he now turned his attention to the leftist project which was to become a lifelong obsession.

I was given the book which had started it all, *The Rights of Man* by Thomas Paine, a slim volume which Dick had received as a teenage birthday present from his father. Having started to read reluctantly, expecting a convoluted eighteenth-century treatise written in fusty prose with f's instead of s's, I immediately found myself engrossed.

Paine had been condemned to death and hanged in effigy for daring to put forward in plain unvarnished English a series of proposals which, to the modern reader, were indisputable. As long ago as 1791 and long before they were implemented, he'd argued for individual liberty and equality under the law, free education, old-age pensions, rights for women, fair taxation and the abolition of hereditary power.

This same former customs officer had gone on to inspire colonial Americans to take up arms in the War of Independence, had helped to frame the US Constitution and later become a pivotal figure at the heart of the French Revolution, nearly losing his head to the guillotine. At the end of his life he'd retired to a farm near New York and died there, shunned and penniless. Posthumously declared a hero, his bones had been dug up for reburial in England but mysteriously disappeared on arrival, never to be found.

I could well understand why Dick was so attracted to this extraordinary story. It had epic scale and a crusading hero; two elements which had always held immense appeal. But, perhaps even more compellingly, this was a subject which would also speak to the craving for parental approval which had driven so much of his career.

His screenwriter of choice was the highly regarded socialist firebrand, Trevor Griffiths, a blunt class warrior from Yorkshire who'd co-scripted Warren Beatty's controversial film, *Reds*. According to his agent, who supplied Dick with the phone number, Trevor was holed up in a rented cottage and must only be disturbed at certain prearranged times. Their conversation, as later relayed to me, went something like this:

'Hello, this is Richard Attenborough. May I please speak to Trevor Griffiths?'

'Trevor here.'

'I know you're very busy and I do apologise profusely for disturbing you but I'm hoping you might kindly agree to write a script for me.'

'What is it?'

'Well, you see, I'm potty about Tom Paine . . .'

Silence.

'Hello? Mr Griffiths? Are you still there?'

Heavy breathing.

'Are you all right, Mr Griffiths?'

Eventually, choked with emotion, came the explanation: 'Looking for a razor.'

'I beg your pardon?'

'To slit my throat.'

Mr Griffiths, it emerged, would give his lifeblood to script *Tom Paine* but had just accepted a commission to write two teleplays about the miners' strike – a subject equally close to his heart – which would take him at least twelve months to complete. Bowled over by the sheer drama of the writer's reaction and, as they talked further, by his scholarly knowledge of Paine, Dick offered to wait.

In my view, this was dangerous. For the past two years we'd both been paid by Universal under the terms of our first-look development deal, and had yet to come up with a viable project.

'What we need, and quickly,' I said to Dick, 'is a backup. Just in case.'

'Don't be silly, darling. You can't come up with another subject just like that.'

Dick can't resist enthusiasm; I can't resist a challenge. Waking up the following morning, I knew precisely what our backup should be. Wickedly, I also knew exactly how to sell it to my partner.

First, I had to make a formal appointment to see him but refuse to give any reason. Then I had to resist the wheedling and grilling which would inevitably follow. Finally, having driven him crazy with curiosity, I had to make a bold pitch which would grab and hold his attention.

At the appointed time, I walked into his office and handed him a single sheet of paper. There were no words on it, just a silhouette of that world-famous icon, the Little Tramp.

He studied it in silence. Then he looked up and grinned.

'Chaplin,' I said.

'Not Chaplin, darling . . . Charlie.'

RA— It was my father who performed the introduction. We'd travelled up to London for a twelfth-birthday treat which began with a visit to the National Gallery in Trafalgar Square. Once inside, the Governor made a beeline for a newly displayed post-Impressionist work, then the subject of much controversy: Seurat's *Bathers at Asnières*.

To this day, I can still hear his loud, almost orgasmic shout of pleasure as he caught sight of the unframed canvas, still recall the disapproving glares from other visitors, still recapture the shared joy as we drank it in together.

At home our walls were covered in a whole range of paintings the Governor admired, all reproductions he'd saved up to buy from the Medici catalogue. But here was an original in every sense of the word, simple in composition yet breathtakingly complex and so large it occupied the whole end wall of the room.

And, unlike any reproduction, this canvas actually glowed with the ambiance of a lazy, hazy summer's day; young men and boys on a river-bank with boats, trees and factory chimneys shimmering in the distance.

We stood in front of it, the Governor and I, for a long time, him telling me that one critic, in his ignorance, had dubbed this master-piece 'vulgar, coarse and commonplace'. Then, looking at his watch, he announced I was about to encounter another genius.

We walked to Piccadilly and arrived at the colonnaded London Pavilion just in time for the matinee performance of *The Gold Rush*. Although it was eight years after the advent of talkies, this was a revival of the silent version, made in 1925. And, like the Seurat, it was a revelation.

I was astonished by the sheer scale of the film, particularly the epic shots of gold prospectors struggling through the snowy wastes of the Sierra Nevada. But what I remember most is the juxtaposition of conflicting emotions this other genius, Charlie Chaplin, was able to engender so apparently effortlessly. Here was someone who had the ability to make me feel incredibly sad and then, in an instant, with just one look or a gesture, make me howl with laughter. Even more extraordinary, this was a shared experience. Magically, everyone else in that darkened auditorium was feeling those same emotions at the same time; their laughter making me laugh all the louder, their sombre silence intensifying my own sense of heartache.

I emerged from the London Pavilion determined to be an actor when I grew up.

More than thirty years were to pass before I met Charlie in person and again it had to do with my birthday. Every summer during the

1960s, Sheila and I took the children to a *pension* in the South of France, close to a sandy beach. And every summer on or around 29 August, we would drive to the Madoura Gallery in Vallauris to choose my birthday present. This was always a ceramic piece designed by Picasso – who I had the joy of meeting just once – and, as time passed, we assembled a sizeable collection.

After one such expedition, we decided to lunch at a restaurant in Villeneuve Loubet which had just been awarded a star in the *Michelin Guide*.

I recognised him instantly. Charlie Chaplin was sitting close to the door at the only occupied table with his wife, Oona, and some of their eight children. I remember going hot and cold; part of me desperate to tell him how much I admired his work, the professional part determined not to intrude. Professionalism won and, on being shown to our own table, I deliberately sat with my back to him so I would not be tempted to stare.

Halfway through our meal, the sound of scraping chairs told me the Chaplin family was leaving. Then, I felt a hand on my shoulder and turned to find him smiling down at me. 'Mr Attenborough?' I managed to nod before he bowled me over completely. 'I just wanted to tell you that, in my estimation, you are a very fine actor.' Before I could muster the words to express just how much that meant to me, he was gone.

Charlie and I met for the last time a decade later. Having received his long overdue knighthood the previous year, he had returned to London with his wife to attend the opening of BAFTA's new premises in Piccadilly and receive a Fellowship from our president, Princess Anne. As vice president, it fell to me to brief the Chaplins beforehand.

I went to his customary suite at the Savoy and found him, at eighty-seven, sadly diminished. By then he was confined to a wheelchair and, Oona told me, spent hours gazing out of the hotel window, holding her hand as he recalled his extraordinary childhood on the other side of the Thames.

As always on their visits to London, a hire car had taken them earlier in the day to tour the streets of Lambeth, where the infant Charlie and his brother, Sydney, had lived precariously in lodgings and, briefly, in a workhouse before their mother had been committed to the pauper lunatic asylum at Cane Hill, leaving the two boys to fend for themselves.

When Oona had finished telling me this, she left the room. I sat close to Charlie, explaining what was to happen at BAFTA the following evening. Although he appeared to be listening, I noticed his eyes never left the door his wife had closed behind her, his whole being willing her to return. When Oona finally reappeared, the relief was palpable, leaving me in no doubt that, of all the women in his life – and there were many – this was the one he absolutely adored.

Charlie died on Christmas Day the following year at his home in Switzerland. Oona never recovered. Her grief was exacerbated when a Pole and a Bulgarian dug up her husband's coffin and attempted to coerce her into paying a ransom of £400,000. Oona flatly refused, saying, 'Charlie would have thought it ridiculous.'

DH— I chose to omit this macabre postscript from the synopsis Dick asked me to write in order to pitch our Chaplin project to Universal. As he had decided at the outset, our film was to be called *Charlie*, and *Charlie* it remained throughout all our many trials and tribulations until a perverse last-minute ruling by the Motion Picture Association of America forced us to adopt the far more sombre *Chaplin*.

Embarking on my detailed film treatment, I faced the problem of condensing a long life filled with extraordinary incident into just over two hours of screen time. Simplistically, Charlie's story fell into three distinct chapters: the impoverished East End childhood; the period of fame and fortune in early Hollywood; and, finally, the uneventful twilight years after his expulsion from America, spent quietly *en famille* in Switzerland. The first two were crammed with so much drama, humour, scandal and creativity that Dick and I immediately agreed to exclude the third.

I drew heavily on Charlie's *My Autobiography* and *Chaplin: His Life and Art* by David Robinson. David, formerly *The Times* film critic, was a walking Chaplin encyclopedia and the only person ever to be granted access to the family's extensive archive. After we had acquired screen rights to both books, he became our poacher-turned-gamekeeper consultant, offering at the outset a piece of seemingly excellent advice: 'Write the review you'd like to receive and then write the script.'

From the point of view of someone who'd spent most of his working life viewing and reviewing the output of the world's film-makers – good, dire and indifferent – this made perfect sense. But, as David was to learn during the long years of development hell which followed, it's never that simple.

Soon after I'd completed my treatment, Trevor Griffiths delivered the first draft of his Paine screenplay, an amazing tour de force. Written in longhand and typed up by his partner, Gill, *These Are the Times* came in at a whopping 285 pages. The accepted rule of thumb, used throughout the film industry, equates one page of a script to one minute of screen time. By this rough yardstick, Trevor had written a four-and-a-half-hour film. But, on closer examination, it proved to be even longer.

One huge historical scene – which would take at least five minutes of screen time and cost an absolute fortune – had George Washington overseeing the decisive Battle of Trenton during the War of Independence. This Trevor had scripted in three lean sentences:

WASHINGTON, on high ground, watch in hand. The two armies launch a synchronised surprise attack on the sleeping ENEMY. Half-dressed HESSIAN hurtle into the narrow streets with muskets and cannon, attempt defensive action; OTHERS simply run off by the thousand.

In order to maximise box-office receipts, distributors and their exhibitors demand movies that allow for two separate evening performances; the optimum running time being no more than 135 minutes. However, remembering *Gandhi* had screened at over three hours and that Frank Price had accepted this without demur, Dick was not, at this initial stage, unduly worried about length. His overwhelming concern was cost; on a first reading, Terry Clegg had guesstimated the budget for Trevor's script at an eye-watering $50 million.

Under the terms of the development deal established by Frank Price, Universal had paid for Trevor's first draft. What Dick now needed was the agreement of his successor, Tom Pollock, to underwrite the cost of the further refining drafts he was eager to commission.

We flew to Los Angeles; I to hear the fate of my *Charlie* treatment, he to talk up Trevor's screenplay. Marti Baum picked us up from the Beverly Hills Hotel and drove us across Coldwater Canyon to the forbidding Black Tower, executive headquarters of MCA, Universal where, in the words of the official studio guide, 'scripts are read and careers are made or broken'.

The penthouse floor of this glowering landmark was occupied by the legendary Lew Wasserman, a former agent, now all-powerful president and CEO of the whole vast conglomerate. By his decree, everyone working under him had to be formally dressed and these almost exclusively male minions were referred to dismissively by the people who actually made films as 'the suits'.

Unlike the reserved Frank Price, Tom Pollock was extremely outgoing and jovial. But, disconcertingly, one of his eyes rolled alarmingly in its socket. I remember whispering to Dick, clad in his usual jeans and denim bomber jacket: 'Better pick an eye and stick with it.'

As chairman of the Motion Picture Group, good-cop Tom was naturally suited and booted. So too was his bad-cop sidekick, Casey Silver, the man in charge of the script department. In this set-up, after some introductory pleasantries, it fell to Mr Silver to trash Trevor's wonderful screenplay. It was, he said, far too long, far too intellectual, far too complicated and, of course, far, far too expensive.

Dick fought eloquently. He spoke at length about the subject's historical importance. He waxed lyrical about Dan Day-Lewis, who he hoped would play Paine, and the host of other players, all of them major stars, who had expressed their eagerness to appear, even in minor supporting roles. When none of this elicited a shred of discernible enthusiasm, he jumped to his feet and acted out a couple of scenes. This Pollock evidently enjoyed while Silver remained resolutely impassive.

It fell to good-cop Tom to summarise the meeting. Universal loved Dickie, of course they did, and they really did want to continue working with him. But unfortunately a life of Thomas Paine was not a movie they felt able to pursue. *Charlie*, however, was a different matter.

Over the next decade, Trevor Griffiths was to write four more drafts of *These Are the Times*. Jake Eberts paid for two of them and Dick himself paid for two more. By the time the last was delivered, the cost of the film was $100 million and rising.

In 2004, Trevor finally gave up any hope of seeing his script made into a film and published it in book form. Dick, however, has never given up hope. *These Are the Times* is always his next project.

RA— Back in 1960, my next project involved Johnny Mills and his author wife, Mary Hayley Bell. While we were shooting *The League of Gentlemen*, Mary had sent me a copy of her latest book, an intriguing novella called *Whistle Down the Wind*, inspired by her three children, Juliet, Hayley and Jonathan.

Johnny and Mary had just returned from Hollywood where they'd been chaperoning Hayley, then aged thirteen. Having made a phenomenal screen debut opposite her father and Horst Buchholz in J. Lee Thompson's acclaimed thriller, *Tiger Bay*, their younger daughter had been put under contract by Disney, achieving huge success in *Pollyanna* and being awarded a special Oscar while completing her third film, *The Parent Trap*.

Bryan agreed that a combination of Mary's book and Hayley as the eldest of the three child characters would make a terrific next project for us. Indeed, so taken was he with the idea that he became determined not only to write the script, but to direct the film as well. Although he had no experience, this made perfect sense to me. I knew, being an actor, he had a finely tuned sense of performance and also, being a crazy collector of every kind of camera, that he also had a terrific eye for composition.

However, although we were all friends, I wasn't sure Johnny and Mary would see it this way. Hayley was a hot property at a crucial stage in her acting career and I feared they might be unwilling to entrust her to any rookie director.

Deciding to take things one stage at a time, I contacted the Millses' illustrious agent, Laurie Evans, to discuss the acquisition of film rights to Mary's book. These negotiations having been successfully concluded, the two of us met for a celebratory lunch with Forbsie who, having described his plans for the script, suddenly and disastrously started to talk about directing. The inscrutable Laurie didn't so much as bat an eyelid.

On the drive back to Richmond, Bryan was jubilant, convinced he'd won him over without even a skirmish, let alone a battle. I, however, felt distinctly apprehensive. Sure enough, later that same afternoon, a formal letter from London Management was hand-delivered to Beaver Lodge. It stated that the Millses required director approval and would only accept one of the people named on the enclosed list, ambitiously headed by David Lean. Needless to say, Bryan's name was not included.

He was deeply wounded and more angry than I had ever seen him, so angry that in high dudgeon he immediately excluded himself from the whole project and went off to write another vehicle for Cary Grant. Missing him intensely, I continued alone, engaging Guy Green, whose name was on the list of approved directors, and commissioning another partnership, also approved by Johnny and Mary, to write the script.

Willis Hall and Keith Waterhouse, both originally from Leeds, had first met as teenagers. After each had found success – Willis as a playwright, Keith as a novelist – they'd teamed up to write the groundbreaking stage production of *Billy Liar* and were now regularly contributing to the irreverent *That Was The Week That Was* on television. It was their idea to transpose Mary's story, set in the genteel countryside of the Millses' Kent farmhouse, to the more rugged terrain and temperament of Lancashire. This, I believed, was a wise move which served, in large measure, to mitigate any element of cloying sentimentality.

While Willis and Keith were producing their first draft, Forbsie was travelling all over Europe, being given the runaround by Cary Grant. It ended badly. When, at the end of 1960, he delivered his script, it was immediately and unceremoniously shelved.

Soon afterwards, we took *The Angry Silence* to America and the rift between us was healed. Then, only weeks before the start of shooting, Guy Green suddenly announced he was pulling out of *Whistle Down the Wind*, having received a considerably more lucrative offer from MGM. With the crew hired and the art department already at work in Clitheroe, I had no director.

Johnny, Mary and I held a council of war at their farmhouse in Cowden. Tentatively, I suggested Bryan might replace Guy. But, astonishingly and totally out of the blue, Johnny announced they'd had a much better idea: they wanted me to take over.

Knocked for six, I said I'd like time to think about it and, on the drive back to Richmond, did think long and hard. I was flattered and tempted, of course, but I'd never had any ambition to become a director. What I enjoyed most about life on the other side of the camera was being in charge of the organisation; negotiating, raising the finance, troubleshooting and putting together a homogenous crew. In short, I was happy being a producer. Forbsie, on the other hand, yearned to direct. And what I really wanted, more than anything, was to put our partnership back on the old harmonious footing.

On reaching home, I phoned Johnny. Having thanked him for his faith in me, I told him I had to decline. Although we desperately needed a new director, I did not believe I was the right person to take over. Would he and Mary at least agree to meet Bryan? Johnny said they'd discuss it. Ten minutes later, he called back, inviting us both to supper the following evening.

Back at Cowden, with the ground already prepared, the Millses listened intently as Bryan took them through the script. As the evening wore on, I could see them responding to his vivid imagery and unbounded enthusiasm. Finally Johnny, having absented himself briefly, returned bearing a bottle of champagne. We toasted the film and then we all drank to Bryan's success as a director. I heaved a huge sigh of relief.

Forbsie and I went on to make two more films together. The first of these was *The L-Shaped Room* which he adapted from Lynne Reid Banks' novel and directed for James Woolf's company, Romulus. I was out of work at the time and, knowing I needed the money, he loyally arranged that I should oversee the day-to-day business of production and share a producer credit with Jimmy.

Our final collaboration was *Séance on a Wet Afternoon*. Again, Bryan wrote the script and directed. I produced and played the male lead, complete with prosthetic nose, opposite the wonderful but complicated American method actress, Kim Stanley.

Then for many years, our professional paths diverged, although the friendship remained strong. Sheila and I were on holiday with Nan and Bryan when I read the Gandhi biography which changed the course of my life and made me determined to become a director. Having made that decision, Forbsie was naturally the first person I approached to write the screenplay. However, after some initial research, he declined on the grounds that he'd taken a dislike to the Mahatma and I was out of my mind even to contemplate such a project.

I should have remembered this twenty-five years later when Universal gave *Charlie* the go-ahead. They were keen to appoint an American writer but I was determined that the commission should go to Bryan; not only because he needed the job, but because I sincerely believed no one else could turn in a better screenplay.

What I didn't appreciate until far too late was that he also strongly disapproved of Chaplin, considering his passionately held political views naive, his oeuvre vastly overrated and much of his personal life despicable. Determined to portray him warts and all, Forbsie began his script with black humour, depicting the botched theft of Charlie's coffin, a sequence I knew Oona, then terminally ill, would find distressing.

Each of Forbsie's drafts – and he was to write four over the course of the next year – had to be submitted to Universal in order to release the next tranche of his fee. And each elicited a raft of increasingly unpleasant and destructive comments from Casey Silver's script department which it fell to me to convey, as tactfully as I was able, to Bryan.

The crunch came in May 1990. A further meeting in the Black Tower resulted in what I then believed to be one of the worst days of my life. I was bluntly informed the choice was mine: either abandon *Charlie* or get another writer. When eventually I screwed up the courage to tell Forbsie I felt obliged to get another writer, it felt as if I was murdering our friendship, and during the interminable period of bitter silence which followed, I missed him more than I can say.

It was he who generously made the first move towards a reconciliation. And, on the morning of 26 December 2004 – which really was the very worst day of my entire life – of all our many friends and acquaintances, it was Bryan and darling Nan who immediately came rushing round to comfort me and Sheila.

DH— The next writer to tackle the *Charlie* script was the distinguished novelist William Boyd. It was during one of our regular trips to Hollywood to discuss the latest of Will's drafts, and hopefully move a little closer to actual production, that Marti Baum begged Dick to do him a favour. One of his fellow agents at Creative Artists had a client who was desperate to meet him.

The client proved to be a bizarre American youth, clad head to toe in black biker gear with equally black hair contorted into spikes. Compulsively twisting one of the spikes, this apparition mumbled he'd heard Sir Attenborough was making a picture about Charlie Chaplin and should be aware he was the only actor on earth capable of bringing him to life. Taken aback, Dick lied through his teeth extremely courteously, promising that, when the time came, he would be considered.

There was someone else working in Hollywood, who was also determined to play Charlie. This was Kenneth Branagh, then directing and starring in *Dead Again* with his wife Emma Thompson. He invited us onto the set, showed us some footage and came to lunch at the Beverly Hills Hotel to make his extremely persuasive case.

Back in England, film critic David Robinson had yet another leading man in mind, doing his level best to persuade Dick that he should cast Michael Jackson. 'But David, darling, Charlie was white.' To which David responded: 'When did you last see Jackson?'

Dick, however, had an unusual idea of his own and approached the eminent South African-born Shakespearean stage actor, known to be gay but yet to come out, Antony Sher.

When, after a screen test, Dick and Sher mutually agreed not to proceed, Terry Clegg set up further tests for three unknown but up-and-coming young American actors at the old Raleigh Studios in the heart of Hollywood. Almost as an afterthought, we included as a fourth candidate the spiky biker.

At the end of a long and dispiriting day, he was the last to stand in front of the camera. With his dark hair now waved in a reasonable facsimile of the young Chaplin, he gave an excellent reading in a totally believable English accent. Concealing his surprise, Dick said he'd get back to his agent after viewing the rushes, but the young actor asked if he could be granted a little more time.

He left the stage and came back with a stepladder. As the camera started to turn, he embarked on a extraordinary silent routine; clowning his way through a series of ham-fisted attempts to set up the ladder, tripping, trapping his hand, getting his head stuck between the rungs and, when he did finally reach the top, swaying alarmingly before performing an amazingly acrobatic pratfall.

'Cut.' Dick was laughing so hard the tears were running down his face.

He knew it. I knew it. The whole crew knew it. He might be mad as a box of frogs but Robert Downey Jr was as close to a reincarnation of Charlie Chaplin as we were ever likely to encounter. We never had any doubts.

However, although they hadn't yet reached us, rumours about Robert's recreational activities were already beginning to circulate in Tinseltown and at Universal there were doubts aplenty.

With our leading man grudgingly approved, we began to cast around for a leading lady to play two key roles. It was my idea that the same person should play both Charlie's tragic first love – a teenage chorus girl called Hetty Kelly – and Oona, his last and most enduring love of all. We needed a star name and dark-haired Winona Ryder, then one of Hollywood's hottest properties, bore a remarkable resemblance to Oona. However, her agent was determined to secure an enormous fee and negotiations continued, back and forth, interminably.

By the beginning of 1991 – four years after I'd come up with the idea for *Charlie* – Will Boyd had delivered his final shooting script, and although Universal were proposing to engage yet another writer 'to sharpen up the dialogue', they'd given us an amber light and all the funding we needed to embark on pre-production.

Well ahead of schedule, a super-efficient American construction team had all but completed two key sets among the orange groves of the Santa Clara River Valley. The first was a rudimentary open-air stage with muslin drapes to filter out the fierce sunshine, the second an exact replica of the more advanced film-making complex Charlie had commissioned in 1917 at the junction of Sunset and La Brea.

The axe fell on Friday 1 February, just six weeks before we were due to start shooting. Dick, Terry and I were scouting beach locations at Malibu. At that time, we depended on car phones, so Dick, who was expecting a call to say Winona Ryder's fee had finally been agreed, was not unduly concerned when our driver beckoned him over.

When we saw the blood rush to his face, Terry and I knew it was bad news. A shell-shocked Dick told us there was to be no green light. Universal were pulling out of the whole project and putting *Charlie* in turnaround. Our first-look deal was terminated and all expenditure blocked. Furthermore, if we couldn't come up with a new backer, they would destroy all our sets.

We rushed to the CAA building in Beverly Hills to hold a council of war with Marti Baum. Who on earth would pick up a $27 million project at this late stage in the game? To Marti's way of thinking the only possibility was the man who had instantly decided to buy *Gandhi* and recently been restored to his old job as head of Columbia Pictures. He put through a call and Frank Price kindly agreed to spend the following day considering our project and give us an answer at his home on Sunday morning.

The answer, delivered with great charm and many regrets in Frank's English rose garden, was no.

Terry went back to London and Marti went into overdrive. On the Monday afternoon he took us to see production executives at Twentieth Century Fox where we received an instant and far less charming turn-down. Finally, at the end of Tuesday, having exhausted every other possibility, Marti set up a last-chance meeting with a flamboyant one-man band, regarded by many in 'old' Hollywood as a tasteless upstart.

In many ways, Mario Kassar personified the American dream. He was a Lebanese-Italian who'd started out selling spaghetti westerns throughout the Middle East. After settling in California, he'd become a small-scale film-maker and, with his Hungarian partner, Andrew Vajna, had set up Carolco, a modest distribution company specialising in foreign sales.

Their first taste of success had come in 1982 with the release of the ultra violent *First Blood*, establishing the lucrative *Rambo* franchise. Then, only a year later and for a minuscule outlay, they'd acquired a much derided sci-fi adventure starring an Austrian bodybuilder which had gone on to gross $78 million.

Having split up with his partner, Mr Kassar now occupied a fortress of an office building adjacent to Book Soup on Sunset Strip. Knowing what he did, it seemed unlikely that Dick, with his loathing of gratu-itous violence, could ever work with him. However, he immediately warmed to this rotund Chaplin enthusiast and to his multi-ethnic staff which, unusually, was mainly female.

Mr Kassar listened intently, giving nothing away as Dick made his fervent pitch. Having asked for a copy of Robert's screen test, he said he'd try to view it that evening and get back to us the following day.

Neither of us was overly optimistic during the short drive back to the Beverly Hills Hotel. But, as soon as he entered the lobby, Dick was handed an urgent message: 'Have seen Downey's terrific test. Get your people over here. Mario.'

'Your people' were Dick's young lawyer, Andrew Hildebrand, and Terry Clegg. Both flew over immediately and embarked on a gruelling series of contractual and budget negotiations which would drag on for months. Elsewhere in the Carolco building, Dick and I had the first of our many script conferences with Mario's closest associates, known as the two Cathys.

Echoing their counterparts in the Black Tower, Cathy Rabin and Kathy Summer pronounced our dialogue lacking in sparkle. But their eyes lit up when we named the award-winning playwright Universal had been planning to bring in as an uncredited script doctor. Within a matter of days, the four of us were admiring a splendid view across the Thames from the Chelsea Harbour apartment of our third screen-writer, Tom Stoppard.

However, even after Tom had delivered his witty one-liners, our deal with Carolco hadn't quite reached a conclusion. Only towards the end of June, when Mario invited us to his home, did we finally understand the reason behind the seemingly endless procrastination.

Mario lived with his young family in Holmby Hills, next door to Hugh Hefner's Playboy Mansion, under the protection of the world's most expensive security system and two permanent bodyguards. His spacious and tasteful mansion boasted an amazing art collection in which early Russian icons were juxtaposed with Fernando Botero's exceedingly corpulent nudes.

The real eye-opener, however, was the basement cinema; huge screen, state-of-the-art sound system, buckets of popcorn, reclining chairs uphol-stered in butter-soft leather. Here we were treated to a preview of the newly completed film which was to determine our fate. *Terminator 2*, aptly subtitled *Judgment Day*, was Mario's lavish $100 million sequel to his cheap 1983 sci-fi pickup and, he announced as the lights dimmed, the most expensive movie ever made.

It was loud, brash and violent – not the kind of film Dick and I would normally choose to see – but also beguilingly witty and self-mocking. Linda Hamilton was no bimbo, but an astute and sinewy heroine. Schwarzenegger, although resolutely wooden and muscle-bound, displayed an endearingly wry sense of humour. However, it was James Cameron's special effects and advanced computer-generated imagery which literally took the breath away; massive explosions, sensational chases, a whole city incinerated and the amazing regeneration of molten pools of metal.

This was the single project on which Mario had gambled pretty much everything he possessed. If it did well, *Charlie* was on. If it failed, we'd be booking the next flight home. Hollywood can gauge the level of a movie's eventual success or failure from the box-office take during the first Saturday and Sunday of American release. *Terminator 2* grossed an incredible $31.7 million over the first weekend of July 1991.

All the *Charlie* contracts were agreed and signed by the end of the month.

A film can have many producers. An executive producer's involvement is usually purely financial, the co-producer's input is supervisory and an associate producer is answerable to the person wielding overall power, who is, simply, The Producer.

Originally, Terry Clegg was our co-producer, I was associate producer and, in addition to directing, Dick was the sole producer. We had assumed, as was his custom, that Mario would take the executive producer credit. However, with his future no longer in jeopardy, he turned his full attention to *Charlie*, appointing himself joint producer with Dick and taking a late but controlling hand in the script.

Aided and abetted by the two Cathys, Mario insisted the film must include the last chapter of Chaplin's life. This being the element Dick and I had long ago decided should be excluded, we should have stuck to our guns and refused. But, persuasion having failed, we found ourselves in yet another make-or-break confrontation. And, having spent the last four and a half years of our lives fighting to make this film and being at risk of losing Robert who had put his career on hold to play Charlie, we gave in.

Our fourth screenwriter was Dick's friend William Goldman, author of the definitive Hollywood exposé, *Adventures in the Screen Trade*, and the man Joe Levine had brought in sixteen years earlier to script *A Bridge Too Far*.

It was Bill's idea to introduce a fictitious editor, to be played by Anthony Hopkins, who would travel to Switzerland to question the elderly Chaplin about his forthcoming autobiography. Although this device satisfied Mario's desire to depict the final phase of Charlie's life, it meant that the bulk of our story would have to be conveyed in a series of somewhat disjointed flashbacks. It also meant that Robert would have to age from teenager to octogenarian within the space of little more than two hours.

9

ABOVE THE TITLE

RA— JUNE 1980. HE was living on a fifteen-acre ranch out at Santa Paula. I was on a flying visit to the West Coast. We'd arranged to meet at his favourite haunt, the old Brown Derby at Hollywood and Vine.

Because he was always so punctual and I'd been delayed, it seemed strange not to see him when I arrived. About to sit where I could keep an eye on the door, I caught sight of the ravaged old man beckoning from one of the bar stools right at the back. A shiver ran through me: the old man was Steve.

How do you say farewell to one of your closest friends? What do you talk about the last time you meet?

I'll tell you. We ribbed each other about the day he scared the shit out of me on his motorbike. We traded the usual boasts about our sons; his Chad, my Mike. He reminded me about the time I dragged him to a football match at Stamford Bridge. I reminded him about the formal dinner at Paul Newman's house where, instead of fine wine, the white-gloved butler served us cans of Budweiser on a silver salver. And then, when the conversation lagged, we relived the endless rain-sodden months we'd spent together in Taiwan.

Steve and I sat at that bar and we talked about everything under the sun except the one thing that was uppermost in both our minds. I never thanked him for landing me the part of Frenchy Burgoyne. He never mentioned he'd been given only six months to live. And when we hugged on the sidewalk outside, neither of us said goodbye.

Six months later, I was in India, about to start work on *Gandhi*, when I received the news I'd been dreading: at the age of fifty, Steve McQueen was dead.

I first met him during the summer of 1962 in Bavaria where John Sturges was shooting *The Great Escape*. This was my big international acting break-through and just three members of the all-male cast were billed above the title: Steve as the Cooler King, Jim Garner as the Scrounger and me as Big X. And right from the outset, both on-screen and off, there was this intense macho rivalry between the Brits and the Yanks.

It came to a head when the two separate groups were lounging around in the sun during an early break from shooting. As always when time hung heavy, Steve was riding his 500cc Triumph, zooming off between the POW camp huts and returning to skid around us Brits in ever decreasing dusty circles. Finally, those piercing blue eyes hidden behind dark glasses, he came to a halt beside me and sat there, twisting the throttle provocatively. 'Wanna ride?'

Fatally, I hesitated. It was thirty years since I'd ridden pillion and, having been rushed to hospital as a result, had sworn I'd never ever do it again. But national honour was at stake here and I knew I couldn't refuse the challenge.

'You bet,' I said heartily, climbing on behind.

Although they cemented our friendship and united the cast, the fifteen minutes which followed, as I clung on for dear life, were the most terrifying I can remember.

Steve was a speed freak. He was devastated when the film's insurers ruled against him performing the most famous motorbike stunt in movie history but never took the credit for it, always being careful to point out it was performed by his pal and double, Bud Ekins. What did give him immense pleasure was dressing up as one of the Germans chasing Bud towards the wire.

There's a perception that Steve was anathema to screenwriters, always angling to make his parts bigger. That, in my experience, is completely untrue. In fact, he was a minimalist, forever fighting to cut lines because he knew, better than anyone, that one telling look is worth any amount of dialogue.

The other thing about Steve, in additional to his phenomenal loyalty, was his almost spiritual affinity with anything mechanical. There's a telling scene in *The Sand Pebbles* when he first goes below decks on the *San Pablo* and introduces himself: 'Hi, Engine, I'm Jake Holman.' And, throughout the long shooting schedule, whether he had to strip something down, repair it, oil it or put it back together again, there was always this supreme competence.

Why would anyone in their right mind cast an English actor to play an American sailor called Frenchy in a film set in China to be shot in Taiwan? The answer, I am sure, although Bobby Wise who directed *The Sand Pebbles* was far too gentlemanly ever to say so, was that Steve, my co-star, rooted for me.

I valued his friendship profoundly and still miss him more than I can say. He was one of the great screen actors of all time.

DH— June 1992. Dick and I are the first to arrive at this small German recording studio in the middle of nowhere. Our scowling star, Robert Downey Jr, is uncharacteristically late. Understandable really; he's in the middle of a well-deserved European holiday with his new girlfriend and this is the fifth or sixth time we've had to ask him to re-record his voice-over.

Charlie, now in the final stages of post-production, is exceeding the contractual length and Mario Kassar has demanded cuts. To paper over the cracks, Bill Goldman has written yet more lines to be spoken by the octogenarian Chaplin.

As we prepare to record them, I'm with the Germans, who normally work with singers and musicians, trying to explain the requirements for film. Dick, meanwhile, is in a small soundproofed booth, talking earnestly to Robert, who stands in front of the microphone, scanning his page of dialogue for less than ten seconds before casting it contemptuously aside.

The engineers connect me with the booth. I ask for some level. Robert snarls in his old-Chaplin voice: 'If you're happy and you know it, clap your hands.'

I say we're ready when he is. As the recording light goes on, Dick retrieves the script and replaces it, face up, on the reading stand. Robert defiantly turns it face down. Staring expressionlessly through the glass, he then proceeds to deliver every one of his lines; each exquisitely timed, totally in character and, amazingly, word-perfect.

We just about have time to thank him before he climbs into his waiting car and is driven off into the night. Staring at the disappearing tail lights, Dick says: 'Would you believe it? The little bugger can act, sing, dance, play the piano and compose like an angel. And, as if that wasn't enough, he's got a photographic memory.'

My mind goes back to an early morning in California last October when we were on location among the orange groves of the Santa Clara River Valley.

The sun was only a glow on the horizon when 26-year-old Robert arrived promptly for his dawn call. I remember watching in dismay as the most multi-talented artist I had ever encountered emerged from the chauffeur-driven car, unshaven and glassy-eyed; a stumbling wreck falling into the waiting arms of our second assistant director.

An hour and a half later, costumed, made up and bright as a button, the other Robert was on set, ready to rehearse. While he and Dick blocked out the first shot, Terry Clegg and I were conferring worriedly on the sidelines.

'He's got to talk to him,' Terry said for the umpteenth time.

'He won't. God knows I've tried. As long as Robert turns up on time, knows all his lines and keeps on giving a wonderful performance, Dick's not going to bring everything to a halt by having a showdown.'

Our young star, as Terry and I well knew, was then in the process of splitting up with his previous live-in girlfriend of five years, Sarah Jessica Parker. We also knew from telltale sources that he went home at the end of the shooting day and drank a whole bottle of vodka in an effort to get a full night's sleep. Waking only a short time later, he would drive round one of the less salubrious areas of Los Angeles until he managed to hook up with an alley dealer. Then, having had his fix, he again tried to sleep until it was time for the fifty-mile drive out to the location and another long day in front of the camera.

Intimation that this brilliant and endearing boy was, to say the least, a little bit strange had come a few months earlier. Dick and I had been invited to dinner at his office, which turned out to be a small house, reputed to have belonged to Charlie Chaplin, way up in the Hollywood Hills.

We'd arrived after dark to find the entire place glowing with hundreds of candles. A violin recording of the romantic theme music Chaplin had composed for *Limelight* was spilling into the narrow street, accompanied by an amazing voice, not unlike that of Nat King Cole – Robert singing, 'I'll be loving you eternally . . .'

Inside, although only the three of us were to eat, the table had four place settings. At its head was an eerie presence: a tailor's dummy dressed head to toe in a Little Tramp costume.

Robert, convinced of his spiritual affinity with Chaplin, went on to approach the task of reincarnating him for the film with a dedication which, at times, bordered on fanaticism.

Having bought the little house in the Hollywood Hills, he'd learned to play tennis and the violin left-handed, as Chaplin had done. During the interminable delay while we were negotiating with Mario Kassar at Carolco, he'd studied the work of all the great stage and film mime artists. Then, weeks before the start of shooting, he'd travelled to London with the express intention of acquiring Charlie's original accent, spending hours with Dick's cockney chauffeur, Bill Gadsdon, until he could mimic him perfectly.

Nothing, however, could have prepared Robert for the week he was to spend in Switzerland right at the end of our shooting schedule. This was where Chaplin had lived out his final years in a white, twenty-room villa overlooking Lake Geneva with Oona, their eight children and numerous staff, including two nannies. He'd died there, surrounded by his family, on Christmas Day 1977, and when we arrived, fifteen years later, the whole place was in a time warp – exactly as he'd left it.

On entering the Manoir de Ban, Robert was in Chaplin heaven. He lay on Charlie's bed, sprawled on the sofa which had appeared in *City Lights* and was taken by the family's executrix, Pam Paumier, into the cellar archive where he was able to see, touch and smell the assembled memorabilia of his alter ego's working lifetime.

Then came Chaplin hell. To become the octogenarian Charlie, he had to sit immobile in a make-up chair throughout the night. First, his entire head was painstakingly encased in the bald cap, wig and the delicate latex moulds of ageing skin created by an American prosthetic artist, John Caglione. Then came the delicate colouring process: hooded eyes, sparse eyebrows, thinning lip line, jowls, wrinkles and liver spots;

all delineated with fine sable brushes. In all, this transformation took eight hours.

However, excellent though it was, the prosthetic make-up would not stand up to bright light or extreme close-ups and required constant running repairs. It was also extremely delicate. Robert was able to drink through a straw but eating was out of the question. Come early afternoon, when it became evident he was quietly going mad under the latex, Dick would announce a wrap and Robert would immediately claw at his face, tearing it off in strips.

Deservedly, he received a Best Actor Oscar nomination for his reincarnation of Chaplin. That he didn't win was our fault. Had we stood out against Mario Kassar and refused to tell Charlie's story in flashback, the film would have been far more coherent – although it would almost certainly never have been made at all. And had we fulfilled expectations by including more of the comedic Little Tramp and less of his progenitor's dark and complicated life story, we would undoubtedly have attracted better reviews.

Would winning an Oscar have provided the impetus Robert needed to kick his drug habit? I doubt it. Despite his subsequent short-lived marriage to Deborah Falconer, the birth of their son, Indio, and a number of further acclaimed screen appearances, he was arrested in 1996 for possession of heroin, a gun and crack cocaine. A month later, he was arrested again for trespass, having blundered into a neighbour's home in the middle of the night and fallen asleep in a child's bedroom. When ordered to enter a supervised rehabilitation programme, he escaped through a window. On other occasions he repeatedly failed to turn up for mandatory drug tests.

And so it went on. Hauled before the same exasperated judge for the fifth time, Robert confessed: 'It's like I've got a shotgun in my mouth and I've got my hand on the trigger and I like the taste of gunmetal.'

Sentencing him to three years in the California State Penitentiary, the judge added harshly: 'I'm going to incarcerate you and I'm going to incarcerate you in a way that is very unpleasant.'

Robert was not forgotten during his time in prison. Dick stayed in touch as did most of the loyal and admiring friends he had worked with over the years – including Sean Penn, Michael Douglas, Johnny Depp and Mel Gibson. Despite many setbacks after his release, this most captivating, infuriating and creative of actors, has continued to work ever since. He is now in his early forties, recently remarried and, hopefully at long last, clean.

RA— 'We decided we needed someone who knows absolutely everything or someone, like you, who knows bugger all.'

Although I've had quite a few backhanded compliments in my life, this – from one of my closest friends – was undoubtedly the most surprising. It was delivered on a Saturday morning in 1967 when I rang John Mills to talk about the script he'd left for me at Old Friars the previous evening.

Johnny answered the phone immediately and without any preamble demanded: 'What do you think?'

The script was an adaptation of Joan Littlewood's wonderful stage musical, *Oh! What a Lovely War*, reconceived for the screen by the celebrated thriller writer, Len Deighton.

I said: 'It's absolutely terrific, Johnny. A phenomenal piece of work. I'm so touched that you and Len should think of me. What would you like me to play?'

He was completely matter-of-fact. 'Oh, we don't want you to act. We want you to direct it.'

For once incredulity rendered me totally speechless. Lacking any previous experience and having rejected Johnny's earlier suggestion that I should direct *Whistle Down the Wind*, this was the last thing I'd expected. Even on first reading, it was evident that *Oh! What a Lovely War* was not only extremely complicated, but a totally original, surrealistic and highly-stylised film subject.

Eventually I said: 'Johnny, forgive me, but this is a massive undertaking. Oughtn't you to be looking for someone very experienced?'

It was then he explained that he and Len, his partner, had taken this extraordinary decision because, knowing 'bugger all', as he so graciously put it, I would come to their project with a fresh eye and a completely open mind. Was I willing to do it?

At a low ebb because, after five years, *Gandhi* was still in the hands of David Lean and Robert Bolt, I said fervently, 'I'd adore to do it.' And went on to pose the all-important question: 'Have you got any money?'

'No, we haven't got any money.'

'How are you planning to go about it?'

Back came the sheepish answer: 'We thought we'd ask you.'

One of the people I consulted was Bud Ornstein, the genial American who headed United Artists in London. Having heard me out, Bud said: 'A First World War subject full of singing and dancing? Are you out of your mind? Only a fuckin' lunatic would back it.'

Then, after a short pause, he added: 'Come to think of it, there's a stinking rich American lunatic on his way over here right now. Just bailed out Paramount and crazy about movies. Known as the mad Austrian of Wall Street – Charlie Bluhdorn.'

When Bud got me an appointment to see him, this shirt-sleeved enthusiast, variously described as irrepressible, rapacious and ruthless, had taken up temporary residence in the Dorchester.

Having done my homework, I knew Charlie was the son of Jewish refugees, whose first job had been with the New York Cotton Exchange on a salary of $15 a week. He'd gone on to buy a small spare-parts company called Michigan Bumper and parlayed this modest investment into the powerful conglomerate, Gulf & Western, which owned, inter alia, publishers Simon & Schuster, Madison Square Garden and, providentially – Charlie's most recent acquisition – the moribund Paramount Pictures.

He proved to be three years younger than me and in every way larger than life; huge personality, huge charm, huge bulk. He kicked off by asking about the film. What was so special?

I told him it was absolutely unique and great and moving and so on. When he failed to react, I got to my feet and started to sing and dance my way through some of the musical numbers: 'They Were Only Playing Leapfrog', 'Hold Your Hand Out, Naughty Boy', 'Oh! Oh! Oh! It's a Lovely War' ...

Finally, when I came to a somewhat breathless halt, Charlie threw out: 'Who's gonna be in it?'

Stupidly, I enthused. 'Well, the important thing is to have totally unknown people playing the Smith family.'

'Unknowns! Are you crazy?'

Swift change of gear: 'Well, of course I intend to have major stars playing all the important cameo parts – the Kaiser, Emperor Franz Josef, Field Marshall Haig, Sir John French, et cetera, et cetera ...'

'Gimme me some names.'

It was then, not having approached a single actor, that I started to lie through my teeth. Starting with John Mills – a safe bet – I confidently reeled off Kenneth More, Jack Hawkins, John Clements, Maggie Smith, Dirk Bogarde, Vanessa Redgrave . . .

When I paused to gauge his reaction and still none came, I knew I had to up my game. 'And of course,' I bragged, 'I will also be casting a number of our great theatrical knights: Sir Laurence Olivier, Sir Ralph Richardson, Sir Michael Redgrave, Sir John Gielgud . . .'

I came to a grinding halt and, after a long pause, Charlie said: 'Mr Attenboro, get me just five of those names and I'll give you the money.'

'But Mr Bluhdorn, you haven't asked what it's going to cost.'

'You're making it here, aren't you? Sign a slew of those English sirs and you're in business.'

On that we shook hands. I left the suite on cloud nine, doing my high-kicking dance from *Dr Dolittle* all the way to the lift.

When I told Sheila what I'd done, she said sagely: 'Well, darling, you'd better go and see Larry.'

Our foremost theatrical knight had gout, very bad gout. Sir Laurence Olivier was holed up in a sort of garret at the top of his elegant Regency house on Brighton's Royal Crescent. Having climbed the narrow wooden staircase, I found the great man in his pyjamas, bandaged foot elevated, lying on a narrow bed strewn with scripts. He told me he couldn't move.

When I explained about the film and said I'd been asked to direct, he couldn't have been more enthusiastic. He'd adored Joan Littlewood's stage production and he passionately believed in actor-directors. That was the reason he'd agreed to set up the National Theatre – a job he would eventually ask me to take over and which I did not in any way feel equipped to accept.

Encouraged by his initial reaction, I went on to tell Larry about my meeting with the mad Austrian of Wall Street, confessing I'd brazenly trotted out a cast list that not only included his name, but that of every other distinguished actor in the country. He didn't rebuke me but immediately asked: 'Who do you want me to play?'

When I suggested Field Marshall French, Larry said: 'I'll play him, of course I will, because you really ought to direct. I know you can do it. Just make sure you surround yourself with the best technical people you can find.'

Having thanked him profusely, I took my leave and had almost reached the floor below when the invalid miraculously abandoned his bed to hobble onto the landing and project an incredibly generous after-thought into the narrow stairwell.

'Dick,' came that mellifluous voice, 'who else do you want?'

I called up that I particularly hoped to secure his great friend Ralph Richardson and, with any luck, John Gielgud.

'Make sure you tell both of them, particularly Ralphie, I've already agreed to appear for Equity minimum and they must do the same.'

And that's how I mustered all five of the theatrical knights, I'd so rashly promised Charlie Bludhorn. Purely because of Olivier. If I'd started with anyone else, they'd have said they needed to think about it or they had to consult their agents, but once I had Larry and, through him, Richardson and Gielgud, everyone else followed. I can truthfully say it was the most glittering cast ever assembled for any British film.

DH— August 1992. Now approaching seventy and a member of someone else's cast, I could sense that Dick was unusually nervous. After a fourteen-year absence, he was about to make his acting comeback, billed above the title to play the eccentric John Hammond in Steven Spielberg's dinosaur epic, *Jurassic Park*.

The two men were due to discuss his portrayal in a camper van, parked outside Stage 24 at Universal Studios where set building was already in progress, but Spielberg was late, very late. When someone finally tapped on the door, Dick was surprised to find himself confronted by an elderly prop man bearing a vast array of spectacles. They came with a message. Apologising for his tardiness, Spielberg was suggesting that, while he waited, Sir Richard might like to choose the eyeglasses he considered most in keeping with his character.

At first, he seemed reluctant to abandon the heavy tortoiseshell frames which had become his visual trademark. Then, beginning to experiment with the different styles on offer, he became excited at the prospect of reinventing himself and, in the process, regaining some of his long-lost anonymity. Going from one extreme to the other, he finally plumped for professorial thin gold rims.

Another knock at the door; again not Spielberg. This time it was a young assistant director bearing another abject apology and three large tubs of Ben & Jerry's ice cream. The absent director, still unavoidably detained, was asking Sir Richard to select the flavour that Hammond would eat in one of the film's early scenes.

Impressed by this attention to detail and unable to resist one of his secret vices, Dick dived into Chocolate Chip Cookie Dough. Having demolished the whole pint in a matter of minutes, he turned his attention to Super Fudge Chunk and, after he'd wolfed that down, generously invited me to share the remainder.

Returning half an hour later and seeing all three tubs scraped clean, the tanned and toned assistant managed to conceal his amazement as he shepherded us into a waiting golf buggy. Steven's third request, again accompanied by many apologies, was that Dick should join him at his new headquarters on the far side of the studio lot.

Spielberg's hugely successful production company had been named after the first short he'd filmed on 35mm stock with $15,000 borrowed from a friend. *Amblin'*, a twenty-four-minute tale of two itinerant hippies, had so impressed Sid Sheinberg – then in charge of Universal television – that he'd immediately hired the young director at the princely sum of $275 a week.

No doubt mindful that his subsequent full-length features, *Jaws* and *E.T.*, had grossed the company a staggering $835 million on an investment of $19 million, Sheinberg had recently wooed his errant protégé back to Universal by creating a luxurious suite of offices to house the now mighty Amblin Entertainment Inc.

Nothing could have been in greater contrast to the Black Tower, Sheinberg's own forbidding workplace. Amblin's staff of fresh-faced kids, all apparently dressed for summer camp, occupied a sprawling single-storey hacienda, boasting a series of shady courtyards and wide, cool corridors adorned with superb Native American artefacts.

At the centre of it all, the office of the boy genius, now in his mid-forties, was laid-back too; earth colours, Navajo rugs, original Tiffany lamps, family photographs and, reflecting his own affinity with everyday American life, a couple of original works by Rockwell.

Dick and Steven had first met nine years earlier when both were in contention for the prestigious Directors' Guild Award. Convinced that his younger rival not only deserved to win, but undoubtedly would win for *E.T.*, on hearing his own name announced for *Gandhi*, Dick had felt impelled to acknowledge the loser with a hug before making his way to the podium.

Now, meeting him again as an actor, he was surprised to find that, although shooting was to start on *Jurassic Park* in less than a fortnight, Spielberg's whole attention was focused on a completely different project.

He explained: This was the Holocaust story which had haunted him for over a decade, a film so far removed from anything he'd ever done before that he'd tried to palm it off on three other directors – Wilder, Scorsese and Polanski – until, inexorably, it had come back to claim him – heart, heritage and soul. And, despite spending the whole afternoon putting through an increasingly passionate series of calls to Europe, he'd just been refused permission to film in the former concentration camp at Auschwitz.

Dick, all too familiar with such obsession, instantly switched into supportive film-maker mode, explaining about Helga and Irene, the two little girls his parents had helped to save from Nazi Germany. Spielberg was later to say of him: 'Dickie was the only person who really understood what I was trying to do.'

It was this, several months later, which would prompt the unusual request that Dick should take over the direction of *Schindler's List* when Spielberg was obliged to return briefly to Hollywood. By then, however, and totally unexpectedly, Dick was shooting another film in England.

Following the success of *Gandhi*, he'd continued to receive unsolicited ideas for films at the rate of five or six a week. Some people sent in books, others long impassioned letters. Still more, hoping to tap into Dick's known preference for biography, drew his attention to a whole host of sung and unsung heroes. Sadly, almost without exception, their ideas were totally unsuitable for mainstream cinema; either ill-conceived, derivative or just plain bonkers.

Then, on the afternoon he was due to fly to Hawaii to start work on *Jurassic Park*, an unacknowledged script, accompanied by a letter from an established English producer asking Dick to direct, was discovered under a pile of correspondence during his habitual last-minute flurry of 'tidying up'. Since the sender was pressing for an answer and Dick would be away for three weeks, I was asked to read it immediately.

So, as the Attenboroughs finally set off for Heathrow, I took the script back to my office at Twickenham Studios.

I remember it so vividly. Here, set out in professional form, was the work of a truly inspiring screenwriter, someone who not only understood period, pace and drama, but also had the ability to present real people as intriguing characters and make you care about them. I read the whole thing straight through, smiling in many places. Then, to my total amazement, on reaching the last page, I realised I was crying.

Shadowlands was the saddest subject Dick and I would ever make together and, paradoxically, the happiest film-making experience of our entire working relationship. No other production ever came together so easily. When he phoned me on his arrival in Hawaii, I told him William Nicholson's screenplay was one of the best I'd ever come across and, unlike any other, had reduced me to tears.

He read it on his return to London ten days later and, of course, he cried too.

Within a week, a meeting was arranged with Brian Eastman, who owned the subject, at which he and Dick got on so well they immediately agreed to enter into a producing partnership.

A few days later, Tony Hopkins, who adored music, had invited himself to a *Chaplin* soundtrack recording session at Abbey Road Studios. As he was leaving and without telling him anything about it, Dick handed Tony a copy of the *Shadowlands* script. He rang first thing the following morning to claim the part of C. S. Lewis.

Brian Eastman then travelled to Hollywood where he immediately found an enthusiastic backer. This was the decisive Frank Price, who, as head of Columbia, had bought worldwide rights in *Gandhi* on the strength of a single screening and later, as head of Universal, had agreed to finance *Cry Freedom* during a chance meeting with Dick at an airport. Fortuitously for us, Frank was now in the process of setting up his own production company, Price Entertainment.

With $22 million of funding in place, Dick and I flew to Los Angeles to find our leading lady. He interviewed just one actress, very briefly.

Debra Winger had read the script, done her research and was utterly determined to play Joy Gresham. The only downside, as far as Dick was concerned, was her reputation for being 'difficult'. He sat her down and told her that he would not stand for any tantrums. Having given him an assurance that she would behave impeccably provided he always told her the unvarnished truth, adding flirtatiously that he would adore her by the time they finished working together, the forthright Miss Winger departed.

Dick, still in two minds, went out onto the hotel balcony and stood there until he saw her emerge below. Having studied Debra's quirky gait as she walked to her car, he came back into the room and phoned her agent to say she had the part.

An unexpected codicil came the following Sunday. It was election year in the States and we'd been invited to a Democrat fund-raising brunch at the home of Mike Medavoy, then chairman of TriStar, who was trying to involve Dick in a screen version of *Les Misérables*. After the speeches, we queued at the buffet and, knowing no one except our host, took our plates to one of the vacant tables.

The seat on Dick's other side was immediately occupied by another, even more 'difficult' and determined American actress. Then knocking fifty but looking a good ten years younger, Barbra Streisand proceeded to harangue him for the next twenty minutes. Having somehow got hold of our script, she was strenuously insisting she was the only actress on God's earth who not only could, but absolutely had to play Joy Gresham. It took every scrap of Dick's considerable diplomatic skill to convince her the role was no longer available.

One major part remained to be cast. Again fortuitously, Dick had encountered the perfect child to play Joy Gresham's son, Douglas, during the making of *Jurassic Park*. This remarkably perceptive nine-year-old went by the name of Joseph Mazzello III.

On 23 April 1993, just seven months after we'd first read the script, *Shadowlands* went into production.

Dick had assembled a unit that contained many reliable talents and familiar faces, including the indispensable Terry Clegg, Simon Kaye, who had been his original sound recordist on *Oh! What a Lovely War*, his long-term production designer, Stuart Craig, the superb composer, George Fenton, and his all-time favourite editor, Lesley Walker. Among the new recruits was Pat Clayton, dependable and rock-steady as first assistant director and a brilliantly innovative cinematographer from

Leicestershire, Roger Pratt. Both would go on to become highly valued and irreplaceable members of this close-knit team.

Throughout the whole of the shoot, there was a sense among the exceptionally homogenous 200-strong cast and crew that this was more than just another job. It emerged that elements in the story had touched the lives of almost everyone involved; be it an alcoholic relative, falling in love late in life or a diagnosis of terminal cancer. For Dick, too, this was a special film, the one that came closest to fulfilling his demanding self-imposed criteria, the work he considered his best as a director.

For six glorious rain-free weeks we worked, from dawn to dusk and often before and beyond, in a series of quintessentially English locations. We started in Oxford where, due to the kind collaboration of its president, Anthony Smith, we were able to film within the chapel, cloisters and quadrangles of centuries-old Magdalen College. Then it was on to the famous 'Golden Valley' beauty spot at Symonds Yat in the Forest of Dean. To the delight of our male technicians, this sunlit odyssey also took us to the last remaining mainline steam railway, operated by amateur enthusiasts at Loughborough.

Then it was down to earth and back to London where, on an overcast Sunday morning in June, we'd obtained permission to shoot in a dingy backstreet behind Camden Town Hall. The scene required rain. When Dick and I arrived at 7.30 a.m., he was told the crew needed more time to rehearse this special effect and was quickly shepherded into a camper van where his usual breakfast – two pork sausages and a dollop of HP Sauce – was, unusually, ready and waiting.

Having consumed his bangers in a trice, he was becoming tetchy about the unexplained delay when our second assistant Michael Stevenson, looking decidedly conspiratorial, finally came to collect him.

All was explained as he rounded the corner. A cheer went up from the grinning technicians, all wearing rain-sodden paper coronets in celebration of Dick's life peerage, announced the previous day.

RA— It had all started just over a year earlier. In March 1992, after an unremitting decade of Thatcherism, the new Conservative Prime Minister, John Major, had called a general election and, to my great joy, the opinion polls were at last beginning to show a significant swing to Labour. When Neil Kinnock asked if I would again be willing to campaign, I readily undertook to do anything he wanted.

Some weeks later, I was to speak at a rally in Manchester and went up there accompanied by a couple of up-and-coming young MPs. On our arrival back at Euston, the three of us crossed paths with Neil who was about to travel north. Having exchanged news with their leader – all of it highly optimistic – my two companions, the sober Scot and his effervescent friend, went off to find a taxi. Watching them go, Neil ruminated in his sing-song Welsh accent: 'If I get knocked over by a bus one of those boys will lead the Labour Party. Though which will be Prime Minister and which the Chancellor, I don't know.'

The 'boys', of course, were Tony Blair and Gordon Brown.

Election heartbreak followed. Amid a huge debate about taxation, came claims that an emotive Labour broadcast highlighting unacceptable inequality in healthcare, dubbed 'Jennifer's Ear', had been rigged. While John Major received plaudits for speaking from a humble soapbox, the right-wing press roundly condemned Neil for mounting a huge, 'triumphalist' rally in Sheffield. The biggest and lowest blow of all was delivered by the tabloid reaching almost a quarter of the adult population. On the morning of the election, the *Sun* came out with the excoriating headline: IF KINNOCK WINS TODAY WILL THE LAST PERSON IN BRITAIN PLEASE TURN OUT THE LIGHTS.

Kinnock did not win and, after a period of stunned mourning, we embarked on a further five years of Tory government, determined that next time round it would be a different story.

It was at this low point that I received an unexpected lunch invitation from Lord Cledwyn, a dedicated politician and leader of the opposition in the Upper House. Cledwyn and I had known each other since boyhood – his father and mine had been friends – and, after we'd reminisced about long-ago summer holidays in Beaumaris, I looked around, catching snatches of conversation. The Lords dining room was not the fusty geriatric watering hole I'd half expected, but a lively hotbed of erudition.

As I thought to myself this is where the brains are, I heard Cledwyn asking if I might agree to accept a life peerage. This was completely unexpected and, in the light of recent events, I think it's worth saying that, save for a few thousand pounds in party dues and contributions, I had never donated any significant sum of money to Labour.

Seeing my astonishment, Cledwyn went on to explain there were two ways of entering the House of Lords: either on the basis of professional expertise and achievement, or through something called the political list. Should I accept, I would be on the Labour Party list, one among many so-called working peers expected to enter the Lords that year.

Becoming a working peer implied a full-time job. My mind went immediately to my Thomas Paine project. Despite being hugely flattered by what was on offer, I knew I would never stop trying to make *These Are the Times*.

When I explained this, Cledwyn said, 'Look, we're not asking you to give up your career and we understand we may not see as much of you as we will of those who have no other commitments. Look at it this way: if twelve new Labour peers are appointed and only ten can make it to a particular vote, we will accept that. We won't demand your attendance. But if there's a three-line whip, obviously we'd hope you would make every effort to be here.'

I asked if I could go away and think about it. 'Of course,' he said, 'but don't take too long. The Birthday Honours are announced in the middle of June and there isn't much time before we have to put forward our definitive list.'

If I hadn't been an actor, I would have liked to be a politician. So, when I met Cledwyn again, after long discussions with Sheila, I told him I'd be honoured to accept.

And so it was on. However, not long afterwards, I had a phone call from Charles Clarke, then Neil Kinnock's Chief of Staff. Charles told me: 'Neil wants to have dinner with all four of you before the Prime Minister's letters go out.' And I said: 'What do you mean, all four?'

He was flummoxed: 'Oh, Jesus, hasn't anybody told you? We only have four Labour appointees.'

'Then I can't be one of them. You can't have one in four not turning up because I happen to be off somewhere making a movie. It's out of the question.'

'But everybody will understand.'

'It's not a question of everybody understanding, Charles. I simply can't do it. It wouldn't be correct.'

He quickly fixed up a meeting and I went to see Neil in his House of Commons office. 'I'm terribly sorry,' I told him, 'I know I accepted but I'm determined to go on making films until I drop off the perch. If there were to be a dozen or more new Labour peers, that wouldn't be a problem. But with so few others, I'm afraid it's out of the question.'

'We think you're making a big mistake,' Neil said, 'but, if that's your decision, we have to accept it.'

I meant what I said. The honour didn't matter to me. The important thing was to do the job they required and if I couldn't do it properly, I wouldn't become a peer. And, as far as I was concerned, that was that.

Then, completely out of the blue a whole year later, after Neil had resigned and John Smith had taken over as shadow leader, I received a formal letter from John Major saying the Conservative government wished me to accept a life peerage. This was not a political appointment, but for services to the cinema. How it came about, I haven't the faintest idea.

I'd put the idea of entering the House of Lords completely out of my mind, it hadn't obsessed me, but this time, on this basis, I felt able to accept and, although non-political life peers often sit on the cross benches, I also elected to take the Labour whip.

Over the course of my long acting career, I've assumed almost a hundred different identities, starting at the age of six as Fleta, a female fairy in *Iolanthe*. On-screen, I've laboured under nicknames which have included Frenchy, Whitey, Knocker, Dripper, Pinkie and Bunter. Known variously at home as darling, Dick, Tut and Pappi, away from home I've been a knight, an ambassador, a president, a commandeur and a chevalier, several kinds of chairman, a university chancellor and a school governor. At school I was Atty, at RADA – much to my annoyance – I became Dickie and during the war I was merely a number.

A place was one thing I had never been until I encountered the formidable Conrad Swan, Esq., CVO, PhD, FSA, Garter Principal King of Arms. Garter – as he was known for short – wrote to me in June 1993 saying it would be necessary to sign 'certain papers stating what designation you wish to take for your Life Barony'.

I went to see this Canadian scholar at the imposing College of Arms where we agreed that I would 'henceforth be styled', as he put it, Lord Attenborough of Richmond-upon-Thames. Garter was very insistent that I should also commission a costly coat of arms, an offer which, since it was not mandatory and held absolutely no appeal, I firmly declined.

My next encounter was with a retired admiral, Sir Richard Thomas, formally known as the Gentleman Usher of the Black Rod, an office dating back to the fourteenth century. As is well known, his duties included summoning MPs to the Lords for the State Opening of Parliament and having the doors ceremoniously slammed in his face before striking three times with his ebony rod to gain admittance.

However, as Sir Richard kindly explained, he was also responsible within the House of Lords for accommodation, works and services, for keeping order, maintaining security and – I received a severe look at this juncture – arresting any lord committing a breach of privilege.

Since it was also part of his remit to guide me during my formal introduction to the Upper House, Sir Richard proceeded to outline a ceremony that sounded mind-bogglingly complicated – what with renting the right hat and robes, remembering to bring my Writ of Summons, entering and kneeling before the Lord Chancellor at the Woolsack, swearing the Oath of Allegiance, signing the Test Roll, being escorted to the Labour bench, sitting and getting to my feet three times, putting on and doffing my hat, also three times, and finally making sure I bowed again before making my exit.

An actor faced with so many complicated moves would have required numerous blocking rehearsals. But for a nervous novice peer there were none.

And so, on the last day of October 1993, extremely apprehensive but ably supported by two very dear friends, Lord Cledwyn and the eminent neurologist, Lord Walton, I was received into the House of Lords.

On leaving the chamber I was given a slim scarlet dispatch case covered in deerskin which contained an imprint of the Queen's Great Seal attached to an illuminated document, known as Letters Patent, which, in exquisitely executed and totally unpunctuated calligraphy stated:

ELIZABETH THE SECOND by the Grace of God of the United Kingdom of Great Britain and Northern Ireland and of Our other Realms and Territories Queen Head of the Commonwealth Defender of the Faith to all Lords Spiritual and Temporal and all other Our Subjects whatsoever to whom these Presents shall come Greeting

Know ye that We of Our especial grace certain knowledge and mere motion in pursuance of the Life Peerages Act 1958 and of all other powers in that behalf its enabling do by these Presents advance create and prefer Our trusty and well beloved Sir RICHARD SAMUEL ATTENBOROUGH Knight Commander of Our Most Excellent Order of the British Empire to the state degree style dignity title and honour of BARON ATTENBOROUGH ...

DH— January 1995. Since his elevation to the peerage, Her Majesty's trusty and well-beloved Baron has had very little by way of gainful employment, having spent just three months appearing as a twinkly Santa Claus in *Miracle on 34th* Street. During the same fallow period, despite all our unpaid efforts, he and I have failed abysmally to set up no less than eight different films.

Heading this list, as always, is his cherished and prohibitively expensive Thomas Paine epic, *These Are the Times*. Drawing on our experiences with *Chaplin*, I've argued till I'm blue in the face that it's madness to insist on including both the War of Independence and the French Revolution. In addition to the huge costs involved, I'm convinced no audience will sit still for a film that runs over four hours. But can I persuade an obdurate Dick? No way.

When we'd been turned down by all the major studios, Marti Baum produced a couple of Japanese television executives who said they'd put up the money if Dick was willing to shoot in some complicated new-fangled format, this at a time when virtually no one had heard of high definition. The executives returned to Tokyo, lugging Trevor Griffiths's weighty script, and never made contact again.

Next, the indefatigable Marti introduced us to an ostrich farmer from Texas who wore cowboy boots crafted from ostrich skins. He was, we were assured, a multimillionaire, eager to diversify into the movie business. However, at each of our meetings he brought along a different group of wide-eyed and raucous Texan buddies, all armed with cheap throwaway cameras, all demanding to be photographed hugging Dick. I relayed this to Marti, he investigated further and confirmed with chagrin that the ostrich farmer was not a serious player.

Back in London, Dick came up with the cost-saving idea of shooting the whole Paine script and then dividing it into two separate films, doubling the potential for profit. This brainwave bit the dust when distributors pointed out that if the first release flopped, they'd be stuck with double losses.

Undaunted, Dick then went to the BBC, proposing an expensive but groundbreaking television series. Nice noises, no luck.

During all these negotiations, a proposal that he should produce and direct *Les Misérables* was bubbling away in the background. This fell by the wayside when the show's composer and lyricist insisted on retaining all the original recitative. Convinced a film version could never succeed without any spoken dialogue, Dick walked away from the project.

For similar reasons, a screen version of *The Phantom of the Opera* also failed to materialise, as did *Mountains of the Moon*, a film about the Victorian explorer Richard Burton, eventually to be made by the writer/director, Bob Rafaelson.

At this juncture, David Matalon, one of the New York-based Columbia executives who'd enthused over *Gandhi*, came to us with an exciting idea for children called *Seventh Heaven*. This was about miniature people living clandestinely in an American apartment block and for nearly a year we collaborated on several drafts of the script: all to no avail.

We also worked with two other screenwriters, one of them Trevor Griffiths, on *The Sailmaker*, a fictional tale set in a Mexican desert, featuring a spectacular prison break – another subject which failed to attract any finance.

One of my own pet projects was an adaptation of *Some Other Rainbow*, based on the best-selling book by John McCarthy and Jill Morell. I was certain this political love story, involving a young couple who had both found themselves imprisoned – he in Beirut by Islamic jihad, she in London by her loyalty to him – would make a terrific film. But when we finally met the delightful John and Jill, it was evident that Britain's favourite twosome were no longer a couple. Moreover, John was already committed to making a different film with his Irish cell mate, Brian Keenan.

I found our eighth and most testing project in, of all places, my GP's waiting room. Leafing through a tattered copy of *Country Life*, I came across a photograph of an imposing Red Indian chief, clad in the full regalia including a huge eagle-feather war bonnet. From the accompanying story, I learned that, before he was exposed as an imposter in the late 1930s, this extraordinary character – real nationality English, real name Archie Belaney – had toured Britain under his assumed Native

Canadian identity, lecturing, among other venues, at the De Montfort Hall in Leicester.

Doctor's appointment over, I rushed across Richmond Green to ask if Dick had ever heard of him.

'Heard? Darling, Dave and I were there! We would have been about eight and ten at the time. He, of course, was only interested in the animals – the lecture was all about baby beaver. But what bowled me over was the man's phenomenal stage presence. We pooled our pocket money afterwards to buy his book and queued together for absolute ages to get it signed.'

Reminded of his share in this joint purchase some sixty years later, Dick picked up the telephone, demanding to know if his younger brother still had the book. Amazingly, David was instantly able to tell him he did and, possession being nine-tenths of the law, fully intended to hang onto it. Both brothers, it seemed, had inherited the hoarding gene.

And so began the saga of *Grey Owl*.

We roped in an enthusiastic Jake Eberts, himself Canadian, to amass the necessary funding and commissioned Bill Nicholson, who'd scripted *Shadowlands*, to write the screenplay. Several drafts later, we felt sufficiently confident to embark on a winter recce in Quebec, accompanied by our long-standing sheet anchor and budget expert, Terry Clegg.

The whole of the province being under umpteen feet of snow, the resourceful Terry took us to a specialist shop in Montreal to get kitted up for the journey which lay ahead. We bought boots, hats, gloves, thick socks, pocket hand warmers and, for Dick, a high-visibility scarlet parka.

Early next morning, Terry had a helicopter take us from Montreal to a potential location site way up the St Lawrence River. Diverting en route to pick up Jake Eberts from his lakeside fishing cabin, this was to be a 500-mile round trip. Terry sat in front with the pilot, Dick and I behind; he bundled into his scarlet parka and woolly bobble hat.

For me, the flight was exhilarating, not unlike a fairground ride. The chopper would fly straight towards a rocky outcrop covered in snow, then, just as we seemed likely to crash into it, hop nimbly over the top. However, some twenty minutes into the flight, I realised that Dick's face had taken on an ominously greenish tinge.

I couldn't believe it. For years, I'd accompanied him all over the world, clocking up hundred of thousands of miles, treating Concorde like a handy if highly expensive bus, with never a queasy moment. Then I remembered him telling me how nauseous he'd been when flying over Germany during the war.

I leaned forward to shout in the pilot's ear, 'Where are the sickbags?' His response was a very French-Canadian shrug.

I looked at Dick again. If push came to shove and provided I could whip it off in time, that bobble hat would make an excellent substitute. At this point, he managed to unclench his jaw just long enough to ask how long it would take to reach our first destination. The pilot said he was encountering an unusually strong headwind and it would be at least an hour.

Two hours later we landed on a frozen lake and a jolly Jake came out of his cabin to meet us, proudly announcing he'd laid on some Skidoos for a sightseeing trip through the forest. Not knowing a Skidoo was essentially a motorbike on skis, Dick – then seventy-one and an unwilling pillion passenger at the best of times – gamely professed enthusiasm.

Skidoo trip over, Jake, Terry and I packed into the helicopter with a very subdued Dick. Only when we were airborne, did the pilot suddenly announce he was not licensed for night flying and it was too late to take us on to our original destination. To be sure of landing in daylight, we must turn back, pick up some fuel and return directly to Montreal. With the advantage of a tailwind, he said, there shouldn't be any problem.

The watery sun was low in the sky when we'd refuelled. Knowing his time of trial was almost over, Dick even managed to smile when Terry took a photograph. However, before we took off, the pilot informed us the capricious wind had turned a full 180 degrees and was now blowing more strongly than ever.

Night fell quickly and the little chopper was soon enveloped in total darkness; not a pinprick of light visible anywhere in all the wild terrain below. We flew on and on with the pilot leaning forward to peer intently through the windscreen, presumably keeping his eyes peeled for the same jagged peaks he'd hopped over so nimbly that morning.

Then, suddenly, he relaxed back in his seat and I saw the object of his search. There, ahead of us, was a motorway crowded with tiny cars, their headlights providing the welcome little beacons which would guide us back to Montreal.

Continuously overtaken by the miniature vehicles beneath, we struggled on against the headwind for what seemed like an eternity before finally putting down at Dorval very late at night.

Come spring, the complicated co-production deal which Jake had been carefully stitching together suddenly fell apart. Three years would elapse before *Grey Owl* finally went into production.

RA— Following that setback, Di and I are slumped on a row of red plastic chairs under the glare of neon strip lights. We're waiting for the last plane out of Marco Polo, one of the world's most romantic airports. But, at this hour, no sleek speedboats bob at the jetty outside and, across the water, Venice is cloaked in an oily mist.

After an arduous seventeen-hour day of location hunting, we look like a couple of tramps. The coffee bar is closed and, for once, we don't even have the energy to talk.

There's only one other passenger in sight, a lone circling man who's doing what polite English people do when they think they've spotted a celebrity. Eventually he plucks up the courage to accost me. 'Is it really you, milord?'

When I summon a smile, he says, 'I can't believe it. You, sitting here, like anyone else. I thought you'd be having tea with the Queen and opening shops and things.'

The actuality is rather different. Di and I are locked in combat with a Hollywood company which has approached me to produce and direct a film about the young Ernest Hemingway. This intriguing story, based on the little known love affair which inspired his debut novel, *A Farewell to Arms*, is set in northern Italy during the First World War.

However, in their eagerness to take advantage of cheap Eastern European labour, the executives at New Line are insisting it has to be shot in Hungary. Immune to our protests that the architecture and topography surrounding Budapest are completely wrong, they've presented us with an ultimatum in the form of an impossibly low ready-made budget.

Without the expertise of Terry Clegg, now engaged on another film,

Di and I have set ourselves the task of proving that *In Love and War* can be filmed almost as cheaply in the authentic Veneto region. To this end, we flew in at crack of dawn this morning to join forces with an experienced local production manager.

Once on the autostrada, it quickly became apparent the charming Guido was blessed with an unnerving ability to steer with his knee while smoking, gesticulating and conducting a series of impassioned conversations on his *telefonino*.

It came as a huge relief when he turned into the countryside. At first the scenery was a huge disappointment, seeming to consist of uninspiring roads flanked by ugly little factories. But that all changed as we approached the Dolomites and stopped to explore a whole series of wonderful location sites, including, after a long climb, the extraordinary fortifications on Monte Grappa, a tiny jewel of an opera house, a series of gorgeous Palladian villas, and the medieval town of Bassano, where the young Hemingway had lodged while serving as a volunteer ambulance driver with the American Red Cross.

And then it was back to Venice. There can be few sights more magical than the Grand Canal in winter sunshine. But, more magical still, Guido took us into one of the few waterside palazzi available for rent and on to visit the huge rope shed in the Arsenale, the gondola repair yard at Dorsoduro and the silent cemetery island of San Michele.

Over a late dinner, we worked on the figures.

Now, trudging exhausted but vindicated towards the waiting plane, Di and I are in total agreement: Noël Coward was right. Work *is* more fun than fun. This beats opening shops any day.

DH— Our pleasure is short-lived. By the end of the same week, we're in West Hollywood. New Line Cinema, best known for *The Return of the Texas Chainsaw Massacre* and *A Nightmare on Elm Street*, operates out of an unassuming office block on North Robertson Boulevard. Here nobody wears a suit and most of the employees are women.

Four of them have been placed in charge of our project and, although they won't be much in evidence once we go into production, each will receive a screen credit as executive producer, associate producer, production executive and executive in charge of production.

It's the executive in charge of production, an attractive blonde from Kansas, with whom we must do battle over our budget. Despite compelling evidence amassed during our recce with Guido, she continues to maintain there aren't sufficient funds available below the line to shoot in Italy. However, there is enough above the line to hire an A-list star to play the Red Cross nurse who falls disastrously in love with the hobbledehoy Hemingway.

At the executive producer's behest, we fly to New York to meet Julia Roberts. She's charming, says she loves the script and really, really hopes 'her people' will be able to reach an agreement with 'our people'.

We fly back to Los Angeles where Dick gets on the phone to Julia's agent. Her fee is $10 million. New Line are wildly excited and, after consultations with an unseen higher authority, the amount is agreed. Dick relays this to the agent who promises to get back to him shortly.

When he does call back half an hour later it's to announce that Julia's fee has just gone up to $12 million plus a specified number of return journeys to and from Europe by private jet, guaranteed employment for her numerous assistants and, of course, a luxury trailer to be available at all times.

The Hollywood grapevine eventually comes up with a reason for this outrageous volte-face. No A-list actress has yet commanded more than $10 million a picture and Julia's many managers, all on a percentage, are determined to set a new benchmark. This time it's way too rich for New Line and they pass.

Next, we're inducted into the absurd process of scripting by committee. Having abandoned two previous writers, our New Line mentors decide to audition new candidates via a series of telephone conference calls.

We assemble round a table, Dick and I, the executive producer, the associate producer who is also New Line's script editor and yet another producer, Dimitri Villard, who is the son of the man who co-wrote the book on which the film is based.

We squirm as a series of jobbing screenwriters are grilled about their 'vision' of the project. In addition to six varieties of producer, the film will eventually carry a total of seven writing credits: two for the book, two for the story, three for the screenplay.

RA— It's a basic rule of film-making: you can't make a good film from a bad script. And a good script does require vision, preferably the vision of a single writer who is passionate about the subject and sufficiently collaborative to understand the director's need to visualise every scene in his mind's eye, set-up by set-up, long before he starts shooting.

There were too many cooks at New Line, all well intentioned, all desperate to make a creative contribution, all believing the script could be immeasurably improved by yet another writer. The end result was a spoilt broth without a driving through line, without any true identity.

After protracted negotiations – during which I somehow kept omitting to sign my contract – *In Love and War* was made in the Veneto with a cast of my own choosing and a superb Anglo-Italian crew.

Agnes Von Kurowsky was played by the beautiful Sandra Bullock, one of the finest and most subtle actresses I have ever come across; hard-working, down to earth and professional to her fingertips.

Playing opposite her was Chris O'Donnell, epitomising the headstrong, idealistic teenage Hemingway before he became the hardbitten, hell-raising literary giant.

These actors, in my view, gave exquisite performances. But, although both had embarked on the film in the hope of changing their image, there was a depressing reluctance on the part of critics and audiences alike to accept them as anything but the sassy girl from *Speed* and the baby-faced Robin from *Batman Forever*.

I have in front of me a glossy photograph. It was taken at the Odeon Leicester Square on 12 February 1997. The occasion is the charity premiere of *In Love and War* which was to benefit the International Red Cross. I am in black tie, escorting a beautiful girl in a long evening gown. She is our guest of honour, the 35-year-old Princess of Wales.

She has reached the end of the receiving line and is shaking hands with Chris O'Donnell. A moment or two later, she will turn to the little girl in a party dress who stands on the left of frame, waiting to present her with a bouquet and souvenir brochure. This is my darling younger granddaughter, Lucy.

How poignant it is to see them on the only occasion they ever came together; the vibrant young woman, so soon to die, and the beloved child, then six years old, now lost to us forever.

IO

ANY OTHER BUSINESS

RA— PRINCE CHARLES WROTE to me in Richmond towards the end of 1984. I was away at the time, shooting *A Chorus Line*, and while his first letter was being forwarded, he sent a second to the Regency Hotel in New York.

So within a matter of days I received two letters from Highgrove. Both were handwritten and quite long, the second apologising for 'prestering' me in America. The prince was explaining that his young wife had never made speeches prior to their marriage and the prospect was causing her a great deal of anxiety. Could I recommend someone discreet who would be willing to give her some tuition? There was a particular occasion – a ship she was due to launch – which made this a matter of some urgency. I replied that I'd be glad to help the princess myself as soon as I returned to London.

We met at Kensington Palace in February 1985, four years after her marriage and six months after she'd given birth to her second son, Prince Harry. My appointment was for eleven o'clock in the morning. We drove into Kensington Gore, stopped at the police barrier and were directed into a courtyard. I was met at the door by a butler in a tail-coat who was accompanied by liveried footman. The butler's name was Burrell.

He showed me into a ground floor waiting room. Shortly before the

1977: Watching the newly knighted Sir Charles Chaplin receive the BAFTA Fellowship from the Academy's President, Princess Anne

Chaplin, 1992: The Little Tramp as reincarnated by Robert Downey Jr.

Filming *Chaplin*, 1991: Directing Robert in one of the early scenes

The Great Escape, 1963: With Steve McQueen

Oh! What a Lovely War, 1969:
With Larry Olivier

Filming *The Flight of the Phoenix,*
1965: Sheila and the children in
Hollywood with Jimmy Stewart

Filming *Shadowlands*, 1993: With Tony Hopkins and Debra Winger

The Bliss of Mrs Blossom, 1968: Married to Shirley MacLaine

Filming *Jurassic Park*, 1992: On location in Hawaii with Steven Spielberg

2004: Sheila and Doctor at Old Friars

(*Overleaf*) RA as some of the many characters he has portrayed in film. See detailed caption on Page 292

Filming *In Love and War*, 1996: On location in the Veneto with Chris O'Donnell and Sandra Bullock

Grey Owl, 1999: Pierce Brosnan as the phoney Red Indian chief

Premiere of *In Love and War*, 1997: Princess Diana about to be presented with a bouquet by my darling granddaughter, Lucy Holland. (*Left to right*) Lucy, Chris O'Donnell, Dimitri Villard, Kay Hawkins, Di and the princess

To Dickie.

With fondest love from the other
lady in your life ...!

Diana.

The last picture of us all together, taken to mark my 80th birthday in the summer of 2003

Back row left to right:
Son-in-law, Michael Holland, daughter-in-law; Karen, son Michael
and son-in-law, Graham Sinclair.
Centre left to right:
Grandson, Sam Holland; elder granddaughter, Alice Holland; younger granddaughter,
Lucy Holland and daughter, Jane Holland (both died in the tsunami); younger
daughter, Charlotte Sinclair; grandson, Will Sinclair; grandson, Tom Attenborough.
Front left to right:
Grandson, Toby Sinclair; grandparents Richard and Sheila Attenborough;
grandson, Charlie Sinclair.
(Photograph © Tommy Hanley)

appointed time, I was ushered up into a rather formal drawing room on the first floor. Diana entered at eleven on the dot.

No, I didn't bow – we shook hands – and I don't recall what she was wearing; some sort of floaty skirt, I think. But I do remember she was ravishingly beautiful and very unsure of herself. Then, and for quite a while afterwards, until she became Darling and I became Dickie, we addressed each other as Ma'am and Sir Richard. Having established a rapport, we continued to meet every fortnight, always on a Wednesday, always at the same time.

There were two main problems. First and foremost was the shyness – her habit of dropping her head and looking up at you through that fringe. The other hurdle was the formal nature of the speeches she was required to deliver. No one in the royal family ever spoke off the cuff; they always read from a pre-prepared text and the result, inevitably, was somewhat aloof and stilted.

My task, as I saw it, was to persuade the princess to abandon her script whenever possible and get her to fix on a single person in the audience, speaking directly to him or her, straight from the heart. In common with actors on a film set, I also had to convince her she was the one person on earth who could do this successfully.

During the next twelve years, Diana would write me over forty letters in her generous cursive hand, all liberally sprinkled with little sad or smiley faces. With two exceptions – the first and the last – they all came by registered post, enclosed in a Buckingham Palace envelope with her identifying initial D scrawled in the bottom left-hand corner.

The first communication I received from her was a printed telemessage. It is dated 29 March 1985, a few days after our third meeting. Obviously composed soon after she'd delivered the speech we'd rehearsed, it contains no less than two exuberant exclamation marks and proudly draws my attention to her 'Oscar-winning perfect-pitch performance' at Northampton that morning, going on to inform me she fully intends to collect her award in person.

That was the start. Over the years which followed, despite an age gap of thirty-eight years between us, I became her friend, sounding board, cheerleader and, on occasion, her admonitory Dutch uncle.

When we met, the world still believed she and Charles were a fairy-tale couple. And, for a while, I believed it too. But gradually, over the weeks and months which followed, she confided the heart-breaking truth.

This had been a naive and romantic teenager, selected for her virginity and breeding, who fell head over heels for an older man, believing her feelings were reciprocated in full measure. When asked if they were in love following the announcement of their engagement, Diana had instantly replied, 'Of course,' while Charles had equivocated: 'Whatever love means.'

Putting this gaffe down to embarrassment, she had no inkling of the actual situation until her wedding when the shock of learning there were to be three people within her marriage had all but unhinged her.

There were, nevertheless, some happy times. She and Charles had delighted in the birth of their sons and both were excellent and extremely loving parents. In the summer of 1988 Diana wrote from Balmoral, where all four were on holiday, to wish me a happy birthday. This is the only letter in which the habitual 'I' becomes a joyful 'we', giving a glimpse of the contented family life which, sadly, would otherwise elude her.

Knowing I would disapprove, Diana never informed me she was collaborating on a revelatory book with the author Andrew Morton. Not long after the hoo-ha surrounding its publication, she was devastated when transcripts of her private telephone conversations were also released into the public arena. Sheila and I took her to one of our regular lunches and comforted her as best we could. She responded by sending me a photograph on which she'd written: 'To Dickie with fondest love from the other lady in your life.'

At another lunch some months later, Diana reiterated her disapproval of my Garrick Club tie. Handing me a gift-wrapped box, she cheekily announced our relationship would be at an end if I persisted in wearing 'those ghastly cucumber-green and salmon-pink stripes'. Henceforth, whenever we met, I was under orders to appear in the tasteful navy replacement she had chosen at Hermès.

Soon after the terms of the royal divorce had finally been hammered out, in writing again to thank Sheila and me for our concern and support, Diana added with what then seemed like optimism: 'The last months have been a nightmare but there *is* light in the tunnel.'

The year of her death was, for me, one of extraordinary highs and lows.

In January 1997, 'the other lady in my life' visited Angola under the auspices of the International Red Cross to witness at first hand the appalling injuries caused by long-buried landmines. Having been filmed – symbolically as it turned out – walking through a minefield, she elected to defy convention by publicly calling for an immediate international ban. I was so proud of her. At long last, Diana had found her voice.

In a despicable response, Earl Howe, the Tory's junior defence minister, labelled her an ill-informed 'loose cannon', to which the Labour defence spokesman, Dave Clark, rightly and gallantly responded: 'I think we should welcome the fact she has tried to warn the world of the dangers of these terrible weapons.'

A little later, Diana attended the charity premiere of *In Love and War*, which was to benefit the Red Cross. Lucy, the younger of our two granddaughters, was to present her with a bouquet. But, just before the princess reached her, someone threw the six-year-old into confusion by shoving a brochure into her other hand and Lucy forgot the all-important curtsy.

I was telling Diana how upset she was as we approached the doors to the dress circle. Although the whole audience was already on its feet, waiting to applaud her, she immediately turned back to comfort Lucy and ask for a private demonstration, pronouncing with typical sensitivity: 'That's easily the best curtsy I've ever seen.'

Then, on 1 May 1997, came that most historic of post-war general elections. Frustratingly disenfranchised, like all peers, for the first time in my adult life, I was unable to vote. After the polls closed, Sheila and I sat glued to the television, switching between those Richmond boys – David Dimbleby on BBC, brother Jonathan on ITV – as the famous swingometer started to creep inexorably away from the blue and into the red.

A phone call summoning us to a celebration, quietly arranged weeks in advance, came in the early hours of the morning. We drove into central London, still following the results on the car radio. Almost unbelievably, after eighteen years of Tory rule, major figures such as Portillo, Rifkind and Lamont had been ousted and seat after seat was falling to Labour. We crossed Waterloo Bridge to find ourselves in a minor traffic jam, surrounded by hundreds of other jubilant supporters, all heading for the Royal Festival Hall.

Inside, hastily summoned, was the biggest political party ever. The first person to mention the magic word 'landslide' was the architect Richard Rogers, there with his wife, Ruthie. I remember we linked up with David and Patsy Puttnam and were briefly joined by that other New Labour architect, a remarkably calm and collected Peter Mandelson. From him we learned that the Blairs were still on their way from Sedgefield.

John Major had conceded defeat and the sky outside was tinged with pink by the time a boyish and ebullient Tony strode onto the stage to receive a rapturous reception that went on and on and on. Grinning, arms outstretched, he captured perfectly the mood and the moment when he declared: 'A new dawn has broken!' adding over our cheers: 'And it's wonderful.'

Two weeks later, I was cheering again under the twin towers of the old Wembey Stadium.

Apart from my family, I have just three passions in life. First and foremost comes film-making. Second comes politics. And last, but by no means least, is the utter joy and total relaxation which is football.

I wholeheartedly agree with Bill Shankly, one of the great managers of all time, who famously said: 'Some people think football is a matter of life and death ... I can assure them it is much more serious than that.'

For me, the only thing that could surpass watching Chelsea win at Stamford Bridge on a Saturday afternoon was seeing them carry off the FA Cup for the first time in twenty-seven years. This they did against Middlesbrough on 17 May 1997.

As I had long been a director of the club before being appointed life vice president, Sheila and I were privileged to have seats in the royal box. In contrast with the yelling crowd of some 80,000 fans decked out in club colours of blue and red, our official party was required to be soberly suited and booted. Somewhat incongruously, I nevertheless felt impelled to sport my lucky tweed hat.

It didn't let us down. Just forty-two seconds into the game, Di Matteo caught Ben Roberts completely off guard, shooting from twenty-five yards to score the quickest ever goal in the history of the final. Twenty

minutes later, Middlesbrough's best striker retired injured, and towards
the end of the first half, what could have been an equaliser was, to our
huge relief, ruled offside.

The second half was electric. Scenting victory, our supporters were
urging the team on with every fibre of their being, singing, among other
more scurrilous ditties:

> Blue is the colour, football is the game
> We're all together and winning is our aim
> So cheer us on through the sun and rain
> Cos Chelsea, Chelsea is our name.

Magically, just seven minutes before the final whistle, that genius
Gianfranco Zola flicked the ball to midfielder Keith Newton, who
steered it into the net with his left foot, underlining our victory with
a second triumphant goal.

That year, it fell to the Duchess of Kent to present our captain,
Dennis Wise, with the coveted trophy. Having always been puzzled by
the hiatus between the final whistle and this ceremony, I was intrigued
to learn that it was to allow sufficient time for our blue-and-white
ribbons to be attached to the handles and, more importantly, for the
name of the winning team to be engraved on the cup itself.

Ten days later, Princess Diana did me the most tremendous favour.
I'd been involved in raising funds to create a new arts centre, specifi-
cally designed for people with disabilities, on the campus of Leicester
University where my father had spent most of his working life. The
new building was now complete and, when I asked her, the princess
kindly agreed to perform the opening ceremony.

She came by helicopter which landed in a field close by. I was there
to greet her, wearing her tie, of course. Pleased that I had remembered,
she took my hand as we walked towards the waiting crowd.

Once inside the new building, she made a short but perfectly judged
speech, casting mischievous little looks seeking approval in my direction, before unveiling the commemorative plaque.

I then took her on a conducted tour. She met a woman, blind since
birth, who was painting a picture, surrounded by artists who were frail,
lame, deaf, mentally impaired. She met others making music and still

more in the sculpture studio. Diana spoke to each of them, refusing to be rushed, and all too soon we reached the appointed time for her to leave. I accompanied her back towards the helicopter, telling her about another group who'd also been hoping to meet her.

'I really would like to see them,' she said and loped ahead in her high heels to tell the pilot their scheduled departure would be delayed.

Back in the building, I took her into a room where seven profoundly disabled youngsters, all with cerebral palsy, proceeded to show her how they could dance in their wheelchairs.

Here I witnessed Diana's greatest gift; a unique combination of touch, loving compassion and empathy. It was no coincidence that she had been the first royal ever to take the hand of an Aids sufferer or to cradle the face of a leper. She genuinely wanted – and needed – to connect with the damaged, the disparaged and the unwanted. Finally freed from the constraints of protocol and fully aware of the power of her unprecedented celebrity, her aims in life were to find happiness, to make the world a better place and, above all, to provide a stable and loving home for her two sons.

We finally parted beside the helicopter with a kiss on my cheek – she on her way to London, I returning to the new building for further celebrations.

Having driven back, it was close to midnight when Sheila and I finally arrived home. Promising myself I would write to thank Diana first thing in the morning, I was taken aback to find, already awaiting me, the last letter I would ever receive from her.

Hand delivered from Kensington Palace earlier that evening, it began: 'Dearest Dickie, I was so proud to be standing beside you today.' Amazingly, *she* was actually thanking *me* for asking her to travel all the way up to Leicester to open 'your wonderful new building'. She continued: 'You and Sheila are hugely kind and supportive towards me and I do cherish that welcome gift.' Ending with an expression of her fondest love and devotion, the second page was signed, as always, 'Diana X'.

Towards the end of August that year, while Sheila and I were relaxing at our home on the Isle of Bute, she phoned from somewhere in the Mediterranean. She was on a huge and very glamorous yacht, Diana told me, and having the most wonderful time. On her return to London within a matter of days, she would phone again and we would arrange another meeting.

Many of my generation can recall precisely where and when they heard that JFK had been assassinated. Desperately trying to get *Gandhi* made, Sheila and I were in Bombay just after my second meeting with Prime Minister Pandit Nehru. I remember walking out of my hotel to find the normally clamorous street cloaked in utter silence save for the eerie sound of an Indian woman wailing.

And so it was with Diana. Although there was no sense of foreboding, I still know exactly where I was standing on that summer Sunday morning when the phone rang. Our younger daughter, Charlotte, was calling to tell us Diana had been fatally injured in a car crash. Where? The Pont d'Alma tunnel in Paris.

Shocked and grieving, Sheila and I turned on the television. We watched as Diana's boys, palpably stunned, dutifully took part in the royals' habitual church parade at Balmoral. Then came a sombre Tony Blair, outside another church in his County Durham constituency. Again perfectly capturing the mood and the moment, he spoke eloquently of the loss to the nation, dubbing Diana 'the people's princess'.

By the Monday afternoon, a long queue was waiting patiently to sign a book of condolence close to where her body lay at St James's Palace. Hundreds more – bearing bouquets, teddy bears, candles, all kinds of personal tributes – were converging on Kensington Palace.

By the Tuesday, further books of condolence were being made available all over the country. Outside Diana's home, the sea of flowers grew ever larger while a mute but increasingly hostile crowd kept vigil in front of Buckingham Palace. Now questions were being asked. Why was no flag flying at half mast? Why no plans for a state funeral? And why was the silent Queen still hidden away in Scotland?

The following day, I received a call from Broadlands, the stately home in Hampshire where Diana had spent her disastrous wedding night. Knowing how close I had been to her, my film-producer friend, John Brabourne, husband of Countess Mountbatten, was phoning to console me. We went on to discuss the growing public unrest, which we both feared, if left unchecked, could pose a threat to the monarchy. John, who was in daily contact with Balmoral, told me the whole place was 'in a state of total turmoil'.

I said that, in my opinion, the Queen should be persuaded to make some kind of public statement and the question of the flag needed to be addressed. John agreed about the statement but explained that protocol, precedent and continuity all dictated the royal standard must never be flown at half mast, even on the death of the monarch.

I said, 'Protocol and precedent be buggered, John! It seems to me this is getting totally out of hand. If it can't be the royal standard, get them to fly the Union flag. That's the very least she deserves.'

John said he would try and on the Thursday came an announcement that the Queen was to speak to the nation and a Union flag would be flown at half mast on the day of Diana's funeral. This was accompanied by a statement that the royal family was hurt by suggestions they were indifferent to the country's sorrow.

On the Friday, they finally returned to London and the Queen, making her first live televised appearance, paid a very moving tribute to her late daughter-in-law. We watched as she and Prince Philip – both seeming unusually unsure of their reception – emerged from Buckingham Palace to interact with the waiting crowd.

Sheila and I returned to Old Friars that evening. Dressing for the funeral on the Saturday morning, I was reaching for the black tie kept for such occasions when, with a sudden lump in my throat, I remembered Diana's laughing instruction to wear the one she'd selected whenever we met and put that on instead.

In Westminster Abbey, seated next to the piano where Elton John was to sing 'Candle in the Wind,' we missed the historic moment when the Queen bowed to Diana's coffin as it passed Buckingham Palace.

What I most remember about the service is the young Earl Spencer's passionate eulogy. As it came to an end, I heard an extraordinary sound, like the beating wings of a huge flock of birds. It took a few moments to realise it originated outside the abbey. Beyond the open doors, thousands of people were applauding what they'd just heard over the loudspeakers. More extraordinary still, that infectious applause was being taken up by the mourners inside, starting at the back and rippling up the nave until, caught up in the emotion of the moment, I was clapping too.

Looking back, I can understand why Earl Spencer's tribute could be interpreted as an attack on the royal family. But at the time I didn't perceive it as lese-majesty. Quite the contrary. To me, he was talking about ensuring his sister's greatest legacy: her beloved boys and their future role in a modern monarchy, fit for the coming millennium and beyond.

Although, out of insecurity, Diana often hid behind the fallacy that she was 'thick as two short planks', I considered her, in many ways, wise beyond her years. It was not on a whim that she so often took her sons, unannounced and incognito, to local shops, theme parks, hospitals and hostels for the homeless.

She knew, if William was ever to be king, and remain so, he and Harry must not brought up surrounded by sycophancy and circumscribed by the privileged assumptions of a bygone age. It was not enough to make scheduled appearances where every traffic light turned green at their approach and all evidence of life in the raw had been scrupulously tidied away. If they were to understand and connect with the people, they had to see, hear and experience life for themselves.

DH— Our car wasn't going very fast. And the Canadian at the wheel was a highly experienced film driver; devoutly Catholic and teetotal.

It was March 1998, six months after the death of Princess Diana. While Dick had been playing the sixteenth-century statesman Sir William Cecil opposite Cate Blanchett in Shekhar Kapur's *Elizabeth*, Jake Eberts had been busy reassembling the funding for our own aban-doned project. After a three-year hiatus, *Grey Owl* was finally on again.

Sitting in the back of the Chevrolet station wagon, neither of us wearing seat belts, Dick and I were on our way to our first Quebec loca-tion, a frozen lake in the middle of a nature reserve. I glanced out of the window. To one side of the country road, some fifty feet below, was a winter-petrified stream. Ahead, the road veered left to cross it.

As soon as we were on the bridge, the car locked into a skid, heading straight for a flimsy parapet, no more than a couple of feet high. In that instant, registering our momentum and clearly seeing the abyss below, I knew, we all knew, we were about to die.

None of us uttered a sound and that instant lasted an eternity.

Then – how or why I don't know – we were gliding towards the opposite parapet, then left, then right again at a less acute angle, before finally coming to rest, bonnet-deep, in a snowdrift on the far side of the bridge.

The driver switched off the engine. Utter silence followed. He was the first to speak. To my surprise, he didn't thank his God but muttered, 'Fuck, fuck, fuck . . .' very quietly like a mantra.

I looked at Dick. Dick looked at me. Ever uxorious, he said, 'Whatever you do, don't tell Sheila.'

What I most remember about the aftermath, however, is how intensely alive I felt and how miraculously the crystalline snow glistened under that heavenly blue sky.

All in all, *Grey Owl* was a tough shoot.

We were based in Montreal which boasted the only film studios in Quebec but was hundreds of road miles from all our other locations. A further difficulty was that we had to depict all four seasons within a tightly budgeted nine-week schedule. And, come what may, we had to finish before mid-June when swarms of blackfly and man-eating mosquitoes would be seen on camera, drawing blood on the actors' faces.

Pierce Brosnan, a keen environmentalist, was to play Grey Owl. He came to us fully prepared, having diligently researched the real-life impostor, Archie Belaney, and taken the time to master the arts of canoeing and running in snow shoes.

Now in his mid-forties and fresh from his triumphant debut as James Bond, this incredibly charismatic Irishman caused a sensation wherever he went. He'd waited a long time for this kind of celebrity and handled it with never-failing patience, courtesy and charm

Cast opposite Pierce was eighteen-year-old Annie Galipeau, a totally inexperienced but very beautiful Algonquin Canadian whose dark eyes and mobile face mirrored her every thought. The problem was that she spoke very little English and, having learned her lines parrot fashion, was unable to provide the verbal nuances Pierce and Dick required.

Dick at seventy-four was as bullish as ever, leading from the front, oozing energy and enthusiasm, refusing to sit on set and stoutly refusing to acknowledge gout, diabetes or deafness despite the eighteen-hour days. During the winter shoot, bundled up in his scarlet parka and cocooned in layer upon layer of thermals, he marched resolutely through the woods accompanied by a young minder whose sole job was to haul him out of the metre-deep snow holes. His only concession to old age came during our one-hour lunch break when, after a light snack in his camper van, he would nap for precisely thirty minutes.

For me, at sixty sleep – or lack of it – became a major issue, as did a recurring back problem and, with the arrival of spring, a massive allergic reaction to the insect repellent with which we liberally doused ourselves and the surrounding vegetation.

Our so-called rest days were few and far between. Between viewing rushes and editing, Dick was helping the Diana Memorial Fund and a cash-strapped RADA by fronting a fund-raising documentary about the Academy's former president, Princess Diana. This television production was being backed by another flamboyant and equally indomitable septuagenarian, Robert Halmi.

Hungarian by birth, Halmi had in his youth twice been sentenced to death: first by the Nazis as a member of the resistance movement, and subsequently by the occupying Russians for his espionage activities on behalf of the United States. On both occasions he had escaped by the skin of his teeth and gone on to become a well-known writer-photographer for *Life* magazine.

By the time we met him, Robert was an American citizen and the multimillionaire chairman of Hallmark Entertainment, a company which specialised in adapting great works of literature for television. When work on the Diana documentary was completed, he summoned us to a mysterious meeting, sending an executive jet to Montreal.

Of all the many privileges that come with the celebrity lifestyle, this form of air travel has to be the most luxurious: no queuing, no ticket, no check-in, no passport control, no trudging along endless corridors. You are driven straight to a sleek little plane, climb three or four steps and sit wherever you please.

On this occasion, having landed at a private airport in New Jersey, we were directed to a small room. Robert, who'd recently stumbled on the stairs of a Budapest cafe, was waiting on crutches to greet us. The room contained just three chairs and a small coffee table dwarfed by a leather-bound book. Wasting no time, our host indicated this huge tome. 'You wonder why I bring you all this way? This, my dears, is your next project.'

It was the Bible.

Even Dick was the tiniest bit daunted. But Robert soon put our minds at rest. He wasn't proposing we should film all of it; merely the Old Testament.

'Think of it,' he said. 'Together we turn five thousand years of human history into twelve hours of prime time.'

We stayed with him for more than an hour, gradually talking ourselves – the Darwinian and the agnostic – into this mad undertaking. Finally, having agreed to start when *Grey Owl* went into post-production, we returned to Montreal.

Back in London that summer, I found myself battling a whole series of seemingly unconnected ailments – double vision, choking, mysterious swellings – as we started to work with four eminent and highly individualistic writers.

Peter Barnes, hailed as one of the unrecognised geniuses of English theatre, was responsible for most of Genesis. Armed with pen and pad, his unlikely creative workplace of choice was McDonald's in Leicester Square. The also late and very lovely Jack Rosenthal – the second Jewish writer of the quartet – tackled Jacob, Esau, Joseph and Moses. Peter Whelan, veteran of the Royal Shakespeare Company, was assigned the parting of the Red Sea, the handing down of the Ten Commandments and the walls of Jericho. The maverick atheist charged with bringing the Old Testament to a close was the erudite and bawdy John Mortimer.

During the ensuing months, amid ongoing arguments regarding the ethnicity of Adam and Eve, successive drafts were bandied back and forth across the Atlantic until, ominously, twelve hours of programming were suddenly reduced to eight. Finally, a year after our airport meeting with Robert, having learned three other networks were planning to screen 'Jesus miniseries', NBC called the whole thing off.

For me, it was in many ways a relief. Although Dick was determined to go on making films until he keeled over, I was no longer physically able to put in long hours, due to the range of ailments which none of the specialists I consulted was able to explain. Only recently, have laboratory studies linked the insecticide used on our Canadian locations to Gulf War syndrome.

However, my much disparaged retirement was to be short-lived. Forty years and umpteen films after our first meeting. I was finally about to witness Lord Attenborough in chairman mode.

This was the man in the grey flannel suit, who, when not acting, producing or directing in denim, spent a week of every month presiding over an amazing variety of businesses and charity board meetings.

Among them was the Royal Academy of Dramatic Art. As the Academy's chairman since 1973, Dick was now committed to rebuilding his alma mater's bomb-damaged and dilapidated headquarters in Bloomsbury. Having successfully applied to the Arts Council Lottery Fund for a grant of £24 million, he'd undertaken to raise a mandatory further £8 million in match funding himself.

I was co-opted to help, and as a former student – albeit very briefly – became a member of the academy's ruling council and other committees directly involved in finance, design and redevelopment.

Never having attended a formal meeting, it took me a while to get to grips with the various protocols. Dick always arrived promptly, took his seat at the head of the table, laying out and meticulously squaring off his papers before removing his wristwatch. This he placed in front of him, face upwards; a reminder that grandstanding was not permitted and his time was precious.

I soon realised he regarded conducting a meeting as film directing in another guise. Those of us gathered round the table were his cast to be called upon, each in turn, to play our lines and sometimes be subtly played off, one against another. Given that most of RADA's council were professional actors, this produced some fascinating performances.

But it was in the other meetings, involving a disparate mix of entrepreneurs, accountants, project managers, architects, lawyers, theatre designers and drama teachers, that Dick the tactician really came into his own; able to compact a whole raft of divergent opinions into an agreed and succinct summary. Very occasionally, when faced with an absolute impasse, he would appear to lose his temper. This always achieved the desired effect.

Privately, our dealings with the Arts Council's lottery officials often caused him to lose it for real. Of course it was right that a public body, charged with making grants amounting to millions, should require assurances they would be properly spent. However, the endless form-filling, impossible deadlines, nit-picking, political correctness, bullying, disbelief, incompetence, interference and sheer lack of communication were unbelievable. I spent the whole of one Christmas editing and rewriting a huge and complicated submission which had to be delivered on 2 January. We waited weeks before it was even read.

Dick, meanwhile, was arm-twisting everywhere he went in order to raise the other £8 million. But, with a host of other lottery projects also hell-bent on inveigling every philanthropist in sight, this was a near impossible task. Nevertheless, he managed to do it, by the skin of his teeth, with a final munificent donation from Alan Grieve of the Jerwood Foundation.

In the summer of 2000, with the new building almost complete, we received a visit from the Arts Council's Director of Capital Services, Moss Cooper. Having delivered a dire warning that without a root-and-branch overhaul of its staffing, fee structure and day-to-day finances, RADA would be forced to close, he took me to one side. Was I aware, he asked, that as a member of the council and charitable trustee, this meant I could lose my home and everything I possessed? Angry and shocked, I asked if he was aware that the time I had donated was worth somewhere in the region of £100,000? He shrugged.

Worse was to come when Mr Cooper, formerly attached to the Wolsey Theatre in Norfolk and Townsgate Theatre in Essex, was taken to inspect the magnificent new 200-seater Vanbrugh Jerwood auditorium.

Based on a classical seventeenth-century concept by Inigo Jones, this was a masterpiece of flexible design, unique in its ability to offer the drama student every possible stage configuration from proscenium through apron and thrust to theatre-in-the-round. As the man from the Arts Council was leaving, I asked his opinion, expecting at the very least a modicum of enthusiasm. Instead he pronounced dourly: 'It'll make an excellent carpet showroom.'

RA— Until I took on Capital Radio, all my chairmanships had been in the voluntary sector.

It had begun during my early thirties when Noël Coward, who was about to become a tax exile, tried to persuade me to take over his presidency of the Actors' Orphanage. When I declined in favour of Laurence Olivier who had far more clout, celebrity and standing, Noël invented the post of working chairman. And this I agreed to accept, going on to become chairman, patron or president of more than a dozen charities. Then, at the end of 1971, I was introduced to a dentist from Weybridge with the unlikely name of Barclay Barclay-White.

Some twenty years earlier, the advent of commercial television in the UK had proved so lucrative it had famously been hailed as 'a licence to print money'. Now the newly formed Independent Broadcasting Authority was about to award two licences to set up London's first commercial radio stations.

Eager to seize what appeared to be a once-in-a-lifetime opportunity, the dentist decided to apply for the general entertainment licence. Knowing no one in radio, he somehow obtained the address of what he considered the next best thing – a film-maker living in neighbouring Virginia Water – and wrote outlining his plan to my friend and former partner, Bryan Forbes.

Forbsie was about to tear up what appeared to be a crank letter when his wife, Nan, urged he at least follow it up, saying: 'What have you got to lose?' So Bryan met Barclay Barclay-White and, having been seduced into his crazy get-rich-quick scheme, went on to seduce me.

Frankly, I didn't take much wooing. It was then two years since I'd last appeared on-screen as the necrophiliac mass murderer, John Reginald Christie, in *10 Rillington Place*, a plea for the permanent abolition of the death penalty. And *Young Winston*, my second film as a director, was long since finished and delivered. With *Gandhi* still in the hands of David Lean and my coffers empty, I quickly immersed myself in this new venture.

The competition was stiff; Capital was up against nearly thirty other applicants, many from the now illegal but still hugely popular pirate radio ships. In our camp, Barclay came with no broadcasting background whatsoever, and although in our youth Bryan and I had both briefly been BBC presenters, what we knew about running a radio station could have been written on a postage stamp.

The first company director we recruited was the genial and highly regarded broadcaster, David Jacobs. Next we roped in our music guru in the person of George Martin, known as 'the fifth Beatle,' and, a little later, the Labour peer and creator of *Dixon of Dock Green*, Ted Willis. On the business side, we were joined by four men representing the local and national newspaper groups which would provide our start-up finance.

We were, however, unable to comply with the mandatory precondition in the IBA application form which required us to name our chief executive – all the best candidates having already been snapped up by our rivals. And here, having been asked to become the fledgling company's chairman, I stuck my neck out, proposing we should take the most monstrous gamble. Instead of settling for second best, we'd go all-out to win and, should we be successful, appoint the best CEO from one of the losing consortia.

The gamble paid off. Capital Radio having been awarded the general entertainment licence, we were able to secure the services of the excellent and very experienced John Whitney.

John and I immediately rolled up our sleeves and set to work. The ten months before we went on air were among the most challenging and exciting I can ever remember. Although I was chairman and this was a business, I also saw myself as the impresario responsible for overseeing the whole design and ethos of the new station.

Above all, we wanted Capital to be the antithesis of the BBC – helpful, down to earth, totally accessible and with none of the pomposity of nation loftily speaking peace unto nation; just friendly people playing music and chatting one-on-one to our listeners.

After much searching, we rented space in the newly built Euston Tower, then one of London's tallest buildings. Unable to afford more than a reception area at pricey ground level, we also leased the whole of the first floor. The problem was that the two came unconnected and, for many months during the fit out, a wobbly twenty-foot ladder was the only means of accessing our studios and offices.

It was then I came up with the idea of creating a spectacular Busby Berkeley staircase which, because it would cost an arm and a leg, quickly became known as 'Dickie's folly'.

As always, there was a last-minute scramble to get everything ready. We worked through the night, and at four o'clock on the all-important morning, I was still in my shirtsleeves, vacuuming the blue carpet adorning the new treads and risers.

Then, just before five, I was in front of a microphone – jacket on, heart pounding – as the red hand on the studio clock jerked away the remaining seconds. On came the cue light. Taking a deep breath, I informed Greater London: 'The date is 16 October 1972. The time is 5 a.m.'

After a drum roll, came all three verses of the national anthem, played by the London Philharmonic and sung so stirringly by members of the Royal Choral Society that I was impelled to stand up and conduct them, grinning at my exhausted colleagues on the other side of the glass.

Cued again, I sank into my chair to announce: 'This, for the very first time, is Capital Radio.' On came our catchy jingle, followed, all too prophetically on that gloriously upbeat morning, by the very first item on our playlist, Simon and Garfunkel's 'Bridge Over Troubled Waters'.

Less than a month later, Britain's miners and electricity workers had announced an overtime ban and the Heath government was forced into declaring a national state of emergency. As the crisis deepened, no vehicle was permitted to drive over 50mph and businesses were compelled to make five days of normal electricity consumption last a fortnight. The final straw was the three-day week.

Far from being a licence to print money, Capital had very few listeners and, in the ensuing economic downturn, our handful of advertisers dwindled away to nothing. All too soon there came a point when John Whitney and I came in on a Monday morning to be told the company was in debt to the tune of £1 million and, come Friday, we would be unable to pay the wages.

Being the ham that I am, I decided a grand gesture was needed. Returning home, I loaded some of my most valuable paintings into the boot of the Rolls and drove them to the City where – as you could in those days – I parked right outside the Bank of Scotland. Inside, I explained the situation to our account manager, telling him, 'Those pictures are worth something in the region of half a million. I'll willingly leave them here if you'll agree to extend our overdraft.'

'Give me five minutes,' he said, disappearing into another room.

He was as good as his word, announcing on his return, 'You may keep your pictures and we'll make the money available.'

Three years later, troubled waters began to recede when Capital finally managed to break even. Within a decade, four million Londoners were tuning in to the station on a regular basis and in 1987 the company was floated on the London Stock Exchange after the most successful and oversubscribed share offering ever achieved by any British media company.

In the same year, I also became chairman of Channel 4 Television.

Lady Plowden, who headed the Independent Broadcasting Authority, had originally tried to persuade me to accept the post in 1980. Her offer, however, couldn't have come at a worse time: after twenty years of ridicule and rebuff, I was about to start shooting *Gandhi* in India.

And so we agreed I would instead accept the position of deputy chairman and the new channel would be headed initially by the assiduous Edmund Dell, a former Labour Paymaster General most recently in charge of the merchant banking group, Peat Marwick.

Of the thirty-odd candidates who'd applied for the crucial post of chief executive, the choice eventually lay between chalk and cheese: John Birt and Jeremy Isaacs. The former promised efficiency and meticulous attention to detail, the latter passion and boundless creativity.

Edmund, a dedicated chess player who had only recently acquired his first television set, was naturally in favour of John. I was determined to have Jeremy. And therein lay the dichotomy between business and show business that would continue to bedevil Channel 4 for many years to come.

Edmund did not give in without a fight but, finding himself the lone dissenter at the decisive board meeting, reluctantly conceded defeat. In awarding Isaacs a five-year contract, he said, we were making 'a terrible mistake'.

One of the many reasons I wanted the ebullient Jeremy was his total commitment to my concept of Film on Four. The only condition I had laid down before accepting the deputy chairmanship was that the new channel should devote significant funding to fostering new work by young British film-makers. The result, under the aegis of our perceptive commissioning editor, David Rose, was a whole string of superbly innovative productions: *Letter to Brezhnev*, *My Beautiful Laundrette*, *Shallow Grave*, *Secrets and Lies*, *Trainspotting* . . .

By the time I took over from Edmund as chairman in 1987, it was evident that, far from being a mistake, Jeremy's appointment was nothing short of a triumph. For the first time, annual revenue from advertising had exceeded our costs, and we were in profit to the tune of £20 million. But, as his contract came up for renewal, the opera-loving Glaswegian was sadly in search of pastures new.

We advertised, not very successfully, for someone capable of replacing the seemingly irreplaceable Jeremy. Coincidentally, the BBC was also recruiting new controllers for BBC1 and BBC2. Although I wasn't aware of it at the time, this process was causing enormous friction between two equally ambitious television executives: the dour Deputy Director General, John Birt, and one of the existing controllers and Managing Director designate, the hugely talented Michael Grade.

I'd known Michael practically all his life; his father, Leslie, and uncle, Lew, the founders of ATV Television, were good friends of mine. So I wasn't surprised when he phoned one evening in early November, ostensibly to give me the BBC transmission date for a documentary about the filming of Cry Freedom.

We chatted on for a while, exchanging family news. The conversation was winding down when, almost as an afterthought, Michael casually enquired about the search for Jeremy's successor.

I said, 'Well, you know, darling, it isn't easy. But we're getting there.'

I heard a slow intake of breath and to my surprise he responded, 'Dickie, I don't know whether this is of any interest to you or not, but I'll say it twice so there's no misunderstanding. If you were to offer me the job, I'd take it.'

'Would you really?'

'I'd jump at it.'

Here, it seemed to me, was the solution to all our problems. Although he was in many ways the complete opposite of Jeremy Isaacs, Michael was an extremely cultured man. This, in my view, coupled with his show-business background, outgoing personality, populist scheduling skills and impressive breadth of television experience, made him our ideal candidate.

Time being of the essence, I immediately rang round to arrange a meeting with the Channel 4 selection panel. This, Michael stipulated, must take place in conditions of the utmost secrecy, it being vital that word of his potential defection did not reach his present employers prematurely.

The impromptu job interview took place at my home on the following Saturday morning. Michael, presumed to be flying to Los Angeles on behalf of the BBC, arrived first and, as arranged, drove straight into my garage. I was already waiting, cloak-and-dagger style, to leap out and shut the car out of sight before escorting him through the hidden office entrance into the house.

Michael couldn't have put on a more impressive performance and, after he'd left the way he'd come, the panel voted unanimously to put his name forward as their first choice for new chief executive. The next step was to inform the IBA, now headed by Lord Thomson of Monifieth, and seek their formal approval. Having been ratified during the Monday afternoon, Michael's appointment was to be announced at precisely 7 p.m. that evening.

He, meanwhile, was writing his letter of resignation to the BBC Director General and making arrangements for it to be delivered a courteous two hours earlier.

My task in this meticulous timetable was to find Jeremy Isaacs and give him advance warning of what was happening. I tried to phone him throughout the morning, without success. It was finally arranged via his PA that we would meet up during the afternoon at the National Film Theatre, where I was to do a series of press interviews tied to the launch of Cry Freedom.

When I told Jeremy who was to succeed him, he exploded and came very close to hitting me. I remembering thinking if he was capable of murder, it wouldn't have been Michael in the firing line – it would have been me.

The two of them finally came face to face in the busy corridor outside Jeremy's office at the end of the week. Michael, resplendent in his trademark red socks and red braces, proffered his hand. Jeremy grudgingly shook it before the pent-up emotion all came pouring out. 'I am handing you a sacred trust,' he snarled. 'If you screw it up, if you betray it, I'll come back and throttle you!'

DH— I'm looking through Dick's diary for 2004; not the office copy, overseen by his beloved PA, Gabriel Clare-Hunt, but the slim, leather-bound version in which he meticulously sets out each day's appointments in that curlicued calligraphy of his, so redolent of a bygone age.

His eighty-first year, the year that everything changed, begins like any other.

Having enjoyed their habitual post-Christmas sojourn in Scotland, the Attenboroughs fly back to London in the middle of January. Dick's first act is to get his hair and beard trimmed at home by the discreet Mr James.

On the Saturday evening he and Sheila attend a theatrical first night. The avant-garde play is *Five Gold Rings*, directed by their son Michael, 53, who, for the past two years, has been in charge of the Almeida Theatre.

Watching the performance with the Attenboroughs is the African teenager, who is their other 'adopted' son, Doctor Mphilisi Dlamini. Named after the bush physician who delivered him, Doctor spends his weekends in the former nursery at Old Friars, replete with the sixth birthday rocking horse Dick has cherished for the past 75 years.

As a clever Swazi child, living in a mud hut with his dying HIV-infected mother, Doctor was singled out by a visiting teacher from Waterford Kamhlaba School who recommended him for a bursary. This was one of many funded by the Attenboroughs through their charitable trust. Now they are supporting his further studies at the American International University close to their home in Richmond. Doctor's burning ambition, eventually to be realised, is to return home and teach in his village school.

Come the last Monday in January, when Doctor returns to campus, Dick devotes most of the following week and, indeed, much of the coming year to Dragon International Studios.

Having been buttonholed at a football match by a fellow Chelsea fan, he became the extremely active chairman of this new company in 2001 and roped me in as an executive director. Together with an assortment of partners, including a Habsburg princess, we are trying to develop a state-of-the-art film studio on the site of a disused opencast coal mine in the Rhondda region of Wales.

Dubbed 'Valleywood' by local press, this is a project which really excites us. However, as we've painfully discovered, it's not only film-makers who can flounder for years in development hell. We've been delayed by a search for non-existent but highly protected dormice, obliged to create special runways for great crested newts and endlessly shuttled between two groups of powerful but apparently incompatible planners.

Then there's the bank, one of the big five. There, our fate is in the hands of a young man called Jeremy, who has a master's degree in the fine art of procrastination. Despite a definitive offer of finance, our all-important legal-term sheet never arrives. Promising much but delivering nothing, Jeremy becomes increasingly elusive until, at the end of April, he completely disappears; gone, desk cleared, colleagues pretending he never existed.

The good news in 2004 is that we've finally achieved full outline planning permission. Dick's diary shows us optimistically flying out to the Cannes Film Festival with our CEO, Stuart Villard, on 13 May. There, armed with glossy brochures, we throw an inaugural champagne party, at which our initiative is warmly welcomed by the Minister for Culture, Media and Sport, Estelle Morris.

Little do we know, Dick having invested major amounts of his own money and both of us our unpaid time, we will still be battling to open the studios four years later.

Meanwhile, following our return from the festival, Dick is beguiling a charming blonde over lunch at his favourite restaurant. The entry reads: '1 p.m. Sue Barker – Ivy.' He's been a regular here ever since he played Sergeant Trotter in *The Mousetrap*, still running an incredible fifty years later at the neighbouring St Martin's Theatre.

Seated at 'his table' – at the back of the room, facing the door – Dick's mission today is to persuade his guest to take over as president of the Muscular Dystrophy Campaign.

Driven by an empathetic need to justify his own good fortune, he has worked tirelessly for this self-help charity since the early 1960s. During that time, he tells Sue, he's attempted to comfort hundreds of parents whose children have wasted away from this cruel genetic condition, some losing several sons in succession. As a devoted paterfamilias – father of three, grandfather of seven – Dick cannot begin to comprehend how they find the strength to carry on. But carry on they do. With inadequate government support, those same bereaved parents continue to raise the vast sums of money needed to fund a programme of ongoing research in the hope it will eventually save other people's children.

Kind-hearted Sue finds it impossible to refuse Dick's request. A press release on 7 June will announce: 'The Muscular Dystrophy Campaign is thrilled to welcome Sue Barker MBE, former world number three tennis player and BBC broadcaster, as its new president.'

Although he's now stepped down from all but one of his working chairmanships, Dick still has no intention of retiring from film-making. Ever.

In June, he asks my opinion of an excellent new script. This is *Closing the Ring*, a love story set in two different countries and time frames, written by Peter Woodward, son of the actor, Edward. Having decided to direct and co-produce with Jo Gilbert, Dick embarks yet again on the eternal quest for funding. The film, starring Shirley MacLaine, Christopher Plummer and Mischa Barton will take him three years to complete.

Meanwhile, in the summer of 2004, Dick and Sheila embark on their annual sunshine retreat, spending the whole month of August in their rustic *mas*, set among Provençal olive groves. There, they are briefly joined by their elder daughter, Jane, and her shipbroker husband, Michael Holland, known as Beau, and three vivacious teenage children, Sam, Alice and Lucy.

Returning to London, happy and relaxed – Dick pink, Sheila brown – the Attenboroughs order their bespoke Christmas card. As always, it features one of the paintings from their collection; this year *Tree* by Craigie Aitchison.

When the thousand cards are delivered, Dick begins the annual task of signing every one of them, adding personal messages to family, close friends and each of the parents he's met through the Muscular Dystrophy Campaign.

The cards have been posted by Sunday 19 December when he records innocently: '12.45, pre-Christmas lunch with Jane, Beau and family.'

The Hollands having departed for sunnier climes, 25 December is spent at Old Friars. Promptly at 11 a.m., following long-established ritual, the Attenboroughs and their younger daughter, Charlotte, together with her two little boys and theatre director husband, Graham Sinclair, exchange presents beside the Christmas tree. By 1 p.m. everyone is in their appointed place at the dining table where traditional turkey and all the trimmings are formally served by the Filipino house staff, Linda and Domin Halunahan. During the evening, Dick and Sheila are joined by his brother, David, and niece, Sue.

The Attenboroughs are contentedly asleep a few minutes before 1 a.m. on Boxing Day morning when a massive earthquake, the second largest ever recorded, erupts thousands of miles away under the Indian Ocean. It triggers hundred-foot surface waves which race towards the coasts of Indonesia, Sri Lanka, India and Thailand.

Contemporaneously, seven hours ahead of Richmond-upon-Thames on idyllic Bang Niang beach in the Thai resort of Khao Lak, the Holland family are enjoying a leisurely breakfast. Beau and his son have a date to join up with some male friends to play golf on an inland course. They set off, leaving behind Jane, Alice, Lucy and Beau's elderly mother, another Jane.

Looking towards the distant sea some time later, one of the golfers notices something very odd: it isn't there any more. Minutes later, Beau sees a wall of water rushing towards him and, grabbing a little boy, races to the clubhouse where, with help from his friends, he manages to haul the child onto a roof before a huge wave engulfs them. As it recedes, sucking out and smashing everything in its wake, the men become desperate to reach their families.

They find a Thai with a minibus who is willing to drive them back to the beach but, after an hour, he refuses to go any further. Beau finally makes it back to Orchid Villas on foot. Of his new holiday home, only the concrete bones of the ground floor remain. The sand all around is littered with hunks of twisted metal, splintered trees and corpses.

Almost immediately, he comes across his drowned fifteen-year-old daughter, Lucy. He then sees his other daughter, still alive but very badly injured, being loaded into a truck. Abandoning the desperate search for his wife and mother, whose bodies will not be identified for many months to come, Beau follows Alice to the local hospital.

It is from there, some time later, that he is finally able to phone his brother-in-law, Michael Attenborough, in London.

The last entry in Dick's 2004 diary is for 26 December. Planning to attend Chelsea's traditional Boxing Day match at Stamford Bridge with Sheila, Michael and Michael's wife, Karen, he's noted the name of the visiting team, Aston Villa.

But this has been savagely scratched out and is now barely legible. Beneath it is written, heartbreakingly: 'Tsunami disaster. Lost Jane, Lucy & Jane Holland.'

RA— My memory of that terrible morning is so completely blank I've obviously buried it very deeply.

All I do remember is that Sheila and I were having breakfast at about nine in the morning when I heard the back doorbell ring. Going to answer it, I saw my son through the glass, looking very odd. I opened the door, knowing something awful had happened. And Michael said very gently, 'Dad, will you go and sit down please?'

He followed me into the dining room where Sheila was and continued: 'I'm afraid I have something dreadful to tell you both. Jane and Lucy have died in the tsunami.'

I'm not even sure we knew what a tsunami was. And then Michael went on to tell us what he'd learned from Beau.

As a family, we have rituals, formalities which have been observed for as long as I can remember. Mealtimes, for instance, are terribly important. Being together for breakfast, lunch or dinner has always been very much part of the way we live. Christmas lunch was always at one o'clock. And you didn't just sit anywhere; we each had our own particular places, seventeen of us when we were joined by Dave and Sue.

So it was never a question of the children just popping in for a visit. Following the 25th, we'd congregate again at Michael and Karen's in Chiswick, or Jane and Beau's in Putney or Charlotte and Graham's in Hampton, moving around between the four different households.

After the tsunami, Sheila and I simply couldn't bear the thought of those two missing faces at our table. So in 2005 we decided to go away on Christmas Eve, and instead of visiting the children's houses, they could come to stay with us at our other home in Scotland. That way the family would still be together but not with this terrible sense of yawning emptiness.

We've maintained that decision ever since. If Sheila and I wanted to cry in Scotland, well, we cried. And if we wanted to laugh because we remembered something funny Jane had said or done and were a bit shocked by our laughter, that was fine too.

As time has gone on, we've found that we're able to talk about Jane and Lucy, recall them, rather than saying they're gone and mustn't be mentioned. We can't do that with other people around but if we're alone we can talk as much as we like and let our emotions well up, spend the whole day with tears pouring down our faces, if need be.

This is how we've managed to cope with the worst thing that's ever happened. It is terrible to lose somebody, for them not to be there, to recognise the fact that they're not only not there, they've completely gone. You ask yourself, over and over, where have they gone? They were here, their being was here. They can't just be wiped out. And yet they are.

It would have been easier if I'd had a religious faith. Overwhelmingly so. It would have been such a help. But you can't suddenly switch faith on. You can say, yes, I try to follow the Ten Commandments, or, yes, I believe in goodness and concern for other people. But you can't suddenly decide, because it suits you, that there is life after death.

Like the parents I met through the Muscular Dystrophy Campaign, Sheila and I needed to find a way of continuing and commemorating those we had lost. Over the years, we had amassed quite a large number of ceramics by Picasso. I can't even think of them without smiling because Jane adored his outrageous sense of humour and found his work wonderfully invigorating.

We have now gifted our entire ceramic collection to the Leicester Museum in memory of our beloved Jane and Lucy.

I've always been aware that it was Sheila, not me, who held us together as a family and, when I look back, I see the whole of my adult life crammed with ceaseless activity. Yet, eternally optimistic and, to a degree, selfish and egocentric, I always believed in a future when I would make it up to the children.

In determining the allotment of my time between public and private, work always took command, work always took precedence. Supposedly, weekends were set aside for the family. But not as conscientiously as I would now wish. If it took me a Saturday morning to conclude some business, then I took it.

When we lost Ginny and Luce that opportunity was gone, never to be recovered. And that has changed my relationship with those who are left to the extent that I will do anything to be with them and we spend much more time together.

I can talk to people about Jane now, although sometimes I can't get the words out. I can also see her. I can feel her touch. I can hear her coming into a room. She comes in laughing or excited or determined, but always full of commitment. That was the very essence of Jane; commitment. And music.

I don't know why, but I haven't been able to play any music since she died but, after we lost her, I started to hear it in my head all the time. Just thinking about her now, I am listening to the *Messiah*. *I know that my redeemer liveth*. How about that? Me, an agnostic.

If anything could convince me of religion as such – which I hate, or the formal manifestation of which I hate – it would be music. Jane never forgot the time we took her and Michael to hear the *Messiah* at the Albert Hall when she was about ten years old. So Handel is Jane. Puccini is Lucy.

I can no longer turn on the radio or listen to CDs because they clash with the music in my head. If I had to give up every other art form – pictures, words, dance – I'd gladly do so, provided I could still have music.

I should have played an instrument, but as a child I was bone idle. Had I put in the effort to learn the piano, I'd have played Beethoven's *Sonatas* till the cows came home.

Music is demanding. Music is absolute discipline. I'd like to have been a musician, really, more than an actor or anything else . . . except a director.

DH— Towards the end of 1991, Dick and I had a meeting with Mike Medavoy, then chairman of TriStar, at Sony Pictures' Culver City studios. Having discussed *Chaplin*, which his company was to distribute, Mike said, 'Come with me. There's something I want to show you.'

He took us into a dimly lit room where a team of earnest young boffins sat hunched over a bank of flickering computer screens. There, Mike announced; 'This is the future of movie making.'

The head boffin explained: once a script had been broken down into its component parts, his team had devised programmes capable of simulating the completed film, down to the very last detail.

He showed us an action sequence in which one matchstick man was being pursued by three others along a railroad track. Another depicted a huge cathedral-like interior filled with more rudimentary figures, all interacting with each other.

'As soon as he has an approved script, the director sits down and blocks out every scene, listing all the camera angles and every piece of equipment he'll need throughout the entire shoot,' we were told. 'That way he works fast, nothing winds up on the editing room floor and no set is ever a foot bigger than absolutely necessary. The savings are fantastic.'

We managed to restrain ourselves until we emerged from the Thalberg Building and stood there in the sunshine, not knowing whether to laugh or cry.

Eventually Dick said; 'If that's the future of movie making, thank God I won't live to see it.'

RA— As we returned to our car, I expressed utter astonishment that someone like Mike, who had nurtured such wonderfully innovative films as *One Flew Over the Cuckoo's Nest*, *Amadeus* and *Mississippi Burning* could so lightly discard the crucial collaborative element of film making.

Then, during the journey back to the Beverly Hills Hotel, I found myself remembering how, fifty years earlier as a callow novice, I first fell in love with directing.

Observing my friend and mentor, the late John Boulting, I came to understand that directing is akin to conducting the *Messiah*; the crew being the orchestra, the actors the singers and the extras the chorus. It is the director who must bring them all to performance pitch, who commands, coaxes and hopefully inspires them, as they in turn inspire him.

Of course he must plan ahead and have a clear idea of what he is trying to achieve. But there is no way any director worthy of his craft can determine the finished film before he has assembled the different skills and personalities that make up his crew or the mosaic of talent that constitutes his ideal cast.

We who have the privilege of working in a film are a breed apart. Contrary to popular belief, it is not the supposed glamour or the prospect of wealth that drives us to work harder and longer than those engaged in any other business. The lure is being integral to a creative team where every individual – be they hairdresser, star, carpenter or cameraman – has a vital contribution to make.

I am now very old, about to celebrate my 85th birthday. Although I have hearing aids in both ears and my heart is kept ticking courtesy of a pacemaker, I am determined to live long enough to direct one last film. That film remains, as always, the story of Thomas Paine, *These Are the Times*.

There is a saying: 'Cometh the hour, cometh the man.' In his turbulent day, Paine was that man. So too at crucial moments in history were my other great heroes: Mahatma Gandhi, Winston Churchill and Nelson Mandela.

Today our fragile planet is full of unrest on almost every level; personal, religious, political. If ever a world needed another such hero, these are indeed the times.

APPENDIX

RICHARD ATTENBOROUGH

FILM PRODUCER/DIRECTOR

Closing the Ring (2007) – producer/director
Grey Owl (1999) – producer/director
In Love and War (1996) – producer/director
Shadowlands (1993) – producer/director
Chaplin (1992) – producer/director
Cry Freedom (1987) – producer/director
A Chorus Line (1985) – director
Gandhi (1982) – producer/director
Magic (1978) – director
A Bridge Too Far (1977) – director
Young Winston (1972) – director
Oh! What a Lovely War (1969) – producer/director
Séance on a Wet Afternoon (1964) – producer
The L-Shaped Room (1962) – producer
Whistle Down the Wind (1961) – producer
The Angry Silence (1960) – producer

ACTOR (Theatre)

The Rape of the Belt (1957–8), Piccadilly Theatre, London – Theseus
Double Image (1956–7), Savoy Theatre, London – David and Julian Fanshaw
The Mousetrap (1952–4), Ambassadors Theatre, London – Detective Trotter

Sweet Madness (1952), Vaudeville Theatre, London – Valentine Crisp

To Dorothy a Son (1950–1), Savoy and Garrick Theatres, London – Tony Rigi

The Way Back (1949), Westminster Theatre, London – Peter Coen

Brighton Rock (1943), Garrick Theatre, London – Pinkie Brown

The Little Foxes (1942), Piccadilly Theatre, London – Leo Hubbard

London W1 (1942), Q Theatre, London, 1942 – Andrew

The Holy Isle (1942), Arts Theatre, London – Ba

Awake and Sing (1942), Arts Theatre, London – Ralph Berger

Twelfth Night (1942), Arts Theatre, London – Sebastian

Ah! Wilderness (1941), Intimate Theatre, London – Richard Miller

ACTOR (Film)

Puckoon (2002) – Writer-Director

Jack and the Beanstalk: The Real Story (2001) – Magog

The Railway Children (2000) – Old Gentleman

Joseph and the Amazing Technicolor Dreamcoat (1999) – Jacob

Elizabeth (1998) – Sir William Cecil

The Lost World: Jurassic Park (1997) – John Hammond

Hamlet (1996) – English Ambassador

E=MC² (1996) – The Visitor

Miracle on 34th Street (1994) – Kris Kringle

Jurassic Park (1993) – John Hammond

The Human Factor (1979) – Colonel Daintry

The Chess Players (Shatranj Ke Khilari) (1977) – General Outram

Conduct Unbecoming (1975) – Major Roach

Brannigan (1975) – Commander Swann

Rosebud (1975) – Edward Sloat

10 Rillington Place (1971) – John Reginald Christie

A Severed Head (1970) – Palmer Anderson

The Last Grenade (1970) – General Whiteley

Loot (1970) – Inspector Truscott

David Copperfield (1969) (TV) – Mr Tungay

The Magic Christian (1969) – Oxford coach

The Bliss of Mrs Blossom (1968) – Robert Blossom
Only When I Larf (1968) – Silas
Doctor Dolittle (1967) – Albert Blossom
The Sand Pebbles (1966) – Frenchy Burgoyne
The Flight of the Phoenix (1965) – Lew Moran
Guns at Batasi (1964) – Regimental Sergeant Major Lauderdale
Séance on a Wet Afternoon (1964) – Billy Savage
The Third Secret (1964) – Alfred Price-Gorham
The Great Escape (1963) – Squadron Leader Roger 'Big X' Bartlett
The Dock Brief (1962) – Herbert Fowle
All Night Long (1962) – Rod Hamilton
Only Two Can Play (1962) – Probert
The League of Gentlemen (1960) – Lexy
The Angry Silence (1960) – Tom Curtis
SOS Pacific (1959) – Whitey
Jet Storm (1959) – Ernest Tilley
I'm All Right Jack (1959) – Sidney De Vere Cox
Danger Within (1959) – Captain 'Bunter' Phillips
Sea of Sand (1958) – Brody
The Man Upstairs (1958) – Peter Watson
Dunkirk (1958) – John Holden
Brothers in Law (1957) – Henry Marshall
The Scamp (1957) – Stephen Leigh
The Baby and the Battleship (1956) – Knocker White
Private's Progress (1956) – Private Percival Cox
The Ship that Died of Shame (1955) – George Hoskins
Eight O'Clock Walk (1954) – Thomas Leslie Manning
Father's Doing Fine (1952) – Dougall
Gift Horse (1952) – Dripper Daniels
The Magic Box (1951) – Jack Carter
Hell Is Sold Out (1951) – Pierre Bonnet
Morning Departure (1950) – Stoker Snipe
Boys in Brown (1949) – Jackie Knowles
The Lost People (1949) – Jan
The Guinea Pig (1948) – Jack Read
London Belongs to Me (1948) – Percy Boon
Brighton Rock (1947) – Pinkie Brown

Dancing with Crime (1947) – Ted Peters
The Man Within (1947) – Francis Andrews
School for Secrets (1946) – Jack Arnold
A Matter of Life and Death (1946) – English pilot
Journey Together (1946) – David Wilton
The Hundred Pound Window (1944) – Tommy Draper
Schweik's New Adventures (1943) – Railway worker
In Which We Serve (1942) – Boy stoker

1 Francis Andrews, *The Man Within* 1947
2 Inspector Truscott, *Loot* 1970
3 Santa Claus, *Miracle on 34th Street* 1994
4 Private Percival Cox, *Private's Progress* 1956
5 Sidney de Vere Cox, *I'm All Right Jack* 1959
6 Squadron Leader Bartlett, *The Great Escape* 1963
7 Probert, *Only Two Can Play* 1962
8 Sir William Cecil, *Elizabeth* 1998
9 Frenchy Burgoyne, *The Sand Pebbles* 1966
10 Tom Curtis, *The Angry Silence* 1960
11 Lew Moran, *The Flight of the Phoenix* 1965
12 Herbert Fowle, *The Dock Brief* 1962
13 Pinkie, *Brighton Rock* 1947

14 Brody, *Sea of Sand* 1958
15 Jack Read, *The Guinea Pig* 1948
16 Albert Blossom, *Doctor Dolittle* 1967
17 Whitey, *SOS Pacific* 1959
18 John Reginald Christie, *10 Rillington Place* 1971
19 Squadron Leader Bartlett, *The Great Escape* 1963
20 Kris Kringle, *Miracle on 34th Street* 1994
21 RSM Lauderdale, *Guns at Batasi* 1964
22 John Hammond, *Jurassic Park* 1993
23 Alfred Price-Gorham, *The Third Secret* 1964
24 Sidney de Vere Cox, *I'm All Right Jack* 1959
25 Francis Andrews, *The Man Within* 1947
26 Silas, *Only When I Larf* 1968

APPOINTMENTS AND AWARDS

1947
Co-opted by Sir Nöel Coward to The Actors' Charitable Trust (TACT)
formerly The Actors' Orphanage: Chairman 1956–88, President 1988–

1949
Equity: Council Member 1949–73

1959
Formed Beaver Films Ltd with Bryan Forbes

1960
Formed Allied Film Makers. Co-director with Bryan Forbes, Basil
Dearden, Michael Relph, Guy Green and Jack Hawkins as Chairman

Royal Theatrical Fund: Board of Directors, Vice-President 1985–

1962
Muscular Dystrophy Campaign (formerly Muscular Dystrophy Group of
Great Britain): fundraising to support scientific research, patients and
their families. Vice-President 1962–71. President 1971–2004. Life
President 2004–

Cinema & Television Benevolent Fund: Council Member 1962–2003,
Vice Patron 2003–

King George V Fund for Actors: Committee Member 1962–73, Trustee
1973–

1963
Royal Academy of Dramatic Art (Levenhulme Scholarship student
1941–2): Member of Council 1963–73, Chairman 1973–2003. Succeeding
past Presidents, Sir John Gielgud and Diana, Princess of Wales. President
2003–

Guns at Batasi – BAFTA Best Actor

1964
Combined Theatrical Charities Appeals Council: Chairman 1964–88, President 1988–

Séance on a Wet Afternoon – BAFTA and San Sebastian Film Festival Best Actor

1965
Royal Society of Arts: Life Fellow 1965–

1966
Chelsea Football Club: Vice President 1966, Director 1969–82, Life Vice President 1993– 2008, Life President 2008–

The Sand Pebbles – Hollywood Golden Globe Best Supporting Actor

1967
Cinematograph Films Council: Member 1967–73

Doctor Dolittle – Hollywood Golden Globe Best Supporting Actor

1969
Gardner Centre for the Arts, Sussex University: Patron 1969–90, President 1990–

Oh! What a Lovely War – 16 international awards including Hollywood Golden Globe and SFTA (BAFTA) UN Award

1970
National Film School, latterly National Film and Television School: Governor 1970–81, President 1977–

University of Sussex: Pro-Chancellor 1970–98, Chancellor 1998–2008

1971
BAFTA (originally Society of Film and Television Arts): Vice President 1971–94, Chairman of David Lean BAFTA Foundation Trustees 1972–2002, President 2002–

1972
Capital Radio: Headed successful consortium applying for new commercial broadcasting licence. Chairman 1972–92, Life President 1992–

Young Winston – Hollywood Golden Globe, Best English Language Foreign Film

1973
The Little Theatre, Leicester: Patron 1973–92, Honorary Life President 1992–

1974
The Young Vic Theatre Company: Director 1974–84

1975
Founded Help a London Child at Capital Radio: Life Patron 1998

1976
Tate Gallery Trustee 1976–82 and 1994–96

Waterford Kamhlaba School, Swaziland: Chairman UK Trustees 1976–2004, Member Governing Council 1987–, President 2004–

A Bridge Too Far – Evening News Best Drama Award

1979
Duke of York's Theatre: Chairman 1979–92

1980
Channel Four Television: Deputy Chairman 1980–86, Chairman 1986–92

1981
British Film Institute: Chairman 1981–92

1982
Goldcrest Films & Television: Chairman 1982–7

Kingsley Hall Community Centre (Mahatma Gandhi lodged there during 1931 visit to London for Round Table Conference): Patron 1982–

Gandhi – 8 Oscars, 2 for Best Film and Best Director, 5 BAFTA Awards, 5 Hollywood Golden Globes, Directors' Guild of America Award for Outstanding Directorial Achievement

1983
Committee of Enquiry into the Arts and Disabled People: Reporting on access and inclusion. Chairman 1983–5

The Gandhi Foundation: President 1983–

Gandhi – David Di Donatello, Italy – Best Producer and Best Film

Evening Standard – Award for 40 years' service to British Cinema

Martin Luther King Jr. Peace Prize

1984
Brighton Festival: President 1984–95

British Film Year: President 1984–6

1987
British Screen Advisory Council: Established as the Prime Minister's Working Party by Harold Wilson in 1975. Became BSAC in 1985. Chairman 1987–96, Honorary President 1996–

UNICEF: Goodwill Ambassador 1987–

Cry Freedom – Berlinale Kamera, BFI Award for Technical Achievement

1988
European Script Fund: Chairman 1988–96, Honorary President 1996–

Orange Tree Theatre, Richmond: Patron with Lady Attenborough 1988–

European Film Awards: Award of Merit for Humanitarianism in Film Making

1989
Arts for Health: Placing works of art in hospitals to aid recovery. President 1989–

European Film Academy, formerly European Cinema Society: Co-founder with Ingmar Bergman, István Szabó, Federico Fellini and Claude Chabrol

1990
Richard Attenborough Centre for Disability and the Arts. Raised funds for new purpose-designed building attached to Leicester University. Opened in 1997 by Diana, Princess of Wales; one of her last public engagements. Patron 1990–

1991
Foundation for Sport and the Arts. Grants from football pool levy. Forerunner of National Lottery grants. Trustee 1991–2003, President 2003–

1992
Chicken Shed: Honorary Patron 1992–

One World Action: Patron 1992–

FVS Foundation, Hamburg: Annual Shakespeare Prize

1993
Shadowlands – BAFTA, Alexander Korda Award for Outstanding British Film of the Year

1994
London Critics' Circle Film Award: Patron 1994–

1995
Satyajit Ray Foundation: Patron 1995–

1996
Oxford University: One year appointment as Cameron Mackintosh Visiting Professor of Contemporary Theatre

Sussex Centre for German Jewish Studies: Patron 1996–

United World Colleges: Member of the International Board 1996–2000, International Patron 2000–

1997
Amnesty International: Patron 1997–

Mousetrap Theatre Projects, dedicated to providing opportunities for disadvantaged young people to attend theatre productions: Trustee 1997–

1998
The Diana, Princess of Wales Memorial Fund: Trustee

Japanese Art Association, Premium Annual Imperiale

1999
Rodin, in Lewes: Patron 1999 and 2008

UK Film Council: Government Advisor 1999–

BAFTA Award for Outstanding Contribution to World Cinema

2001
Sir John Gielgud Charitable Trust: Trustee 2001–

2002
Dragon International Studios Ltd: Chairman 2002–

Themba HIV/Aids Project in South Africa: Patron 2002–

Unicorn Theatre: Patron 2002–

2003
Mandela Statue Fund: Chairman 2003– 2007

2005
St Edward's Oxford North Wall Arts Centre: Patron and Steering
Committee Member 2005–

2006
CLIC Sargent: Ambassador 2006–

Greater London Fund for the Blind: Vice President 2006–

2007
The Richard Attenborough Regional Film Critics Award: Patron 2007–

2008
BAFTA LA – Britannia Lifetime Achievement Award

HONORARY DEGREES

1970
University of Leicester: Hon DLitt

1974
University of Newcastle: Hon DCL

1981
University of Kent: Hon DLitt
University of Sussex: Hon DLitt

1983
Dickinson College Pennsylvania: Hon LLD

1993
King's College, London: Honorary Fellowship

1994
International University, London: Hon DLitt America
Manchester Metropolitan University: Honorary Fellowship

1997
University of Wales: Honorary Fellow

1999
Cape Town University: Hon DLitt

2005
University of Glamorgan: Hon DUniv

2007
Kingston University: Hon DArt

2008
RSAMD, Glasgow: Doctor of Drama

HONOURS

1967
CBE in New Year Honours

1976
Knighthood, New Year Honours

1983
Government of India: Padma Bhusan

BAFTA Fellowship

1985
France, Ordre des Arts des Lettres: Commandeur

1988
France, Legion d'Honneur: Chevalier

1992
Freeman of the City of Leicester: Conferred at joint ceremony with David Attenborough

BFI – Fellowship

1993
Life Peerage: Created Baron of Richmond-upon-Thames

2001
National Film and Television School: Fellowship

INDEX